Theory in Its Feminist Travels

Theory in Its Feminist Travels

Conversations in U.S. Women's Movements

Katie King

Indiana University Press

Bloomington and Indianapolis

Manufactured in the United States of America

Library of Congress Cataloging-in-Publication Data

King, Katie.
  Theory in its feminist travels : conversations in U.S. women's
movements / Katie King.
    p. cm.
  Includes bibliographical references and index.
  ISBN 0-253-33138-2 (alk.). — ISBN 0-253-20905-6 (pbk. : alk.
paper)
    1. Feminist theory—United States.   2. Feminism—United States.
3. Lesbianism—Philosophy.
  I. Title.
HQ1190.K48   1994
305.42'0973—dc20   94-5612

1 2 3 4 5 00 99 98 97 96 95 94

To my Teachers—the first of them, my parents—with appreciation for your support and for your risk-taking

Contents

Acknowledgments

THIS IS MY first book. It feels as if my acknowledgments for it must include acknowledgments for all the elements of the rich intellectual worlds which have created it and myself, although I'm only too aware that forty-odd years of such indebtedness can't possibly be done justice to here. My family—my mother, father, and brother, and my grandparents, aunts, uncles, cousins, and their children—created the living geography that made it possible to move with confidence growing up as an Army brat, and I want to thank all of them for their loving care and for their being my signposts in the world. Until I went away to college I'd never lived in a place longer than two and a half years at a time, so the University of California at Santa Cruz, where I spent most of the next sixteen years, has a special sense of Home in my life. My undergraduate years there were marked by a breathtaking environment, exciting friends, political ferment, and teachers worth emulating. Thank you Vikki DuRee, Chrys DeFreitas, Sylvia Huot, Didi Kaspin, Stephan Ordway, Mark Engel, Luita D. Spangler, Mary Caldwell, Lucy Kemnitzer, Che Sandoval, Moira Lerner, Mischa Adams, Cynthia Sexton, Maggi Veltre, Lisa Aschmann, Peter and Tay Erickson, Val Lucus, Eric Bateson, Harry Berger, Nobby Brown, Richard Randolph, Shelly Errington, Gregory Bateson, Lois Bateson, Gary Miles, Marsh Leicester, Carolyn Martin-Shaw (Clark), John Lynch. And the Cowell fountain. To each one of you my thanks for enriching my life are more far reaching and specific than this bare listing could ever make clear.

I went to graduate school both at the University of Chicago's Committee on Social Thought and at UCSC where I got my degree in the History of Consciousness. I've always been lucky in having people to work with, read with, talk with, think with. Thank you Michael Lavigne, Richie Lewis, Beth Brown, Lillian Doherty, Sharon Traweek, Susan Foster, Alicia Maris, Nancy Heishman, Barry Schwartz, Chris Grella, Val Hartooni, Zoe Sofoulis, Lisa Lowe, Debbie Gordon, Barbara Gottfried, T. V. Reed, Noel Sturgeon, Elizabeth Bird, Gloria Watkins, Lisa Bloom, Caren Kaplan, Eric Smoodin, Lata Mani, Ruth Frankenberg, Marilyn Patton, Yoshiko Miyake, Bill Pietz, Jaye Miller, Rusten Hogness, Donna Haraway, Hayden White, Priscilla Shaw, Michael Warren. Looking now at this list each name radiates a web of stories, some of which intertangle, some lie independent; all these webs leave strands in this book. Lata suggested the subject that tied things together and Caren has listened to, read, and contributed to this book in forms too numerous for me even to properly understand let alone acknowledge.

Books have to have time, space, and material support to come into being. The Women's Studies Program at the University of Maryland, College Park, has been as generous as possible with all three, allowing me an unusual two-year leave to take a postdoctoral fellowship at Cornell, facilitating all my efforts to find time and money, and finally supporting me for tenure. Thank you Seung-kyung Kim, Bonnie Thornton Dill, Lynn Bolles, Debbie Rosenfelt, and especially Evelyn Torton Beck and Claire Moses. Also Laura Nichols. Others have graciously turned up in my life, making things happen for me, speaking well of me at crucial moments, and recommending me for delightful possibilities. Thank you Paula Treichler, Eve Sedgwick, Paul Lauter, Kathleen Martindale, Martha Nell Smith, Marilee Lindemann, Virginia Beauchamp, Bob and Gretchen Dunn. My years at Cornell enlarged my professional network with people who have also become friends and sometime collaborators. Thank you Biddy Martin, Chandra Mohanty, Juliana Schiesari, Falabo Ajayi, Sharon Willis, Harryette Mullen, Ted Pearson, Gerald MacLean, Donna Landry, Elaine Hobby, Irene Zahava. It was while I worked with you all that this book began to materialize. I've had research and writing support for all the pieces that have turned into this book in the following forms: a 1991 Lilly Teaching Fellowship at UMCP (thank you Sandy Mack, Kathryn Mohrman, Ralph Lundgren), a 1988–90 Mellon Postdoctoral Fellowship in Women's Studies at Cornell University (thank you Nelly Furman, Anna Geske, Jonathan Culler), a 1988 General Research Board Summer Research Award at UMCP, a 1985 Regent's Fellowship at UCSC, a 1984 Patent Fund Research Award at UCSC. I especially thank Che Sandoval and Nancy Hartsock for permission to quote from their unpublished work.

This book owes the most to Donna Haraway, to whom I extend my respect and love for many forms of material support, many acts of professional, intellectual and emotional generosity, and for a wide-ranging and much valued friendship.

Introduction

ONE GUIDELINE THROUGH the interweaving arguments of *Theory in Its Feminist Travels* is a focus on the production and reception of theory in U.S. feminism. Such theory is visible as sharply disciplinized, colored by race and racial privilege in the academy, strangely fixed by sexual identity, defined in a division of labor and a generic hierarchy, and consumed within politicized systems of publication and distribution. One argument I make about theory in feminism is embedded in the subtitle of this book; I refer to "conversations" in feminist thinking as a challenge to taxonomized feminist theory, feminist history, or feminism, as a challenge to any unitary history of "the women's movement." My point is to heighten the local aspects of discourse, very much historically—at times almost "momentarily"—located, continually rewritten or reinscribed with new meanings by feminist practitioners and to foreground how the terms, constituencies, and strategies of feminists shift and travel. I don't mean "conversations" are not deployments of power—rather the opposite. I don't mean that everyone gets an equal share in one single conversation we feminists all participate in, but rather that many conversations are going on at once, not every feminist is in all of them—nor would one desire to be—and some people are not in any. Feminists are not always clear about which conversations they are participating in at any time, who and that they are recruiting, making new alliances, new political versions. It is not at all obvious that specific debates may simultaneously inhabit several conversations at once, that objects such as "theory" may travel between and among many conversations, or that multiple objects constructed in different conversations may appear "the same" as displayed under a single sign. "Theory" is sometimes many such political objects mis/dis/played by the single word.

In order to examine "theory" in production and reception I draw upon resources in postcolonial theory, transnational cultural studies, antiracist cultural theory, sex radical approaches to lesbian and gay studies, as well as women's studies and feminist theory and my own work in feminism and writing technologies. Situating theory in its layered histories in U.S. feminism begins the project to address the situation of women's studies and feminist theory in the local/global shifts and tensions that inform our historical moment—what some have called postmodernism, or late capitalism, or transnational culture/s. Developing methodology for such mappings is a need to which my formulation of feminism and writing technologies attempts an answer.

I use "writing technologies" here in a literalization of that seriously playful term "grammatology"—a literalization emphasizing the ideologies of those amazingly productive reifications "the oral" and "the written." Such ideologies are shifting, strategic, and multiple. Feminism and writing technologies investigate specific technologies enmeshed in the multinational sexual division of labor, the neocolonialisms embedded in descriptions of oral and written consciousness, the investments of feminism in specific ethnic/racial/sexual/national literacies, the international systems of publication constructing academic and market values. How are the U.S. and other Euro-centers—overvalued parts of a world economy—delineating particular literacies, including nonwritten ones?

The methods explored or developed in work on feminism and writing technologies, my own and others', enable the examination of the production and reception of theory in U.S. feminism. For example, such methods suggest the question: How can feminists interrogate our locations within the race- and sex-consolidated knowledges of the academy, in the U.S., within a women's studies framework and politics? An approach through feminism and writing technologies—which I see as an emerging "field" in many senses—suggestively places U.S. feminism in a framework that challenges U.S. theorists both to locate "us/the U.S." in transnational systems of power: the multinational sexual division of labor, the cultural hegemonies of the U.S. and the ruptures in that hegemony, and the imperialisms of U.S. feminism. This approach simultaneously challenges theorists to see U.S. feminism as only one small—albeit influential, appropriative, indeed much influenced—strand of globally intertwining activisms. The history of this strand as one of many women's movements is appropriately made and remade from the cultural practices of multicultural feminist critique inside the history of decolonization. Thus, although the book does not center feminism and writing technologies, it does depend upon and exemplify methods emerging from this field. The third chapter in particular will also be a kind of preface to this research area.

At the 1988 MLA panel "Cultural Studies and Feminism," I argued that the subject matter of women's studies *is* cultural studies, and that any "look-back" to the origins of women's studies and cultural studies suggesting that they have prior or separate existences is perverse. An orthodoxy centering cultural studies in the Birmingham School's ideological analyses of popular culture in Great Britain or in the U.S. academic disciplines of communications studies improperly erases each location's constitution within as well as without, and complexly together with particular histories of feminism. Seeing women's studies *as* cultural studies suggests many forms of political engagement in the academy and elsewhere, in theoretical and activist forms together. Indebted to Birmingham and to communications theory, women's studies has yet all along offered a wider range of politically interdisciplinary attachments, all enhancing our work in cultural studies. In 1988 I also argued that one might make an analogy between this way of understanding cultural studies and the revisionary histories of U.S. feminism coming out of the cultural practices of multicultural feminist critique. There we have seen a critique of the "white women's movement" that simultaneously challenges any bogus history that might give over origins or "ownership" of the U.S. women's movement to white women. Similarly, seeing women's studies as cultural studies intervenes into orthodoxies that give over a lamented "ownership" of cultural studies only to a particular network of people and specific schools of thought, institutional locations, and academic strategies. These linkages between revisionary histories—of feminism, of cultural theory, of antiracist centers and influences—are not accidental; histories in which constituencies of feminists, particularly women of color, are seemingly "absent" are also continually renarrativized in current contests for the object "theory" in feminism and oppositional uses of theory in the academy.

Because this book draws upon work in a variety of fields and addresses this currently much-disputed object "theory," I hope it will be read by people in the broad areas of criticism—women's studies and feminist theory, gay and lesbian studies, ethnic studies—and by people with particular disciplinary and interdisciplinary interests—in cultural studies and politics, in postcolonial critique, in literature, history, anthropology. Frankly, I hope that the kinds of mappings I produce will interest those in both self-designated "pro and anti" theory camps, and will make it increasingly difficult to use such labels.

As with other current feminist/academic works, this book is made up of pieces: some written as long ago as 1983–84, some as recently as the revision moments in the processes of publication allow. Discontinuity is the necessary result of such production. If it were possible, I might try to smooth over these discontinuities, especially the revealing semi-redundancies, the errors of insight, rhetoric, and prophecy, the condensed statements of arguments sometimes already made, sometimes yet to be made. If it were possible, I might desire a book more filled out over a glistening structure of spare and elegant logical entailment. Alas, I never write that way, let alone *think* that way. The book is all too necessarily an embodiment of the fields of struggle it's embedded in: debates in feminist theory, as I engage in them politically, talk about them with students, make allies or contend with other women, feminists, colleagues; the attempts to snatch at time to write the book out of the cycles of job-hunting, teaching, committeeing, fellowship writing; the tryouts in the giving of talks and the attempts to fathom the reactions of audiences, coworkers, students, and friends; the book's relation to my life, from the luxury of fellowship time, to the fault lines of family support and friendship networks during the dying of my father and the deaths of dear friends, to the final timelines of hurrying publication before coming up for tenure. All academic books are written in such webs of enabling constraint; some nevertheless appear smoother, more controlled, graceful. This is not one of those books.

Of course I want to make a virtue of such defects. And of course, they are virtues—powers, that is. I energetically and with hope claim a kind of dynamic modeling in the obvious sutures, rewritings with inconsistencies hanging (although I would have "fixed" them if I could have figured out how), in the emphasis on the processes of production in feminist theory, the struggles over what counts as theory.

Is the book itself a pastiche of theoretical tools, a making of theory, simply a discussion *about* theory? Readers have already suggested such differing interpretations. *I* would rather do a lot of pointing, pointing to the instability of the domain of the theoretical. Why does the claim to be a theorist matter so much and to whom? Why is theory so valuable, and why right now?

Many of my own biases and assumptions about theory, my own grounds for understanding theory, derive from my intellectual histories and passions. Supported by both the women's movement of the early seventies and the progressive state educational system in California and its gurus from the same time period, I have arrogantly and gloriously always (always since 1970) assumed that *making* theory was my (second) birthright, a real gas, and already a fruit of politics. Yes, a fruit of politics—as in "by their fruits ye shall know them"; gay "fruits" indeed, for my relation to theory has been on the search for understanding us gay folk; and "knowing them," in the sense that one's theory is only *too* revealing of one's politics. A sense of privilege and entitlement are evident here. At the same time, theory was obviously not something only great thinkers have done/could do, but instead something we all do, both intentionally and unintentionally. I wanted to be intentional, but with rather narrow intentions.

I learned to care about those "great thinkers"—say, Simone de Beauvoir, someone whose work I struggled through in those days—for the *modeling* for making theory that they offered. It never occurred to me that my job was limited in any way to using their apparatus wholesale, as an apprentice. I was always on the lookout for making up my own: rudimentary, Rube Goldberg-ish, often made junk-like out of bits whose history I understood little about, whose baggage I learned about only as I tried to use them for my own purposes and discovered unexpected complications. These bits of history and baggage I found quite interesting in themselves, but only too rarely assumed that they were deeply limiting. These assumptions, while perhaps not entirely without self-criticism nowadays, still leave more than traces tattooed on the body of my work. And my irreverent relation to "great thinkers" reflects both an often-lamented, too superficial understanding of whole bodies of apparatus but also a deep desire to celebrate those theoretical workers who appropriate, misread, transform, and tinker with these bodies of apparatus. My citation practice deliberately attempts to emphasize these trails of junk-people, with whom I identify, and to deemphasize "great men" (even the homosexual ones, with whom I occasionally identify). This is one way to describe an engagement with feminism, structuralism, and poststructuralism from the seventies to the nineties.

First, a Story
What Is an Object?

An assistant professor is describing her work in a pre-tenure meeting with the other members of the women's studies program. She is asked about her book What Counts As Theory in U.S. Feminism?

"Why do you describe theory as an object in this first chapter? Won't this kind of language keep many feminists from reading the book?" "Well... (she sighs)... I want to describe feminist theory as a politics of knowledge-making. The kind of object I mean might be called 'an object of knowledge.' Theory too is such an object.... We produce the things we know...."

IT WAS DONNA HARAWAY who first stunned me with what she called "natural-technical objects of knowledge." In order to know something we first have to make it; or maybe better: we produce the things we know, that's how we come to know them. This came to me as a fabulous fabula, an enabling story intermeshing materialism and social construction. I've returned to this story, "What is an object?" over and over. "The production of facts packaged in objects solid enough to weigh and mail to colleagues" is how I first encountered it, filtered through the materialist feminism of Haraway and my own idiosyncratic interests and idiosyncratic intellectual history.[1] One richly elaborated version of this story is told in several disciplinary registers in Bruno Latour and Steve Woolgar's *Laboratory Life*.[2]

What is an object? I mull over the ways feminists make knowledge and make political identities, mull over them in terms of these constructed objects. I learned to do this in the course of dragging Haraway's apparatus from one set of disciplinary sites to another, noting her own transformations of Latour and Woolgar's anthropology of the scientific lab, and doing my own tinkering here, tinkering there (all in the imagination, of course). Latour and Woolgar argue, time, and detail the construction of a scientific fact: how in January 1968 it begins as an idea that the scientist-producers in this moment of necessary relativism are only too well aware they are constructing; but by January 1970 it has become an object of nature, discovered by now-hardened realists. In a process of "splitting and inversion" the statement about nature splits apart into both a statement and an object of nature. "Before long, more and more reality is attributed to the object and less and less to the statement *about* the object. Consequently, an inversion takes place: the object becomes the reason why the statement was formulated in the first place." In Latour and Woolgar's investigated laboratory the production of a thyroid hormone is ethnographically described as it comes into materialization: from idea to a white powder that can be sent in an envelope in the mail. Such an object is stabilized in the practice of what I call conversations and over the course of shifting alliances and political meanings, which collectively Latour and Woolgar call "the agonistic field."[3]

With this story running through my mind I can't help but notice that feminist objects of knowledge, theoretical objects, political identities are made and materialized over time in political production. In my first work I described how a "poem" is such an object of knowledge, through the editorial and publication processes through which it materializes, through the political meanings it acquires in feminist politics.[4] Want a sharp example? Think for a moment of that feminist theoretical object "Woman" and its production over time within feminist theory. Think of its solidification as a new unitary object produced, first, in its contrast with "Man." Remember the controversies of the early seventies drawing and privileging this contrast in which Black women such as Shirley Chisholm—in the mainstream political arena—or Cellestine Ware—in the nascent groups of radical women—pointedly said (in a strategy to insist on the importance of Woman) that they had been more discriminated against as women than as Black people? Such boundary-making and strategic prioritizing were part of the mechanisms producing and empowering this new unitary object. So too were newly obtained systems of data collection; for example, during the U.N. Decade of Women, new global and national systems for collecting data about women were set into place, drawn upon, or notably absent when needed.

"Woman" with a capital W and singular, essentialized, marks an uneasy moment of stabilization as a new object of knowledge, still contestable within the systems of deconstruction through which it is known again. The critiques of historical romanticization and stereotyping; the specious generic (unmarked) meanings of "white," "heterosexual," "middle-class," "U.S. American," etc.; the reification of (hetero)sexual difference; the analogies to the unitary subject of humanism; the deflection from political communities—all these knowledges of "women" follow upon the construction of the theoretical object. Similarly, "women of color" is made in the course of new political alliances, tentative, unstable agreements within cohorts to strategically prioritize some differences in the name of many differences: nationality, language, religion, class, region, race and ethnicity, community history, politics and so on.

What I look to, in considering what an object is, are especially the moments and histories of its production over time, the contests for meanings within which it is embedded, the political contours that are the circumstances out of which it is fabricated, and the resources and costs of its making, contesting, and stabilizations, some lasting, some ephemeral.

Theory in Its Feminist Travels

1

What Counts as Theory?
Travels through Several Histories
of U.S. Feminism

As a feminist more and more I feel compelled to know something about people's institutional and disciplinary location, because I'm going to get a different sense of feminism if I read feminist development studies grounded in sociology and policy-making, for example, than if I read lesbian feminist poetry written by women who aren't tenured faculty. The places we struggle and resist in relationship to different institutions are also something that we need to know more about when we speak with one another. Our disciplinary and academic locations are part of the context we need to be sensitive to. Otherwise, we run the risk of mistaking the most well-funded of feminist discourses for all of feminism.

Debbie Gordon, *Inscriptions* (1988)[1]

This of course raises the question of what is theory, what is feminist theory. . . . It's a useful question because it takes us back to the seventies, to the history of feminism in this country, to a time when the very term "feminist theory" did not yet exist, and one's critical work as a feminist had to be done in the manner of the double shift: on the one hand, the work in the movement . . . on the other hand, the work in one's teaching and writing context—what was then called "feminist criticism" or "the feminist critique" of theory, of the disciplines. . . . It may not be too much of an exaggeration to suggest that feminist theory became possible as such (that is, became identifiable as feminist theory rather than a feminist critique of some other theory or object-theory) in a postcolonial mode. . . . With regard to feminism, this understanding of a diversified field of power relations occurred, or was brought home, as it were, when the writings of women of color, Jewish women, and lesbians constituted themselves as a feminist critique of feminism, and an intervention in a feminist discourse that was anchored to the single axis of gender as sexual (or rather, heterosexual) difference, however minutely articulated in its many instances, from everyday language use to mass media representations and to all major institutional apparati.

Teresa de Lauretis, "Displacing Hegemonic Discourses: Reflections on Feminist Theory in the 1980s" (1988)[2]

Feminist theory is not recent. The history of feminism is in part a history of theory. . . .

Certainly feminist theory belongs at present to no one; preempting the designation
for one project or another, or contesting the production of theory by feminists, is
considerably less interesting at this stage than seeking to illuminate various
theoretical projects and to position them with greater precision in relation to one
another.

Paula Treichler, "Teaching Feminist Theory" (1986)[3]

I CONSIDER THIS question "what counts as theory?"—positioning it simultaneously
to overlap with my interests in the politics of publication. Concerned with the kinds
of political agencies that are deployed in the interwoven rewritings of theory in
feminism, I intend to examine several "moments" (texts/locations/historical shifts)
in feminism in the last two decades, local moments defined by specific strategies and
stakes in "what counts as theory?" For example, what does it mean for Teresa de
Lauretis to say in 1988 that the seventies was "a time when the very term 'feminist
theory' did not yet exist," when in 1970 Pamela Allen writes a pamphlet describing
the group production of theory in women's liberation, or Cellestine Ware writes a
history of women's liberation in which methods of producing theory mark differing
feminist politics?[4] What are the different investments in the multiple historical objects deployed/displayed under the sign "theory"? What generic or unmarked forms
of "theory" are challenged or altered by, or hide local or marked "theory"? Which
marked forms speciously appear generic, or travel globally?

Several competing/overlapping histories of U.S. feminism offer one geography
for such speculation. In this chapter I do a reading of the "lacquered layering" of
such origin stories; that is, the layerings of instance, of political meanings constrained in particularity, lacquered over so finely that they are inseparable and mutually constructing while distinct. Superimposed (overlapping and nonoverlapping)
histories specify age cohorts, cohorts from specific political movements, marked and
unmarked racially constituted collectivities, the varieties of identities deployed and
constructed within identity politics, people from shared historical moments, geographical unities, and those traveling between, or inhabiting several such groupings.
Over and over these cohorts specify themselves as "the feminists." Teasing out the
threads that connect some and distinguish others is part of mapping out the geography through which "theory" travels.

The texts I will be reading to create one such critical mapping are: Alice Echols,
Daring to Be Bad: Radical Feminism in America, 1967–1975 (1989); Patricia Hill
Collins, *Black Feminist Thought: Knowledge, Consciousness, and the Politics of Empowerment* (1990); Chandra Talpade Mohanty, Ann Russo, and Lourdes Torres, eds.,
Third World Women and the Politics of Feminism (1991); and Jane Gallop, *Around
1981: Academic Feminist Literary Theory* (1992). While centering these texts I will,
of course, be making references or pointing to many other histories, descriptions,
and contestations of and in contemporary feminism, among them: Juliet Mitchell

and Ann Oakley, eds., *What Is Feminism? A Re-examination* (1986); Toni Cade, ed., *The Black Woman: An Anthology* (1970); Cellestine Ware, *Woman Power: The Movement for Women's Liberation* (1970); bell hooks and Cornell West, *Breaking Bread: Insurgent Black Intellectual Life* (1991); Andrew Parker, Mary Russo, Doris Sommer, and Patricia Yaeger, eds., *Nationalisms and Sexualities* (1992); Deborah Gordon, ed., "Feminism and the Critique of Colonial Discourse" (1988); James Clifford and Vivek Dhareshwar, eds., "Traveling Theories, *Traveling Theorists*" (1989); and Hester Eisenstein, *Gender Shock: Practicing Feminism on Two Continents* (1991).[5]

The appearance of Echols's long-awaited book alerted me once again to the layerings of feminist histories. Initially I intended to review Echols's 1989 book side by side with Toni Cade's 1970 book in order to describe and criticize what I've referred to as feminist histories giving over "origins" to white women. However, other histories also needed to be revealed in their layerings. Thus, this chapter emerged, in which I explore what feminisms are named in such texts/histories, what lines are drawn to other movements for social justice, and examine who is included in which histories, what geographical regions are specified, what institutional locations are assumed, and what counts as politics. I think this collection tells enough different, and different enough, stories to *illustrate* but hardly exhaust these "lacquered layerings" I mentioned before, as well as to convey the necessity to challenge and refigure unitary histories of feminism.

To begin to map out some of these nodal points—plural histories, region, institution, cohort, and politics—let's return for a moment to the three epigraphs at the beginning of this chapter and note how attention to the politics of publication begins a process to map out political-theoretical agencies. Gordon's is an informal comment made in the discussion period after several academic "talks" or papers. De Lauretis's is from one such paper delivered during the same mini-conference, although not one of those to which Gordon is replying. And Treichler's is from an essay in a book centering the teaching of theory (understood as a category larger than and encompassing feminist theory). Each epigraph is now in the form of published words with citation histories; the first two from a journal, the second from a collection. Treichler's predates the others by about two years. The degrees of verbal contingency and stability are distinct but hardly adequately distinguished as oral to written, although the first two are complexly "oral" and all are complexly "written." All have been edited in the course of publication, although the editorial processes for this particular issue of this particular journal have probably not gone through as many hands as the editorial processes of the book essay. The issues brought up in each are particularized and heightened by these locations.

Gordon's comment is initially a momentary one, but appropriately generalized within the U.S. academy: "As a feminist more and more I feel compelled to know something about people's institutional and disciplinary location, because I'm going to get a different sense of feminism if I read feminist development studies grounded in sociology and policy-making, for example, than if I read lesbian feminist poetry written by women who aren't tenured faculty." At the time of this in-house mini-conference at the University of California, Santa Cruz, Gordon was still a graduate student, although an advanced one, and special editor of this issue of the journal *Inscriptions*, in which the interchange finally appeared. Also an instructor at Stanford University and later involved in the controversy surrounding the changes in the general education program there that was nationally reported and debated, Gordon spoke with both the passion of her academic-political locations and with longstanding concerns for interdisciplinary scholarship, and for white feminist scholars' accountability for appropriations of multiculturalism. "The places we struggle and resist in relationship to different institutions are also something that we need to know more about when we speak with one another." Only too aware, as an advanced graduate student preparing for the academic job market, of the commodification process involved in disciplinary location, and of both the advantages and disadvantages of having the broad training to teach both feminist development studies and lesbian feminist poetry, Gordon's comments vibrate with the intensity of multiple meanings lacquered together here. "Our disciplinary and academic locations are part of the context we need to be sensitive to. Otherwise, we run the risk of mistaking the most well-funded of feminist discourses for all of feminism." Gordon's own scholarly work at this time both concerned the access of women anthropologists to that distinguishing activity "fieldwork" over several decades of the history of the discipline and within the constraints of race in their productions of what is understood to be ethnography; and also concerned the political histories of some currently valorized male anthropological theorists, whose work she is both indebted to and critical of, such work complexly located in struggles over the meanings of decolonization and political action. Funding, status, academic politics and their knowledge/power relations figure both her location and her scholarship.

De Lauretis's quotation here has many layerings as well. To begin, this talk is one beginning (and, unsurprisingly, there were many) of her influential essay "Eccentric Subjects," published by *Feminist Studies* in 1990,[6] and in manuscript circulated before publication in another early elaborated version. She too offers informal comments in the course of the mini-conference, which situate and rewrite some of the points she makes here. For example, she locates this history of feminist theory as "very much based on my personal history" (145). This qualifying and non-trivial point is worth generalizing in the context of the arguments of this book, especially as "personal" is understood to locate an individual in historical layerings. It was de Lauretis's semiotic work that was first available to academic theorists; her feminist theory followed in the eighties. (This trajectory is also performed in Gallop's title *Around 1981*.) De Lauretis also suggests how her own subject-position is "multiply organized across positionalities along several axes and across mutually contradictory discourses and practices" (in the words in which she describes the feminist subject in her talk [136]), when she makes several points deconstructing U.S. investments and assumptions in the term "Eurocentric" and in complicating the meaning of the location "white non-American woman":

When people here speak of Europe as synonymous with the West, as the homogeneous place of origin of white supremacy and imperialism toward "the rest of the world" (as it is typically put), they ignore the histories of internal colonization, not to mention various forms of class, sexual, and religious oppression, within Europe and within each country of Europe. So that words like Eurocentric (vs. Afrocentric, for example) are highly relative to the U.S. context.... My current understanding of the relation of feminist theory to the critique of colonial discourse is obviously inscribed in my personal history and dis-placements, but has developed in the context of my work in American universities and the particular cultural, racial, sexual, and generational differences expressed by my students and co-workers. (127–28)

De Lauretis's investments in saying "a feminist theory begins when the feminist critique of ideologies becomes conscious of itself and turns to question its own body of writing and critical interpretations, its basic assumptions and terms, and the practices which they enable and from which they emerge" (138)—and locating that moment in the early eighties—differs from other investments I'll be describing in this chapter and book, such as: the investments Alice Echols has in locating as a pivotal moment with theoretical implications the emergence in the late sixties early seventies of "radical feminism" in feminist insistence on maintaining autonomy from the left while remaining connectedly "radical"; the investments Chela Sandoval has in spreading out over several decades, including the seventies, the "third position" that marks the critique of the "white women's movement"; and the investments I have in differentiating between the feminist reception and elaboration in the seventies of theories of lesbianism and of antiracism. These last three also nontrivially mirror personal political histories.[7]

Treichler's quotation positions itself very differently. Rather than contesting to define feminist theory itself, Treichler lays claim to the power to position "with greater precision" feminist theories in the plural. In Treichler's formulation feminist theory is *not* recent. Treichler contests for feminist theory in a terrain somewhat reminiscent of de Lauretis's "double shift"—trying to hold in tension both "academic theoretical writing" and "feminist political theorizing" (58), with the classroom as one privileged location. The questions with which I opened differ in explanatory imagery from Treichler's but also depend upon hers: "What does 'theory' mean? What does it mean to 'do' feminist theory? Can feminist theory reproduce the theoretical pluralism characteristic of U.S. feminism and women's studies and still be 'theory'? Is pluralism an illusion constructed to disguise the real controversies in feminist theory and their potential divisiveness?" (58)

The term *feminist theory* suggests a unity that does not exist. Indeed, the term has become a dense point of linguistic intersection among competing discourses where meanings are produced and almost immediately contested. These contestations are irrevocably built into the deceptively generic rubric "feminist theory." In writing about the teaching of feminist theory, I am really writing about the nature and scope of these contestations, including the tensions between

"feminism" and "theory" that can be heard in feminist voices throughout this essay. . . . (88)

We need to use the principles of feminism, of theory, and of feminist theory, to
place them [diverse feminist theoretical projects] structurally and strategically in
relationship to one another and to the overall enterprise. (99)

My interests in this object "theory" and its travels are political and epistemological. Feminist theory is my "field"; but what sort of field is it with its central
object in such dispute? One of my touchstones in this field is an emphasis on the
"production" in "knowledge production." This is one thread through this chapter,
becoming more entwined and stronger through its second half. However, before I
tackle "theory" as an object head-on, I first take what might appear to be a side step:
I look in detail at the construction of the object "radical feminism" in the feminist
history and polemic of Alice Echols. In this extended discussion, I model the
method I will subsequently use to examine the object "theory" and its constructions. This method highlights the invested interests of particular cohorts in situating
themselves as "the feminists." I too belong to such an invested cohort, and in my
analysis of Echols's book I attempt to locate myself in my political investments. Engaging in this locating process also emphasizes epistemological practices. So examining Echols's history is no side step, but an introduction to what this phrase "epistemological practices" could mean, as well as a way of historicizing myself and of
insisting on elements of contingency as well as agency in producing feminist
histories.

This chapter is an explication of constructions and sometimes of cohorts: as
Echols constructs the object "radical feminism" I name a cohort particularized by
generational and psychological investments in their local object "(feminist) theory";
the object that constitutes my own fundamental tool in examining other objects
"theory." In the second half of the chapter I examine other constructions: Patricia
Hill Collins's construction of "Black feminist thought" and some relations between
"thought" and "theory"; Chandra Mohanty's collective construction of the field
"Third World Feminisms" and her deployment of the object "theory"; and Jane
Gallop's construction of "academic feminist literary theory," in which "academic"
and "literary" as points of contestation shape what can count as theory. Naming a
particular cohort for each object is not always appropriate or possible within this
analysis: it's the *investments* that matter the most to me, and the pieces of them I can
untangle differ with each object "theory." Collins's methods of construction and
her investment in large unities holding together threatened stabilities, such as
"Black feminist thought," require of her the smoothing out of any traces of cohort
investment, but as a result the investments in *construction* become even clearer. In
looking at Mohanty's deployment of "theory" I've not so much named a cohort as
suggested a historical formation, a possible productive unity of effect: the shaping
of women's studies in the United States by international feminists in travel. Gallop

herself works to name her own multiple investments in the object she constructs: she specifies a pivotal moment "Around 1981," in which I see one naming of a rather large but not especially homogeneous cohort. Concerns with the constructions of objects of knowledge, contestations for their apparent unities, and for interested agencies mark this kind of analysis.

Each of the epigraphs discussed above is concerned with interrogating specious unities. Gordon's not only locates the U.S. academy, its insides and outsides, but also its layers: funding, status, academic politics and their knowledge/power relations. De Lauretis's "personal" histories, locating individuals and cohorts in historical layer-ings, deconstruct the seemingly global, but instead quite local, political opposition-ality in the false unity of "Eurocentric." (Her use of postcolonial theory to point out internal colonizations in European histories takes on heightened meaning now as we see the simultaneous breakup of the Soviet Union and the possible new unities of the European Community beginning to be contested.) Treichler's framing of contestation at the *intersections* of this "deceptively generic rubric 'feminist the-ory' " suggests the further question: for *whom* are there these assumed "tensions between 'feminism' and 'theory' "?

So it is with investments in interrogating specious unities and with an eye to mapping out these nodal points of production, that I turn to Alice Echols's history of radical feminism. Indeed, this chapter has its origins in a dialogue with Echols's book *Daring to Be Bad*. Echols strives mightily to smooth out her history into a sin-gle narrative, taking the many materials she has collected and concerned herself with and making a remarkably coherent and very particular sense out of them al-though, indeed, the structure of her chapters preserves separate narratives from the new left and the civil rights movements, with similarly separate hints about gay lib-eration. Perhaps she maintains this separation unself-consciously as part of the meaning of "history," or maybe she's quite conscious of her interests in sharply fo-cusing on and delineating the boundaries of that particular group of people she takes via interviews to define "radical feminism."

As I've worked on my project in this book I've been asked why *my* methodol-ogy didn't include interview material, wasn't more strictly "historical," in order to support my contentions about the differing meanings of theory within historically differing cohorts of feminists. Echols's book is suggestive about the necessary scale of such methodology—how labor-intensive it is, how long it takes as feminist theory eddies on about you, how it realistically requires boundary maintenance to facilitate the scope of the enterprise, how research design appropriately is consolidated rela-tively early in the conceptualization of the project, which itself is quite lengthy, and so on. My own research constraints simply haven't permitted this scale, this "invest-ment" in fact-production, nor have I been willing to pay these particular epistemo-logical costs: (1) such a long production period that theoretical paradigms have sub-stantively shifted between production and reception, (2) requirements that sharply narrow the scope of the project, (3) investments in early stabilizations of the project.

While feminist theory and feminist history are much indebted for the materials Echols has unearthed; the interviews and data she's collected; the literatures she has reviewed and analyzed; the historical and political interpretations she's developed; the connections she's seen, shared, and created; the political debates she produced, participated in, and consolidated—nonetheless, there are limitations to this method, limitations and constraints that produce one kind of facts, one kind of objects of knowledge, and they are often *not* the facts, objects, or kinds of knowledge I am engaged in producing. There is no question that such materials would be fascinating to have around the questions I'm asking and speculating about, and by no means do I intend some wholesale rejection of empirical research. But in this case the "costs" of these materials—for my project—might very well be too high.

My investments in "history"—that flow of events, those writings about the past, the academic discipline, the shifting contexts and subjectivities in which we produce those writings about the past—differ from Echols's. I want instead to produce another historical effect, one of overlayered terrains; in my mind's eye I see a multidimensional grid in which historical narratives flicker and move, changing shape and dimension and space occupied over time, while also altering anew and constantly the "tails" of the past shadowing any present. My science fiction/cybernetic imaginary is showing: History as virtual reality? as mathematical modeling? as fractal geometry? as Lacanian film studio? And borrowing, tinkering with, dragging around the apparatus analyzing and inscribing fact-production is a more necessary part of my intellectual imagination and project.

Culminating in a 1986 publication, Juliet Mitchell and Anne Oakley, together with English-speaking socialist feminists on both sides of the Atlantic, inquired of themselves, "What is feminism?" Academics and activists, policy-makers and advocates, this is a group not especially reminiscent of the "radical feminists" and radical women of the new left that Alice Echols valorizes in 1989's *Daring to Be Bad*, that history of what I would call the political object "radical feminism" in the United States. Older, more deeply institutionalized, with political strategies inextricably interconnected to the state, maybe with more conventional personal lives and more contemporary personal visions, absolutely mired in the academy for good and ill— these women of Mitchell and Oakley's *What Is Feminism?* nonetheless would certainly perceive both continuities and discontinuities between themselves and Echols's radical women, having been radical women—but only in a more extended sense. Certainly none are among those interviewed by Echols, not having inhabited those groups she defines as radical feminism; indeed, some may have defined themselves against those women or that name.

Juliet Mitchell's introduction entangles with her 1966 essay "Women: The Longest Revolution," an essay that mightily influenced women such as those Echols writes about (also the very first essay to be encountered in the socialist feminist reader *Women, Class, and the Feminist Imagination*, mostly collecting materials from and unfolding connections between the journals *Socialist Review* and *Feminist Stud-*

ies).[8] Mitchell doesn't herself locate her essay in any origin story, but rather points to de Beauvoir's *The Second Sex*. A gesture of humility? of anti-sectarianism? an unselfconscious evaluation of de Beauvoir's work, and implicitly her own? Certainly, the setting out of a large, international stage.

Unlike Ellen Willis's partisan and energetic introduction to Echols's book—a book whose person of reference is over and over Ellen Willis—Mitchell situates feminism as embedded in other historical forces on this large, international stage. Willis, as Echols's book might explain in its definition of the meanings of "radical feminism," always privileges feminism, feminism meaning the true heart of "radical feminism," a historically and geographically localized entity only incidentally indebted. More often it is self-defining as, if not sui generis, then at least autonomous, itself the driving historical force of the last twenty years. In contrast, Mitchell sees feminism as embedded in the processes of capitalism, its ability to *steer* the course of historical events non-existent, and while, nonetheless, deeply influential, also dogged by the understanding that its successes are often only the successes of its cooptation by world capitalism. Echols sincerely celebrates and depends upon Willis's vision of radical feminism, even when also plotting for herself a different political course, even a different understanding of historical events. Between Willis and Mitchell lie not only differing allegiances to the left, priorities of Marxist theory, and sides of the Atlantic with diverging economic histories, but also differences in understandings of political agency, of the agencies of feminism as a world historical force.

What is feminism? Here Willis's feminism is not at all nostalgic, even when it remembers with satisfaction and approval earlier revolutionary fervor. Here Mitchell's feminism is not at all self-aggrandizing, even when it renames and builds upon its own contributions with critical insight. Here Echols's feminism is not only partisan even when her history is markedly partisan in its intent and method. To ask the question "What counts as theory?" first starts with noticing what counts as feminism, what counts as feminism's history, its self-consciousness, the drawing of its memberships, its connections to other movements for social justice, its agencies, its geographies.

Echols's book presents itself as transparent. This is not only a particular approach to historical narrative, or a theoretical perspective; most fundamentally it is a claim upon historical authority. "Transparent" refers first to the graceful language in which Echols writes, a style that always points beyond itself, out-there; like a window through which one looks into the past; a window in which scratches, cracks are not visible; in which the frame and sash, curtains and shades are unobtrusive or absent. "Transparent" also refers to the matter-of-fact delineation of event, to how well the facts presented are unquestioningly, authoritatively read. Such transparency does not preclude political partisanship or passion, but it does preclude the palpability of other outcomes. Such transparency is extremely difficult to create. It is one indication of the (maybe momentary) stability of a "fact." The reviews of Echols's book remark upon the perils of describing "recent history." Recent history is unstable. But Echols's defense of herself for embarking on "recent history" is approvingly quoted: the urgency of the possible loss of the valuable memories of the participants in the events themselves. (Note: the events themselves, the participants themselves.)[9] Unlike the earlier essays that appeared in *Social Text*, *Powers of Desire*, and *Pleasure and Danger*, rhetorically the book is remarkably nonpolemical.[10] Perhaps discouragingly so.

While "socialist feminism" in the late seventies and early eighties began to elaborate a discourse on "left culture" (see the "Socialist Feminist Reader" mentioned above),[11] while its histories of the same periods that Echols covers drew heavily on this powerful word "culture" even as it distanced itself from "radical feminism" (defined itself against it—for example, in the person of Catharine Mac-Kinnon), Echols in the mid eighties found herself proselytizing a "radical feminism" in the context of the sexuality debates. Echols promoted a true radical feminism that—with all its excesses and mistakes—was closer at heart to socialist feminism; indeed, radical feminism's very name disclosed its relation (not indebtedness) to the new left, while yet alerting us to its role as the motor for U.S. feminism's most potent theoretical insights.

While "cultural feminism" was as yet the derisive name for, at times lesbians, at times lifestyle feminists, or the approved appellation for feminist art, what Echols calls cultural feminism's period of ascendancy, I would contend, was a time in which it could not be isolated beyond a "tendency"—not yet as feminist sect—for its very power and pleasures lay in its ability to combine with feminisms in the plural. Echols's contribution to feminist theory was to build upon earlier critical uses of the term and define its borders and boundaries, its philosophy and political strategies; all in the course of differentiating it from "radical feminism," for which such a critical and defining discourse already existed: inside socialist feminism. Echols's use of interviews is fundamental to this construction of reality, and socialist feminism is the audience of approval to whom Echols looks, in a move that heals and recasts the politico/feminist splits of the late sixties and early seventies. The sexuality debates are the site from which socialist feminist heterosexuals prove their allegiances to revolutionary sexuality after all—no longer owned by lesbians. Meanwhile the discourse on race—which socialist feminists always claimed, without being able to speak—revs up in the sites of feminist art, especially literature and poetry. (See chapter 5.)

Echols's contribution to feminist theory gives edges and borders to threads of connection: tendency becomes sect. Echols's history—long awaited, maybe a bit dated by the time it is published, maybe already too well-known in spirit if not in detail—while well reviewed, doesn't make quite the splash or raise the ire her polemic did in the early eighties. This very anticlimax is probably one measure of how taken-for-granted her analysis can now be. For many, it will and does appear as undebatable, as simply how it was then and there. For a few it will authorize their centrality to feminism. For most, it will now define "radical feminism." That term will lose fluidity in the successful bid to stabilize it historically (a bid that may not profit Echols personally).

So how does one now contend for this history? How does one insist on histories of feminism that flicker and reshape as one examines them? How does one contend that a single term can refer to more than one political object?

Questions about definitions suggest something of the flux and shift of tendencies becoming political objects, metamorphosing from one possibility to another, and dissolving or budding with time. These terms overlay each other: women's liberation, women's liberation movement, radical women, women's liberationists, feminists, WLM, feminist radicals, radical feminists, radical feminism, the white women's movement, feminism; [a broadly conceived, inclusive] feminism, [a sectarian, tactically specific] feminism, [a historically specific] feminism, [a utopian vision of] feminism, [an intentionally marked] feminism, [an emic—only as named by its participants] feminism, [an etic—conforming to large, categorical imperatives] feminism.

Echols is engaged in making the object "radical feminism." At some point the fuzzy edges of overlapping meanings that make it hard to pin down the multiple possibilities of radical feminism are labor-intensively cleaned up in a methodologically rigorous fashion (such cleaning up is part of the meaning of "good methodology"). As the edges get cleaner, the object pops out; as the cleaner edges reshape our historical memories, the object acquires *a* unique history. This is not bad political history; this is the function of political history in its proper partisanship: the making of political objects and new political meanings.

When I first read about Echols's book, when I first read the polemical pieces that ushered it onto a later stage, when I finally got to read the book itself, at various moments I found myself remembering. It was my own political memory that was energized and activated, my own local, historically specific, politically partisan bits and pieces of memory. Like Echols, I found/find myself revisiting 1967–1975. These years have a sharp claim on me, a sometimes hypnotic focus. It's possible that our reasons for returning have similarities. My own returns suggest a ritualized repetition: as a teenager (fifteen in 1967) and then a young college-age woman (thus, eighteen in 1970, when I arrived at college) many of the events that make up the most celebrated moments of current feminist histories were ones I lived through, and sometimes even felt very much at the center of, but no history names my generation and my geographical region in pivotal, central terms, however pivotal and central I might feel, these moments might feel.

I think I return to remind myself how much *there* I was, in a repetition that overvalues these moments, with a seeming clarity of memory that shows how unresolved yet this loss of my historical presence still is. In our current histories of this period of U.S. feminism, my generation is overshadowed. I'm not drawn to write "the history" of my generation of feminists though; I'm drawn instead to seemingly "set the record straight" about truths that feel absent to me in these histories that I too am drawn to valorize, remembering only too vividly the high pitch of excitement of reading D. C.'s *The Furies* in Santa Cruz, California. When I teach women's studies now I find myself struggling to make it possible for my students to see *themselves* at the center of feminist theory, as I so effortlessly (it seems now) felt it possible to be a center of feminist theory more than twenty years ago.

Also, when I first read about Echols's book, when I first read the polemical pieces that ushered it onto a later stage, when I finally got to read the book itself, at various moments I found myself remembering in particular. One particular I remember is Cellestine Ware's *Woman Power*, the very first book about women's liberation I ever saw, and ever read; I found it in the porno section of a tobacconist's shop near the bus station in Washington, D.C., around the time I graduated from high school. I bought it because my sixth-grade teacher, whom I'd recently visited before leaving the East Coast for college on the West Coast, told me she'd started to become interested in "those women's libbers." Echols tells us:

> Of course, from the early days of the movement there were black women like Florynce Kennedy, Frances Beale, Cellestine Ware, and Patricia Robinson who tried to show the connections between racism and male dominance. But most politically active black women, even if they criticized the black movement for sexism, chose not to become involved in the feminist struggle. Efforts to generate a black feminist movement, which date back to 1973 with the founding of the short-lived National Black Feminist Organization, were less than successful. (291)

This absolutely true statement has a strange, hollow echo in my political memories. *Woman Power*, my first feminist reading, was by a Black woman who represented herself at the very "heart" of what both she and Echols call radical feminism: the heart of its theory-making, the heart of its new political structures, the heart of its activism. A cofounder of one of the four political groups Echols uses to illustrate the varieties of radical feminism, Ware was also this earliest historian of radical feminism. Similarly, the first feminist conference I attended in 1971, where I came out as a lesbian as well as a feminist, had a conventional plenary triumvirate of the time: a white woman representing speciously generic women's liberation, a Black woman representing what we would now call women of color, and another white woman representing lesbians within women's liberation. The race-consolidated meanings are plain in retrospect, and the tokenism palpable, but my political memories of this pivotal moment in the making of my own political identities are of Black women at the center of feminism (which doesn't mean this was the experience of the Black woman who spoke in plenary session). One of the first lesbians I met at the time when "finding the lesbians" was a shaky and adventurous enterprise was Pat Parker, a Black poet, whom I met through her then-lover, a school compatriot.

I certainly didn't know "most politically active black women," indeed, only heard about or met in brief coalition with Black Panther women, for example; was not part of networks of current or longtime civil rights activists; certainly the numbers of Black women were few in the women's liberation groups I attended, in retrospect only very occasionally approximating that magical "12 percent" that signified "proportionate inclusion," a concept invoked within a white norm. The point

I'm trying to make here is about the distinction between the inclusion of numbers of Black women versus the centrality of some Black women. The centrality of some Black women doesn't erase the racism of the white women's movement, but it does slightly reposition it; it also insists that Black women's *contributions* to women's liberation on many "fronts" were central in important ways.

Cellestine Ware's book was far from being as influential as Shulamith Firestone's *The Dialectic of Sex* (although I personally liked it a great deal better, and it influenced my vision of feminism quite a bit more; indeed, it may enjoy a revival), but, for example, it influenced feminist theorist bell hooks, who draws upon it in her definitions of feminist movement and advocating feminism in her 1984 *Feminist Theory: from margin to center*.[12] It also represents a possibility present in early women's liberation that was not built upon and politically elaborated (see chapter 4), but that doesn't mean that other outcomes were not palpable and present just because we can't draw a direct and continuous line between that past and today.

So, forefronting and highlighting the palpability of other outcomes, let's take a brief survey of some anthologies of writings from 1969–1973 women's liberation, where we meet again the four women Echols names in her list of "black women like Florynce Kennedy, Frances Beale, Cellestine Ware, and Patricia Robinson." (This is a survey of the anthologies still present on my own shelves; they represent the materials that managed to stick through my many moves—physical, political, and professional—of the last two decades. They represent my own continuous lines of connection with the past, which I offer as a historical alternative. Thus, I again draw attention to historical contingency.)

Masculine/Feminine: Readings in Sexual Mythology and the Liberation of Women (1969), is an academic contribution to psychological role theory by Betty and Theodore Roszak rather than a "movement" project; still, it prominently includes women's liberation movement texts, and the editors remark that they are "indebted to the Women's History Research Center in Berkeley, California, for the use of its extensive periodicals files and catalogs on women's liberation."[13] (Those were the days when the Research Center consisted of about five large cardboard boxes housed in Laura X's living room. Today, these materials are now available in microfilm, and in this form are owned by many university libraries. Look for Women's Herstory Archives.)

Among the texts is Patricia Robinson's essay "Poor Black Women," introducing "A Collective Statement: *Black Sisters*."[14] The latter ends with a list of authors: "Patricia Haden—welfare recipient / Sue Randolph—housewife / Joyce Hoyt—domestic / Rita Van Lew—welfare recipient / Catherine Hoyt—grandmother / Patricia Robinson—housewife and psychotherapist." In the Roszaks' introducing statement Robinson is identified as a psychiatric social worker, a psychotherapist, and a journalist working with poor Black families. Robinson's essay, without the collective statement, also appears in Toni Cade (Bambara)'s 1970 *The Black Woman* as part of "Poor Black Women's Study Papers" by "Pat Robinson and Group."[15] In Cade the study papers are introduced in these terms:

These are the working papers of a group of women in New Rochelle and Mount Vernon committed to Women's Rights and Power to the People—ideas that are not, cannot be, mutually exclusive or antagonistic to a revolutionary people. Their work consists of, among other things, using criticism and analysis in written form to clarify their own observations, and then using these working papers to further the awareness of other sisters with whom they come in contact. The working papers of Patricia Robinson have appeared in *Lilith*, one of the Women's Liberation Front journals. — T[oni]. C[ade]. (189)

In Cade are also included "Letter to a North Vietnamese Sister from an Afro-American Woman—Sept. 1968," another study group paper, and "A Historical and Critical Essay for Black Women in the Cities, June 1969." The second is signed "Patricia Murphy Robinson for / Robin / Lenise / Marilyn / Dale / Carrietta / Saundra / Maureen / Donna / Aretha / Linda / Celeste / Wanda / Denise / and their beautiful brothers / but the most of all for Vilma Sanchez and Norma Abdullah, courageous women and brilliant theoreticians" (210).

Another version of this essay, considerably different, possibly edited and restructured, maybe less "scholarly," appears in another 1970 women's liberation anthology *Voices from Women's Liberation* and is attributed to "Patricia Haden, Donna Middleton, and Patricia Robinson."[16] There it finds itself in the section called "Theoretical Analyses," among essays on topics such as welfare, political economy, and marriage, and together with another Black feminist essay "An Argument for Black Women's Liberation As a Revolutionary Force" by Mary Ann Weathers. In this same anthology, under the heading "High School Women" are two essays, one attributed to A-Neeta Harris, "Written by a 13-year-old black woman who lives in Mount Vernon, New York (March 1970)," and another to La-Neeta Harris, "Written by a 13-year-old black girl who lives in Mount Vernon, New York (March 1970)," and titled respectively, "How to Get along with Friends" and "Black Women in Junior High Schools."[17]

In *Sisterhood Is Powerful* (1970) is found " 'Statement on Birth Control' [by] Black Women's Liberation Group, Mount Vernon, New York"—the one earlier published in the Roszaks' *Masculine/Feminine* as "A Collective Statement, *Black Sisters*"—without Robinson's introduction, but ending: "Signed by: two welfare recipients / two housewives / a domestic / a grandmother / a psychotherapist / and others who read, agreed, but did not help to compose."

Points to note before moving on: (1) The New Rochelle, Mount Vernon women Robinson is part of and apparently facilitates use differing authorial strategies: from full names to first names to group designations to worker designations and other structural locations and combinations thereof. (2) Notice Cade's political location of the group as "committed to *Women's Rights* and *Power to the People*": slogans doubling as political identities, such as one might shout in the midst of a demonstration or emblazon on a leaflet, poster, or placard; also notice the location of the group in the non-mutually exclusive intersection of these ideas. (3) Cade also elaborates on the meanings and political uses of "criticism and analysis in written form."

An implication is that criticism and analysis also exist in other than written forms; "working papers" are used to clarify observations, to communicate with but also educate other women as well as oneself and one's group.

(4) Robinson was also publishing in the women's liberation journal *Lilith*; notice too the use of the term "Women's Liberation Front" in parallel with nationalist liberation movements. (5) The Mount Vernon women imagine/make connections with women in nationalist liberation movements, such as to "a North Vietnamese Sister" and as "an Afro-American Woman." To what extent do Afro-American women have the possibilities of imagining/making such connections *without* the political or conceptual mediation of the new left and instead with other international connections being forged by Black nationalism in the United States in the midst of many decolonizing movements?

(6) Robinson and the group explicitly conceptualize themselves (and/or compatriots) as "theoreticians" and implicitly mark their working papers as "theory." Notice that Haden, Middleton, and Robinson's paper is explicitly categorized as "theoretical analysis" by the editor in *Voices from Women's Liberation*. This essay and its more multi-authored double in *The Black Woman* deftly appropriate powerful contemporary theoretical work by male nationalists (such as Fanon and Memmi, unnamed in either version) and transform and combine it—sometimes consciously, at other times perhaps without consciousness. Such so-called feminist critique can be deeply appropriative and transformative. What citation apparatus there is exists in the longer *Black Woman* version; it is excised (I speculate) from the shorter *Voices* version. (7) Also note the diversity of linguistic tools and conceptual languages used by the writers of the working papers: they are not all written in one "accessible" language, but in several languages that serve varying purposes and reflect several authorial locations.

Frances M. Beale's essay "Double Jeopardy: To Be Black and Female" appears in several locations, unchanged, with a slight but interesting variant in attribution, and with differing spellings of the author's name. Three anthologies edited by white women spell the name "Beal" and Toni Cade (and Alice Echols) spell it "Beale." In *Liberation Now!* (1971) the essay is copyrighted under the author's name (as in all the other reprintings) but also together with "SNCC Black Women's Liberation Committee."[18] Cade's contributor's notes comment: "Frances Beale—Active in SNCC's Black Women's Liberation Committee, the National Council of Negro Women, and several Black women's study groups. Resides in New York" (253). The essay also appears in *The New Women: A MOTIVE Anthology on Women's Liberation*, edited by Joanne Cooke, Charlotte Bunch-Weeks and Robin Morgan, where it is the only essay explicitly by a Black woman.[19] Indeed, the volume is a reprint of the March/April 1969 issue of *motive*, from the Methodist Student Movement, and Beale's essay was added (along with four others) to the book version. It also appears in Robin Morgan's *Sisterhood Is Powerful*.[20] *Sisterhood Is Powerful* includes it in the section called "Women in the Black Liberation Movement: Three Views" along with the "Statement on Birth Control" and an essay by Eleanor Holmes Norton, "For

Sadie and Maude." Also included in another section, "Up from Sexism: Emerging Ideologies," is Florynce Kennedy's "Institutionalized Oppression vs. the Female."[21]

Beale's essay pairs with the "Statement on Birth Control" by *Black Sisters*. It raises the issue (maybe mostly to a white women's liberation audience) of a large-scale, U.S. campaign for so-called birth control in the service of controlling Black people, using Black women as a "medical testing ground" (349) and "outright surgical genocide" (347). Beale argues that Black women have the right to determine when and whether they bear children "for the struggle" and how many, and how far apart if they desire them (349). *Black Sisters* speaks directly to Black men, including Black men who use the genocide argument to bully Black women, concluding that "birth control is the freedom to *fight* genocide of black women and children" (361).

Beale pointedly uses the term "the white women's liberation movement" (350) and wonders if there are any parallels between it and "the movement on the part of black women for *total* emancipation" (my emphasis, but I think it clarifies the spirit in which Beale is making the distinction). Beale is highly aware that the white women's liberation movement is "far from being monolithic" and suggests that there is no common ground with groups that are not anticapitalist, anti-imperialist and antiracist; no common ground with groups that see male chauvinism as the primary oppression or that are anti-men; no common ground with groups not engaged with the "Black masses"; no common ground "if they do not realize that the reasons for their conditions lie in the System" rather than in men. The essay also includes analyses of sex roles, of the very particular meanings of "work" for Black women within a white conception of "sex roles," that Black women are slaves of slaves (an implicit historical analysis) with a long history "made to our struggle for liberation."

It's evident in these examples that the same essays are reprinted several times; there is a sense of the obligatory but minimal inclusion called tokenism. Although there are other Black women published in these anthologies beyond the four Echols names, we know that only Ware of those four is structurally "at the center" of the formations Echols calls radical feminism, while the others (Robinson and Beale perhaps especially) belong to multiple political locations inside and outside feminist radicalism. Robinson's Mount Vernon poor Black women's group represents another palpable outcome, what at one time was a radical form of feminism, but which is not elaborated, and now not recaptured as radical feminism, because it is not an origin of a line to the cohorts Echols privileges. But in numbers, in published visibility, in current theoretical significance, this group compares strikingly with some of the subgroups Echols narrativizes. The complexity of interests, methods, and political possibilities the collection of working papers and polemics display, the reworking for different locations, and the envisioning of quite differing audiences, real and imagined, need to be kept in mind while we continue looking at these anthologies. Beale's essay, in an unchanging form, seems especially tokenized to me, made to carry too large a burden of representing "Black women" to white women's liberation; while the Robinson and group papers (most contextualized in Cade's *The Black Woman*) are more interactively participating in the collections they inhabit—or at least their "working papers," with their own lively intertextualities, are a broken-up but energetic interconnected collection of work.

One anthology on my shelves has no Black women's writing in it at all. This is 1971's *Woman in Sexist Society: Studies in Power and Powerlessness*.[22] My edition of it (the third printing; the first printing of the paperback was in June, 1972; 1971 was the date of a hardcover edition published by Basic Books) says in tiny letters on the cover: "Current writings by 31 women scholars and activists, including KATE MILLETT • LUCY KOMISAR • SHULAMITH FIRESTONE" and contains three initial pages of rather lengthy quotations from reviews in *Ramparts*, *Saturday Review* Syndicate, *The Nation*, *Publishers Weekly*, *Kirkus*, Minneapolis *Star*, and *Library Journal*. *Ramparts* recommends it for "Women's Studies courses";[23] almost half of the contributors are identified as having university and college affiliations— the "scholars," while the other half are identified as artists, professional women, members of NOW, and women's liberationists—the "activists." There is some overlap. A handful of essays are among the repeatedly reprinted, but most are without reprint acknowledgments; these are less "writings from the women's liberation movement" in its popular front revolutionary form and more writings from an academic arm. (In a possible distancing from this location, Ellen Willis's oft-reprinted "Consumerism and Women" here is authored "A Redstocking Sister.")[24]

Part 4 of *Woman in Sexist Society* is called "Social Issues and Feminism: Education, Homosexuality, Race, and Radicalism" (xii; one essay per each "social issue" and two on radicalism, one of which is the Willis essay). The one essay on "race" (out of 29) is by Catharine Stimpson, " 'Thy Neighbor's Wife, Thy Neighbor's Servants': Women's Liberation and Black Civil Rights" (622–57). A scholarly work, it gives a lengthy and sophisticated reading of the nineteenth- and early twentieth-century intertwined histories of abolition and women's suffrage, "movements [that] use each other, betray each other . . . " (624). The very first paragraph, rather offensively, says, "I respect black liberation, and I work for women's liberation, but the more I think about it, the less hope I have for a close alliance for those who pledge allegiance to the sex and those who pledge allegiance to the skin" (622). Stimpson uses the phrase "white women's liberation" and it layers together several meanings from the historical analysis (of betrayals) that precedes it:

> There are no formal bridges between integrated black civil rights groups and white women's liberation groups as there were in the nineteenth century, as there are in contemporary white radical gatherings. Reliable people also think that surprisingly few of the new feminists were seriously involved in civil rights. More came out of the New Left or in response to discriminatory post–World War II work conditions. The women who were committed to black causes, if they could shake loose from the roles of Lady Bountiful, Sister Conscience, or Daring Daughter, each in its way an archetypal woman's role, gained political and personal consciousness. (645–46)

In this essay Stimpson also powerfully and persuasively critiques the recurrent political uses of a Black/woman analogy. I see this analogy as a historically shared tactic, drawn upon from several political locations, for producing the political object "woman" out of the materials of a discourse on race. Examples from these anthologies of such production include Gayle Rubin's 1969 essay "Woman as Nigger," reprinted from her college newspaper in *Masculine/Feminine* (230–40). It relies, as does Marlene Dixon's "The Restless Eagles: Women's Liberation 1969" in *The New Woman* (49–60), on Helen Mayer Hacker's 1951 essay "Women as a Minority Group," also reprinted in *Masculine/Feminine* (130–48).[25] The Roszaks introduce Hacker's essay in the following terms: "Hacker's paper is an important early recognition of the underlying resemblance of the oppressed, no matter to which group they belong" (131).

The ending of Flo Kennedy's essay from *Sisterhood Is Powerful*, noted above, plays a range of political identities against and with each other this way:

> Dean Willis Reese, a lanky man who talks with a lisp in a shrill voice and walks with a switch, hastened to assure me that I was being refused admission to Columbia Law School in 1948 not because I was black, but because I was a woman. I leaned on the ethnic angle, saying that some of my more cynical friends thought I was being discriminated against because I was a Negro (we weren't saying "black" in those days), and in any case it felt the same. Law-school admission opened the door just wide enough for *me*, but not for my friend Pat Jones, who was a Barnard graduate, with a slightly higher law aptitude level and slightly lower undergraduate average, but white.
>
> Many senior partners, or hiring partners in Establishment law firms still have the nerve to say they don't normally hire women. Some, perhaps most, firms will accept a woman if she is in the upper percentile of her law school class. (So, also, they'll accept supersmart Jews.) (446)

Kennedy's essay begins: "People who have trouble accepting the thesis that women are an oppressed group might be somewhat placated by my theory of the *circularity of oppression*" (438). Features of Kennedy's theory include: examination of a *consent* to oppression and in what circumstances it is possible to withdraw such consent; examination of how oppressed people are used as agents of oppression for oppressors—indeed, who receives a license to oppress; how institutionalized oppression can make it unnecessary for individuals to be oppressors; and includes a critique of "sisterhood," insisting that women too can be "agents of oppression." It's clear that Kennedy's essay intends to produce a theory in which forms of oppression can be understood as interconnected, and that paralleling one with another produces both new politicized groups and new accountabilities among oppressed people. This in the midst of a style in which the possibilities of her own homophobia and anti-Semitism are raised, but made very complex.

But Stimpson's essay occupies a different location and a slightly different historical moment (for Echols this essay might possibly represent a strand of that "tendency" that will become what Echols calls cultural feminism). Stimpson is concerned, on the one hand, about an exploitation by (white) women of this Black/woman analogy. She analyzes the uses of this analogy in Beverly Jones and Judith Brown's "Toward a Female Liberation Movement." (Echols claims: "With *Notes from the First Year* the "Florida Paper" [this essay, written June 1968] was the earliest articulation of radical feminism" [63]. It is also anthologized in *Voices from Women's Liberation* [362-414].) Stimpson says: "The analogy exploits the passion, ambition, and vigor of the black movement. It perpetuates the depressing habit white people have of first defining the black experience and then of making it their own. Intellectually sloppy, it implies that both blacks and white women can be seriously discussed as amorphous, classless, blobby masses" (650). (Hacker's use of the analogy is *not* a discussion of "amorphous, classless, blobby masses"; Stimpson, however, is describing a rhetoric less disciplined.)

On the other hand, Stimpson has more and quite other concerns about the Black/woman analogy: "It permits women to avoid doing what the black movement did at great cost and over a long period of time: making its protest clear and irrefutable, its ideology self-sufficient and momentous, its organization taut. It also helps to limit women's protest to the American landscape. The plight of woman is planetary, not provincial; historical, not immediate" (650). First, and this is a point I want to elaborate later, Stimpson paints the Black movement as better-off than the women's movement: *its* protest is "clear and irrefutable," the women's movement's is not; its ideology is "self-sufficient and momentous," its organization "taut." Cost and time have mattered; "Black" is viewed—rather enviously—as a powerful political object. Second, "the plight of woman" is *limited* by this analogy; the Black movement implicitly is played out only on the American landscape, is provincial, is immediate. Its political organizational power in the United States is forefronted here, but the connections of the Black movement with other global ("planetary") movements for decolonization—historically intertwined through slavery with the early modern emergence of capitalism and colonial expansion and later with industrial capitalism's reconfigurations making rice and cotton culture profitable—this is erased. Black political struggle (intertwined with capitalism) is historically too localized, too immediate. "Woman" as a political identity has to be consolidated in "self-sufficiency"—its specious unity in its very expulsion of Black women from its definitions. As it appears to open up historical ranges, it closes down political interconnections.

I read Stimpson's essay as an apology unapologetically justifying the exclusions that can be called "the white women's movement." I think the word self-sufficiency here and the notion of autonomy in Echols are key to the theoretical exclusions and political fears that accompany an erasure of Black women's history and centrality *in* the so-called white women's movement.

Echols includes as an appendix to *Daring* a transcript piece in which some white radical women argue about Black women and women's liberation. This transcript captured some of the discussion at the Sandy Springs (Md.) Conference, at which twenty women from Chicago, Florida, and East Coast cities—D. C., Baltimore, and New York—met for three days in August, 1968.[26] The discussion began when someone suggested that Black women be invited to an upcoming national women's liberation conference, mobilizing connections to Black women through the Black Panthers and SNCC. Someone mentions that the Black Panthers have a women's group (we know through the earlier discussion of Beale that SNCC at some point had a "Women's Liberation Committee"). The use of the word "women" to mean "white women" is ubiquitous, and especially an anchoring in "our groups, and the people close to us" is recurrent.

Several women are self-conscious about the group's fear of Black women—although some women dispute this characterization. Although someone says "we've had black women in our groups" (and why aren't they part of "our groups and the people close to us"?) it's very clear that for this particular group of white women "our groups and the people close to us" don't generally include Black women. (Were these women "cruising" through the white women's movement?) "Close" means both close in political analysis and agenda and close in friendship and political networks. A range of viewpoints is expressed, and some women continually press to include Black women and to examine white women's own racism, but the pressure is to selectively admit "a few black women who are thinking along the lines we are" (that is, "close" to us). Including those few numbers of such women is however branded as tokenism and "it is worse to do that than not do anything." This group of white women struggles to guess at and interpret the existence and meanings of similar and different concerns among Black and white women: "If there is a black women's movement or momentum or dynamic or anything going . . . "; "if we say if you define women's liberation in the same way we define it, that's a very white racist thing to do"; "if there are black groups which exist. . . . " At what point coalition is necessary is disputed: only after finding "where is it that our oppression lay[s], to see if there is a common bond" or "it's absolutely essential . . . that we have militant black power women in on the formation of our ideology." Indeed, the singling out of Black women in particular is disputed: "I don't understand . . . why you are just picking black, militant women as opposed to all of the other kinds of women with different ideologies."

One powerful thread of fear is that the Black women will "rule the day," will "cow the white women," that they might "interrupt real interchange among white women." Another is that the wrong Black women will attend or will be courted: "Black people may not know that white women don't want them there." "There's going to be a selective process in the kinds of black women who come. And we're going to get the worst kind. Because they are into women's liberation instead of black liberation." (Talk about a double bind!) There is a simultaneous valorization of Black militant women who aren't into women's liberation and a fear of their cowing white women. Echols says it was the so-called politicos (radical women from the new left) who called invitations to Black women into question, and that it was the "pro-woman faction" (which insisted that women were not consenting or complicitous with their own oppression) who were calling the group on its racism.

Notice when considering such a story how the white women's fear and othering of the Black women constructs the white women as a center and the Black women as marginal: needing to be invited, not part of the networks "close to us." Echols

(and my) using the Sandy Springs Conference and its discussion as exemplary constructs it as the part (of women's liberation) that represents the whole. And Echols
suggests this: "This drama would be played out many times in the future, for the
issue of black women's liberation continued to haunt the movement" (106). Echols
also considers the possibility that the white women are right, that if Black women
had been invited to the conference, "they would have guilt-tripped the white
women, making it difficult for white women to feel that they could legitimately focus on their own oppression." Still, she insists that even so, not including Black
women was "a terrible mistake," leading to white women's inclination "to rely
solely on their own experiences when theorizing about women's oppression." But,
she goes on, "it seems less clear how black women would have benefited"; that they
would just have been "educating whites about racism" (107).

But I think this formulation/assumption of white women at the center masks
the other possibility, the one implied by Stimpson's "envious" description of the
Black movement, another evaluation that white women are newcomers, not at all at
a pre-existing center, rather gingerly and sometimes fearfully constructing a tiny
group center on the outskirts of the Black movement and other social justice movements, and of the new left. I think this possibility is palpable in the transcription.
White privilege and radical white women's difficult experiences in the new left combine with Echols's formulation of radical feminism's claims of autonomy to produce
a shifting illusion/reality newly/retrospectively centering white women, in the political imagination of white women's liberationists, as "the feminist struggle."
Echols's question about what Black women would have had to gain suggests this
"palpability" as well, assuming as it does that white women's limitations would cen-
trally take up all political space. Imaginations of Black women at the center figure
at most as teachers of white women.

To get this illusion/reality to "flicker," I read Toni Cade's introduction to *The
Black Woman* alongside the Sandy Springs Conference story:

> We are involved in a struggle for liberation. . . . What characterizes the current
> movement of the sixties is a turning away from the larger society and a turning
> toward each other. Our art, protest, dialogue no longer spring from the impulse to
> entertain, or to indulge or enlighten the conscience of the enemy; white people,
> whiteness, or racism; men, maleness, or chauvinism: America or imperialism . . .
> depending on your viewpoint and your terror. Our energies now seem to be in-
> vested in and are in turn derived from a determination to touch and to unify.
> What typifies the current spirit is an embrace, an embrace of the community and
> a hardheaded attempt to get basic with each other. . . .
>
> Throughout the country in recent years, Black women have been forming work-
> study groups, discussion clubs, cooperative nurseries, cooperative businesses, con-
> sumer education groups, women's workshops on the campuses, women's caucuses
> within existing organizations, Afro-American women's magazines. From time to
> time they have organized seminars on the Role of the Black Woman, conferences
> on the Crisis Facing the Black Woman, have provided tapes on the Attitude of
> European Men toward Black Women, working papers on the Position of the Black

Women in America; they have begun correspondence with sisters in Vietnam, Guatemala, Algeria, Ghana on the Liberation Struggle and the Woman, formed alliances on a Third World Women plank. They are women who have not, it would seem, been duped by the prevailing notions of "woman," but who have maintained a critical stance. (7, 9–10)

The Sandy Springs white women's questioning and imaginings: "*If* there are black groups that exist . . . " "*if* there is a black woman's movement or momentum or dynamic or anything going . . . " suggests simultaneously that the groups Cade names are yet unknown to them, *or also* that they "might not count" to them, even if they did know about them. (And, after all, Cade is published here in 1970, while the conference took place in 1968; this is a period in which many things happen in short time periods.) This range does/will shortly exist among the white women's liberation movement, but radical women will be only a piece of that; a piece understanding itself as the center of revolutionary practice. (Notice that Toni Cade doesn't seem to have any problem placing all these forms of group activity in a revolutionary context.) As radical women separate from the new left and create their independent women's movement (and this is a task taken over time, replayed in various regions, and always contested), what "counts" to them (in the model of radical feminism) would be a similarly becoming "independent" Black women's liberation movement, parallel and equivalent to their own. The "double bind" vision of either valorized Black militant women who are appropriately *not* into (white) women's liberation, or the wrong Black women who want in on (white) women's liberation, could only be settled within this unstated valuing of a Black women's liberation as autonomous on the model of an "autonomous" white women's liberation. None of these three possibilities is what Toni Cade is describing (although all three could mingle with other palpable outcomes). The multiple political locations of Black women Cade is naming don't exist for white radical women whose relations to other liberation struggles are being effectively mediated by the (white, male) left.

Listen again to Echols's description of "black women like . . . " and ask: "*Whose* 'feminist struggle'?" "Must a black feminist movement be *autonomous* to 'count'?"

Of course, from the early days of the movement there were black women like Florynce Kennedy, Frances Beale, Cellestine Ware, and Patricia Robinson who tried to show the connections between racism and male dominance. But most politically active black women, even if they criticized the black movement for sexism, *chose not to become involved in the feminist struggle*. Efforts *to generate a black feminist movement*, which date back to 1973 with the founding of the short-lived National Black Feminist Organization, were less than successful. (291) [Emphasis mine.]

Here, let's go back a bit to look at Echols's method more closely within an understanding of Echols's production of the object "radical feminism," especially to notice how the presences and absences of Black women are positioned methodologically. This requires thinking through the meanings of the interview techniques upon which this historical account is so fundamentally based.

Producing such an object of knowledge costs. The costs are time, resources, contacts, abilities to travel, access to materials, access to people, production of documents, access to publication, abilities to produce audience/s. (This is not an exhaustive list.) These "costs" are political and epistemological. In "Appendix D: A Note on the Oral Interviews," Echols gives us an inkling of some of the costs of producing "radical feminism." The book started out as a Ph.D. thesis; perhaps a somewhat lower-budget school version of what will become the feature-length movie. Originally Echols intended to interview fifteen to twenty women. With oral interviews lasting anywhere from one to six hours and requiring many prior hours setting up contacts, researching individuals, and preparing individualized questions, you can see that this was quite an investment to begin with. However, the project *expanded*, and in the end Echols in fact interviewed forty-two individuals, including conducting two group interviews and two joint interviews. Ros Baxandall in her review of the book in *Socialist Review* remarks on the process of being interviewed by Echols and suggests how much preparation Echols had put into each interview: "Unlike those of most other feminist scholars I've encountered, Echols's interviews were thorough and provocative, as she had read all the literature and therefore had a context for questions and a check on our often-inaccurate memory"[27] (190). Echols started off contacting women whose names she encountered in the literatures she examined and knew. Those women in turn suggested other women, also activists but less well-known, less visible in the documentary record. And in the interview process itself, other women's names came up to be added as possible contacts. Echols says there could have been more names, more interviews, but she then concentrated on activist groups from the pre-1972 days, deciding that the documentary record was not complete for this time period. (One possible informant disagreed with her on the comprehensiveness of the record.)

Now, forty-two individuals interviewed is a very large undertaking. What scale of representation forty-two individuals present out of the range of women activists of the period is less obvious. Limited funding dictated that Echols interview only in three cities: New York, Washington, D.C., and Chicago. All the interviews were done in a fairly circumscribed time period: spring and summer 1984. It's clear that these constraints dramatically privileged a particular set of people. First, it privileged women who remained connected somehow with the cohort that developed during this political period. (This doesn't minimize the fancy detective work Echols undoubtedly was required to do to track some of these people down.) It privileged women in one of the three cities visited, and thus reinforced the priority these cities already had in movement histories, as *publication* as well as political centers. (Of course, the initial contacts from published literatures did this as well.) The decision to focus interview material on radical women active before 1972 (and not to quote interview material from women entering women's liberation after that period or situated in cities other than the three above and Boston) also privileged particular groups and cohorts.

Of course, privileging a finite set of individuals, political groups, and cities as political centers is the way to produce in-depth historical detail. And this the book abounds in. This is and will continue to be a valuable contribution to the history of the women's liberation movement. But, as Baxandall also notes, this book is not a history of the (whole?) movement but rather of the *piece* of it Echols calls "radical feminism." Baxandall asks (having her own answers and requiring us to educatedly imagine Echols's answers): "Why does radical feminism deserve a book, and what were its contributions?" Echols's history is unlike Cellestine Ware's, whose political partisanship (I point out in chapter 4) is more restricted than Echols's, as Ware struggles for the particular ideological positioning *within* radical feminism of the Stanton-Anthony Brigade and New York Radical Feminists *specifically*. Echols, on her side, is engaged in splitting apart a political totality defined later by socialist feminism as its Other: radical feminism. Echols reconfigures this totality as the two objects: radical feminism and cultural feminism. Echols produces these objects by way of what Baxandall calls "an ideological history" (190). Baxandall marvels at Echols's "enormous job of clarifying intricate ideological inconsistencies and splits, but one begins to wonder why they are all so important" (192). They are important as the filaments of fiber that are pulled apart in unraveling the wrong "radical feminism," and they are carefully and intricately repositioned as threads of connection consolidated in the two new political objects.

Echols is very careful to say that this is *not* a history of the women's liberation movement, "rather this is a *thorough* history of one wing of the women's movement" (6). [Emphasis mine.] This very thoroughness is hypnotizing, though. Locating radical feminism at the origins of the women's liberation movement and in this powerful theoretical and political "autonomy" makes it very difficult to distinguish radical feminism from "the women's liberation movement" during much of Echols's historical narrative; especially as Echols does little in description of radical feminism's "outsides" but only elaborates its "degenerations." Meanwhile, white radical women's relationships to other movements for social justice are conceptually mediated through the left.

What to me becomes a rather tantalizing question is why none of the four Black women Echols names as engaged "from the early days of the movement" are interviewed, as this extant interview agenda can only reproduce white women's liberation. Well, we have *one* answer: in appendix D, Echols says she wrote to Florynce Kennedy, who only responded "long after I had stopped interviewing." Good methodology requires an orderly succession of events culminating in the stabilization of the object of knowledge, the production of the facts. The investments already expended in production can be jeopardized. What would it take to destabilize white women at the center of radical feminism? I can't help but wonder if Cellestine Ware's centrality to New York Radical Feminists and to radical feminism as its early partisan historian can be made weighty enough to set some of these constructions toppling. I fantasize that Echols attempted to track Ware down, but that she was no longer connected by those threads of ideological alliance and friendship and political communities. I fantasize because Ware doesn't come up in Echols's interview description; indeed, Ware is referred to rather sparsely in the book. Can a particular instance of structural "centrality" be weightier than numbers? Can "influence" be redefined *outside* the ideological threads that refigure the new "original" radical feminism? Outside white women's publications?

From the materials already examined in my tour of anthologies it seems clear that a number of Black women were deeply immersed in developing theoretical apparatus meant to deal with multiple oppressions and with coalitions among a variety of oppressed peoples and national liberation struggles. Mary Ann Weathers had put it this way in "An Argument for Black Women's Liberation as a Revolutionary Force" in *Voices from Women's Liberation* (reprinted from *No More Fun and Games*, February 1969):

> Women's Liberation should be considered as a strategy for *an eventual tie-up with the entire revolutionary movement* consisting of women, men, and children. We are now speaking of real revolution (armed). If you can not accept this fact purely and without problems examine your reactions closely. We are playing to win and so are they. Viet Nam is simply a matter of time and geography. (304) [Emphasis mine.]

> *All* women suffer oppression, even white women, particularly poor white women, and especially Indian, Mexican, Puerto Rican, Oriental and Black American women whose oppression is tripled by any of the above mentioned. But we do have female's oppression in common. This means that we can begin to talk to other women with this common factor and start building links with them and thereby build and transform the revolutionary force we are now beginning to amass. This is what Dr. King was doing. (306)[28]

Chela Sandoval in a 1991 retrospective dictionary entry (for *The Oxford Companion to Women's Writing in the United States*) defining the term "U.S. Third World Feminism," describes U.S. Third World feminism as based in a "new form of transnational alliance among peoples of color both outside of and within the U.S.," a solidarity across "the social movements of the 1960's and 1970's," bonding "activists of color in the Civil Rights, Anti-war, Black, Chicano, Asian, Native, Student, Encounter Group, Women's and Gay liberation movements."[29] The dates and activisms may very well non-trivially reflect Sandoval's own political histories:

> By 1971 a grass-roots movement of U.S. third world feminists began to form, bringing together women of color who in spite of severe differences in historical relations to power, color, culture, gender and sexual orientation, were surprised to recognize in one another profound similarities. A great number of newsletters, pamphlets, and books were produced by underground publishers during the 1971–1974 period, including separate works by Janice Mirikitani and Francis Beal, both entitled *Third World Women* and meant to affirm and develop the new kind of shared sisterhood/citizenship insistently emerging in the corridors and back rooms where women of color congregated. The burgeoning women's movement, however, could not accept, recognize, or contain this new kind of female alliance. Beal's 1971 essay in *Sisterhood Is Powerful* warned that women's liberation was fast becoming a "white women's movement" because it insisted on organizing along the gender demarcation male/female alone, when, as Sojourner Truth had so

eloquently stressed in 1851, people of color are often denied easy or comfortable access to either of these socially constructed categories. . . . [Sandoval then names "U.S. third world feminist artists, writers, critics, theorists, and activists" of the seventies, such as: Velia Hancock, Toni Morrison, Wendy Rose, Leslie Marmon Silko, Antonia Casteneda, Barbara Smith, Pat Parker, Rosara Sanchez, Maxine Hong Kingston, Lorna De Cervantes, Judy Baca, Teresa Hak Kyung Cha, Azizah Al-Hibri and Margaret Walker.] As Barbara Noda put it, these feminists of color were "lowriding through the women's movement," that is, they were developing the imagery, methods, and theories necessary for the "cruising" through meaning systems which would become the hallmark of a distinctive U.S. third world feminism.

Sandoval is constructing here another political object "U.S. third world feminism" and (1) stabilizing it around a set of names, and thus a set of dates—women of color writing throughout the seventies,[30] although, indeed, some white feminists may have first encountered this body of work in the early eighties; and (2) embedding it within that "new form of transnational alliance among peoples of color both outside of and within the U.S." that in the sixties and seventies was made possible by the multiple events and meanings of "decolonization."

The "flickering" process here, aided by Sandoval and maybe by Juliet Mitchell's introduction to *What Is Feminism?*, places that Sandy Springs Conference and its small (and influential, imaginatively and actively deeply captivating to some of us) constituency onto a larger world stage, much broader historically. Echols's labor-intensive, critical, admiring history and interview technique can be seen as a kind of fabulous "painting in miniature"; the kind of incredible work that must be admired through a lens making what is quite small, very large; indeed, centering as a whole world that bit of artistry (to some of us only too mesmerizingly "whole"). Sandoval's object of knowledge "U.S. Third World Feminism" redraws the scope of political action and recenters what counts as feminism and feminist theory. Rather than a white women's movement at the center of feminism, a white women's movement in a direct line from nineteenth-century U.S. feminism, and in this line continuing a history of betrayal, instead, the flicker flashes this "new form of transnational alliance" in which radical white women, attached and detaching from the new left, are a local eddy, somewhere off-center, working on this seemingly "planetary," but rather local object "woman." Women of color—in a multiplicity of relationships to this object "woman," collaboratively making it, *re*making it, ignoring it in favor of the construction of other political objects—engage in a "theory, method, and praxis" (Sandoval's conflation).

The theoretical contests, and alliances producing theory, in which U.S. Third World liberationists are engaged, are not agreed upon, seen by, or embedded within the white women's movement: "The burgeoning women's movement, however, could not accept, recognize or contain this new kind of female alliance." Checking out a variety of local scenes, or indeed, migrating from one region of the country, the hemisphere, the world, to another required "developing the imagery, methods, and theories necessary for the 'cruising' through meaning systems which would become the hallmark of a distinctive U.S. third world feminism." The white women's movement is another local scene through which to cruise, and being able to mirror it to itself as the center, part of the ability to participate in various local politics.

The discussion I've developed so far—the discussion of the production of the object "radical feminism" and the stakes in its autonomy and its implication in expansion/contraction of the ranges of meaning of "feminism"—sets up the methods I will use for the rest of the chapter in describing the production of the political object "theory" and models my analysis of its ranges of inclusive/exclusive meanings.

I connect Echols, Sandoval, and myself all as members of a generational cohort of feminist theorists and lesbians; however, we are multiply located in other, and very differing, cohorts as well: of region, of political groups and identities, of professional trajectories, and so on. I see us as absorbed in this fascinated return to the late sixties and early seventies, where we insert our absent selves historically by "setting the record straight" (ironic though the word "straight" may be). Locating all three of us as "feminist theorists" might very well be disputed by some (possibly ourselves), and we represent a range of theoretical methodologies, but I hope now to suggest how, within the meanings of this generational cohort, "feminist theory" is what we are all engaged in.

"Theory" occupies a particular place in Echols's construction of radical feminism. From her vantage point in *Daring to Be Bad*'s introduction (at the end of the eighties) it is radical feminism's "theoretical deficiencies," "shortcomings, contradictions, and fuzziness" (10) that led to its degenerated successor cultural feminism. "Some of radical feminism's theoretical deficiencies can be traced to its reactive stance toward the new left," Echols says; in my analysis of the location of Black women I agree, to the extent that this reactive stance overvalues autonomy and detaches radical feminism (and its sometime double "feminism") from other movements for social justice, conceptualized and realized within mediations by the white left. Echols justifies her concentration on radical feminism and especially on the particular cohorts she investigates "because with few exceptions these were the groups that made significant theoretical contributions," having "influence far beyond their numbers" and possessing "a certain awareness of their place in history" (20–21).

One section of Echols's book is titled "Early Theory Building." This section is embedded in her second chapter "The Great Divide: The Politico-Feminist Split," in which "Breaking away from the Left" (chapter 3) is prefigured by the difference within; that is, by the splits between those (eticly inclusive term) feminists who were tied to the left, personally, theoretically, and by activism—derisively refered to by their critics as "politicos," and those (eticly inclusive term) feminists who were "underdogs," "criticizing the left from the left to broaden its analysis of women's oppression" (51–52)—derisively refered to as (local and historically specific term) "feminists."[31] In "Early Theory Building," Echols analyzes papers by Joreen, Anne

Koedt (and reports from *Notes from the First Year*), Evelyn Goldfield, and a joint paper by Beverly Jones and Judith Brown (the "Florida Paper" referred to above), "which illuminate the differences between and within these two camps"[32] (60). The descriptions of splits, in which "shortcomings, contradictions, and fuzziness" are momentarily, if rather illusorily, cleaned up, produce new (if temporary) political identities reifying "theory."

For Echols non-deficient theory is not characterized by "shortcomings, contradictions, fuzziness." Over and over radical feminist theorists themselves attempt to reorder deficiencies by producing new forms of consistency: they break hopefully (with hopeful anticipation) into (what they hope are) coherent and consistent groupings (in which incoherence and contestations break out). The threads of subtle connection and disconnection through the arenas of vigorous contestation are what Echols represents as "theory." Echols's own polemical work, belonging to several overlapping conversations within the so-called sexuality debates, theorizes similarly: her historical representations are explicit theoretical interventions into political groupings and operate to produce new political identities, and what she values are the threads of subtle connection and disconnection reordering deficiencies. Echols's polemical work is filled with the passionate vigor about the possibilities of the present that is crimped in *Daring* without an apparatus in which to value new sites of political resistance, to locate the "outside" of radical feminism, and to take account of new environments and movements of power.

This on the one hand; on the other hand, "theory," understood over a range of years and places in this originary moment, as represented in the variety of occasions I've cruised through so far, can mean (as I analyze and generalize from historically specific materials) explanatory apparatus produced in or distributed through national liberation (anticolonialist and civil rights) movements and thinkers, canonical Marxist apparatus, and feminist appropriations and tinkerings with the above. But it can also refer to products of new feminist practices of production (more and less "purely" feminist, in a dizzying assortment of "feminisms").

Two examples of feminist practices of theory-production are (1) the Mount Vernon poor Black women's study papers discussed before, and (2) consciousness-raising groups (in their variety). Both exemplify complexly intertwined oralities and literacies, and subtly challenge assumptions valorizing written products as "theory." Both are group productions, with representative authors. Both can be conceptualized as "actions." (Contestations over this conceptualization are part of the theory building about consciousness-raising, for example.) I like Echols's term "theory building" and set it next to and against de Lauretis's locution "feminist theory rather than a feminist critique of some other theory or object-theory," emphasizing process rather than realization. Surely theory building is an appropriate epistemological location for the historical periods when feminisms are in obvious and overwhelming flux.

What Echols, Sandoval, and I share, and what I think we take and transform from the meanings of theory in this period, is an investment in the object "theory" *as* those mutually constituting, mutually embedded "actions": theory building, alliance shifting, and political identity production. As a generational cohort continually reinterpreting, inserting ourselves into this early flow of historical events, *we produce ourselves as theorists and remember ourselves at the center(s) of theory building* (certainly we occupied different "centers")—even when canonical histories won't mirror this centrality back to ourselves (and even if our hero worship of some of the canonical, principal players affects our strategies for reinterpretation).

My own memory of the word "radical feminism" is not at all as a particular wing of the women's liberation movement, but as being more "radical" than the other women's liberationists (which might *retrospectively*, after the production of new historical objects, amount to the same thing). What was more radical was in constant flux, and was manipulatable in the movements of personal and group power. Certainly I felt myself then (and feel myself now) to be a person with the power to mold theory (and to produce alternative institutions) in precisely these terms, as well as in other terms in other historical and institutional locations. Much as I myself am invested in the linguistic trails of specific phrases, the idea that "feminist theory" did not exist in the early seventies seems absurd to me, *given* this understanding of the meaning of "theory." Such theory was in the service of producing feminism, therefore it was feminist theory. (I remember the rather dour response of the period when confronted about wearing "men's clothes": "These are my shoes, and I am a woman, therefore these are women's shoes.") My suspicion is that the phrase "*feminist* theory" has a somewhat earlier appearance than suggested by de Lauretis (although I have not tracked its history), but certainly at times, "feminist" could be understood before the term "theory," and sometimes such an unstated understanding could suggest that "feminism" and "theory" were mutually defining—that the only kind of theory one *would* be doing was feminist. What was being *written about* theory, and what was being produced *by* theory, I would contend, at times also reflect differing generational understandings existing simultaneously. My own method for producing theory is anchored in this particular object "theory." This is the object I use for investigating the question "What counts as theory?"

I started off this chapter by asking: What are the different investments in the multiple historical objects deployed/displayed under the sign "theory"? What generic or unmarked forms of "theory" are challenged or altered by, or hide local or marked "theory"? Which marked forms speciously appear generic or travel globally? Patricia Hill Collins's book *Black Feminist Thought: Knowledge, Consciousness, and the Politics of Empowerment* suggests the question "When is it important *not* to display under the sign "theory" and for what reasons?" (The object/s of "display" here I leave in abeyance.)

My questions are meant to pull out threads of divergent and connective meanings, layers of abstraction, of category and element, inclusion and particularity. For Patricia Hill Collins, pulling out threads of divergent and connective meanings (implicitly) begins with generating many alternative words for a "generic" (actually generic or speciously generic?) and a generally unstated, sometimes even conspicuously absent term theory. Here is a list generated in the first few pages of the book, words and phrases that parallel, overlap, or associate with the terms "thought" and "theory": knowledge, higher branches of knowledge, intellectual prowess, ideas, scholarship, minds and talents, collecting the ideas and actions, analytical, analytical foundation, standpoint, distinctive standpoint, intellectual tradition, the knowledge produced, intellectual work, intellectual activism, Black feminist thought, feminist theory, recent resurgence of Black women's ideas (4–9). Collins extensively *stages* (examines) contests for the term "Black feminist" and its constituents "Black" and "feminist" in the section of the book called "Defining Black Feminist Thought," but she largely *performs* fluid interconnections around the words "thought" and "theory."

Collins is very aware of the layers of contestations, political and intellectual, her book engages and contends within. Stabilizing the object "Black feminist thought" is the project of the book, and Collins self-consciously deploys all the powers of representation and authority she can to enhance its stability; at the end of her preface — her most sustained discussion forefronting "theory" — she says:

> In order to demonstrate the existence and authenticity of Black feminist thought, I present it as being coherent and basically complete. This portrayal is in contrast to my actual view that theory is rarely this smoothly constructed. Most theories are characterized by internal instability, are contested, and are divided by competing emphases and interests. When I considered that *Black feminist thought is currently embedded in a larger political and intellectual context that challenges its very right to exist,* I decided not to stress the contradictions, frictions, and inconsistencies of Black feminist thought. Instead I present Black feminist thought as overly coherent, but I do so because I suspect that this approach is most appropriate for this historical moment. I hope to see other volumes emerge which will be more willing to present Black feminist thought as a shifting mosaic of competing ideas and interests. I have focused on the pieces of the mosaic — perhaps others will emphasize the disjunctures distinguishing the pieces of the mosaic from one another. (xiv) [Emphasis mine.]

It is clear throughout the preface that "theory" itself affects the stability of the object "Black feminist thought" (xi-xv). Theory is both appealed to and held to account: clasped together in deliberation (as if they might centrifugally propel themselves apart) are adjectives about the book, such as "intellectually rigorous" and "well researched," on the one hand, and "accessible," on the other — "not less powerful or rigorous but accessible." "I could not write a book about Black women's ideas that the vast majority of African-American women could not read and understand. Theory of all types is often presented as being so abstract that it can be appreciated only by a select few." And again: "the standard vocabulary of these ["theoretical"] traditions ["Afrocentric philosophy, feminist theory, Marxist social thought, the sociology of knowledge, critical theory, and postmodernism"], citations of their major works and key proponents, and these terms themselves rarely appear in the text. To me the ideas themselves are important, not the labels we attach to them" (xii). As

Black feminist thought stabilizes, theory is multiplied but thinned out; generalized, doubled, and de-emphasized; unlabeled.

Yet, theory is appealed to in order to: authenticate Black feminist thought, resource a variety of "theoretical traditions," nominate and validate a "distinctive methodology," "reflect" "the everyday actions and ideas" of Black women and "to see all of these associations with fresh eyes," "reconcile subjectivity and objectivity in producing scholarship" (xiii–xiv). These are some of theory's powers. Theory is also held accountable for: excluding "those who do not speak the language of elites and thus reinforc[ing] social relations of domination"; centering "ideas in ways that are convenient for the more powerful"; and giving priority to "white feminist theorists," "Afro-American men," and others while subordinating Black feminist thought. These are some of theory's indicted powers. "In contrast, I maintain that theory and intellectual activity are not the province of a select few but instead emanate from a range of people" (xii–xiii). Notice that powers and accountabilities are not distinguished as theory as conceptual apparatus, on the one hand (all the good stuff), and theory as illegitimately powerful institution, on the other (all the bad stuff). Black feminist thought is not extra-institutional, but produced by and in a range of people and institutions—people and institutions to be named and to be newly valued (some of this revaluing happens in the dense syntheses that make up the core themes sections).

Theory is not repudiated, but multiply interpenetrated; newly invested, but rigorously unlabeled. What Collins represents as "my choices concerning the volume itself" can also be read as prescriptions for a particular, marked, *strategic* "theory": insisting on accessibility (to preferred audiences), pointedly centering Black women oppositionally, decanonizing individuals and instead emphasizing multiple (and less exchangeable) voices, developing an apparatus for recognizing and generating theory in community, recognizing consolidation as a strategic historic moment, using new tools out of developing apparatus (in this case, the "both/and conceptual stance") to locate oneself in disciplinary/institutional and political values (in this case, the reconciliation of subjectivity and objectivity).

Clearly, Black feminist thought holds together many levels and varieties of an often either absent or deliberately attenuated object "theory." Part of the point of fluidly moving between "theory" and "thought" (or "intellectual activity" or the variety of other terms Collins alternates or particularizes) *is* to get academic theory to release its hold on its illegitimate powers and to include many people and many kinds of action as thinkers (theorists) and thought (theory). Collins has certainly not stabilized "thought" by simply substituting it for "theory": either as its more inclusive equivalent or as mutually exclusive opposites. Fluidly moving between thought and theory (at times allowing first one and then the other to be conceptually contained or embedded *or* to "meta" the other) sometimes allows Collins to pick and choose the contests she wants to engage in, sometimes leaves inchoate a space of nondifferentiation, a repository for yet-unrealized or unimagined patterns of "thought." Both unacknowledged but implicitly engaged in contests for "thought" and "theory" (for although contestation may not figure the language of explanation and imagery of the book, it still inhabits the book quite thoroughly) *and* this space of nondifferentiation are strategies for stabilizing Black feminist thought. Collins has positioned herself in such a way that she cannot be *simply* (although perhaps complexly) appropriated into what one might call "pro-" or "anti-" theory camps. But the fluid movements she performs gather layers of meaning and suggest layers of contestation as they are projected onto a backdrop in which pro- and anti-theory proponents map out mutually exclusive territories. Even more important are the backdrops that dispute the very existence of Black feminist thought, against which the powers of stabilization contest. To resource certain powers theory is consolidated, but in the solvent of new possibilities, theory is dissolved.

In chapter 2 I will discuss in some more detail Collins's development of the notion of "*a* Black women's standpoint" [my emphasis], look at her core themes in light of the notion of "achievement," and examine the framework of the book as a proleptic response to issues of "theoretical adequacy"; in this chapter I want instead now to focus on how Collins intends this book to celebrate, expand, and strengthen Black women's intellectual lives. bell hooks, in her 1991 *Breaking Bread: Insurgent Black Intellectual Life*, shares with Collins concern for the engagement and role of Black women intellectuals; indeed, Collins's book is named in hooks's selected bibliography. (The book is coauthored with Cornel West and involves several intricate elaborations and interweavings of their writings and words.)[33] In the last chapter of *Breaking Bread*, bell hooks insists not only that Black women's intellectual lives be valued, but that the social position "intellectual" be valued and available to any bright, committed Black woman, at any age, inside and especially outside the academy. hooks is insistent that (1) intellectual life is not to be valued only as it confirms women in more or other "service work" (teaching, for example), intellectualism's image as "selfish" must be challenged, Black women intellectuals must be rewarded and recognized for their work; (2) intellectual life involves both isolation and community: that aloneness must be available to and supported for Black women—its risks, difficulties, and pleasures; the assumption that intellectual work estranges women from communities must be challenged by the testimonies and work of Black women intellectuals; that, indeed, intellectual work is often intellectual activism.

hooks is eloquent on both the many pleasures and affirmations of intellectual work and on its skills developed in personal survival struggles, out of abuse and harassment—the very skills that can "enable one to participate more fully in the life of family and community" (150). This is the spirit that Collins hopes most to see "stabilizing" Black feminist thought: participation in intellectual life—a reality and conceptualization that cannot break into hostile pieces the processes and thoughts "themselves" and the institutions and structures that facilitate, reward, and sanction this work. hooks speaks for the possibility of Black intellectual communities—inside, outside, interweaving the academy—just as she carefully teases apart the meanings of academics and intellectuals.

In stabilizing Black feminist thought as coherent and complete, Collins argues for a continuity of epistemology from outlook to support in Black women's experiences, for example:

> The convergence of Afrocentric and feminist values in the ethic of caring seems particularly acute. White women may have access to a women's tradition valuing emotion and expressiveness, but few Eurocentric institutions except the family validate this way of knowing. ... The differences among race/gender groups thus hinge on differences in their access to institutional supports valuing one type of knowing over another. Although Black women may be denigrated within white-male-controlled academic institutions, other institutions, such as Black families and churches, which encourage the expression of Black female power seem to do so, in part, by way of their support for an Afrocentric feminist epistemology. (217)

Collins relies on Afrocentrism to produce long historical and cultural unities grounding Black feminist thought and its sometime equivalent Afrocentric feminist thought. ("Even though I will continue to use the term *Afrocentric feminist thought* interchangeably with the phrase *Black feminist thought*, I think they are conceptually distinct" [40].) The longer passage above marks one of many examples of moments of "stabilization" in Collins's book: where the conceptualization produces the reality and together conceptualization and reality merge. hooks's argument includes much more information about her own experience of abuse and harassment in her own family, as well as within the white-male-controlled institutions of the academy. Eliding this contingency is not romanticization on Collins's part, but rather the production of coherency and completeness in the service of consolidation. Afrocentrism as a unity works to produce coherency and completeness as well. Both hooks and Collins intend and produce new meanings of "institution/community," oppositional meanings within white feminist theory, and signs of nascent realities and possibilities in the process of emergence. Black intellectual communities are modeled and imagined in the figures of Afrocentrism, of Black families and churches as they support an Afrocentric feminist epistemology, in the possibilities of connection suggested by the convergence of Afrocentric and feminist values, and in the deliberate fashioning of form and content in hooks's and Collins's books.

My earlier descriptions and polemic concluding the discussion of Echols's book *Daring to Be Bad*—the situation of the object theory as the mutually embedded actions of theory-building, alliance-shifting and political identity-production—are very different from the investments in autonomy and ideological differences Collins introduces in her core theme section "Rethinking Black Women's Activism." Reminiscent of Sandoval's cruising through meaning systems is Collins's "moving through jobs": "Because the work, and not the particular job, was their focus, they moved on when organizational limits combined with turning points in their self-development. ... Acquiring a focused education by moving through jobs enabled the women to see the bigger picture obscured by working only within one setting." Other concepts, such as "viewing autonomy and coalition as complementary" (161) and "strategic affiliation," suggest simultaneously both fluidity of movement and skills in negotiating between ideological positions, rather than the manipulative transformations of ideological positions:

> I suspect that . . . African-American women in general—are more likely to engage in this strategic affiliation and reject ideology as the overarching framework structuring our political activism. This does not mean that Black women lack ideology but, rather, that our experiences as othermothers, centerwomen, and community othermothers foster a distinctive form of political activism based on negotiation and a higher degree of attention to context. (160)

In the process of stabilization, occurring over time with differing partial moments in which it is unclear whether or not stabilization can or will occur, contingent strategies prioritize some aspects of stability over others. Collins prioritizes coherence: a deliberate, informed overcoherence precedes the exploration of disjuncture. Collins prioritizes transparency of language, rather than, say, the recognition/production of new academic and literary languages: montages, pidgins, and creoles. (Examples of the latter possibilities might be found in the work of Gloria Anzaldúa, Norma Alarcón or María Lugones, or of Henry Louis Gates, Jr.; none are referred to by Collins.)[34]

Collins is fighting for a Black feminist thought not subordinate to white feminist theory and only partially parallel to it, but she is also implicitly arguing for a mutual embrace with (some inclusive and yet to happen) feminist theory. In this formulation the "historical suppression of Black women's ideas has had a pronounced influence on feminist theory. . . . The absence of Black feminist ideas from these and other studies places them in a much more tenuous position to challenge the hegemony of mainstream scholarship on behalf of all women" (7). Note the subtle similarities of intent and distinctions of strategy between this formulation and what could be an alternate conceptualization congruent with formulations by Sandoval spoken of earlier. In these formulations, theory of women of color has a continuity and political (rather than conceptual) completeness over a theoretical activism since the early seventies, a continuity which when centered figures white women as marginal feminist theorists, whose work often at best parallels this work, although in some years and some central theoretical concerns is almost entirely absent from it, and only in the early eighties begins to parallel, recognize, and occasionally encounter and interact with it. Notice the difference of appeal on the one hand, to a continuity across women of color, and on the other, to Afrocentrism.

Collins, at least partially at times, embeds her work to stabilize Black feminist thought within a (sometimes hopeful, sometimes specious) project "to challenge the hegemony of mainstream scholarship on behalf of all women." In other words, Collins moves among "centers": sometimes the center is Black feminist thought quite incidental to anything called "theory"; other times the center is feminist theory, either in its yet-to-be-realized possibilities of inclusion or in its critique as the agent for the suppression of Black feminist thought; at other times, the academy occupies a center of implicit evaluation and sanction; at other times, Black institutions are centered—in their ranges of current historical manifestation, in the imaginative possibilities of knowledge-making they can figure, and in their cultural unity as understood within Afrocentrism.

Third World Women and the Politics of Feminism straddles the eighties in a complexity of political and academic locations. A conference book published in 1991, its conference took place much earlier, in 1983. However, rather than feeling dated or belatedly refocused, the book instead manages its layers of historical specificity with striking rhetorical and conceptual flexibility, taking into account and synthesizing debates and new analyses over this decade. It's possible to imagine (whether erroneously or accurately is another question) that the most polemical pieces making arguments for very particular political programs (say, Nellie Wong's description of the Freedom Socialist Party's platform) are most historically tied to the moment of the conference, but clearly the conference now marks a moment in which new political agendas, conceptualizations, and research programs were connected and then realized over the succeeding time:

> Seven years later, the collection is no longer principally tied to the conference. . . . Historical developments in third world women's struggles, the production and consolidation of transnational corporations and cultures, the institutionalization of discourses of pluralism in the U.S. academy, and the Reagan-Bush years have all intervened to locate us at a very different historical juncture in 1990. The anthology represents our efforts to address these shifts and developments. It focuses on the recent debates over the development of feminist theory and politics by third world women. (ix)

According to the preface, the large themes of the conference, held at the University of Illinois at Urbana-Champaign, were "Colonization and Resistance," "Images and Realities," and "International Women's Movements." These have splintered, reentangled, metamorphosed, and incorporated additional political languages and new academic fields, becoming these thematic clusters in the book: "Power, Representation, and Feminist Critique," "Public Policy, the State, and Ideologies of Gender," "National Liberation and Sexual Politics," and "Race, Identity, and Feminist Struggles." The title of the conference also reflects an earlier focusing of debates and political positions; it was called "Common Differences: Third World Women and Feminist Perspectives," reminiscent of the ground-breaking book by Gloria Joseph and Jill Lewis and suggesting a double meaning, domestic and international, in "Third World Women," a term problematized throughout the conference book.[35] One hundred and fifty people spoke at the conference and over two thousand attended; these numbers indicate the kind of academic/historical takeoff point in feminist theory the conference encapsulates. Literatures over this decade are organized and synthesized in Chandra Talpade Mohanty's stunning introduction, "Cartographies of Struggle: Third World Women and the Politics of Feminism."

In the eighties, U.S. women's studies and feminist theory are marked by new interconnections with and new commodifications and consumptions of international feminisms. What some might conceptualize as two great influences making their powerful impact on U.S. feminist theory in the eighties—poststructuralism (sometimes overlappingly or metonymically named under the rubric "French Feminism") and a multicultural critique inside identity politics—can be alternately described in the scenario of a local and academic U.S. (white) women's movement's somewhat belated discovery of its own embeddedness (and indebtedness) within a large international frame of women's movements, refigured (even mystified) for U.S. academic consumption as a core set of theoretical debates under new influences.

Another form, not yet discussed, in which U.S. (white, academic) feminist theory "discovers"—often not very welcomingly—its relation to other women's movements is through connections with international women scholars coming to U.S. graduate schools to study. Some of these scholars subsequently enter the U.S. academy, others extend lines of connection to academies and political movements in various parts of the world. Within my own graduate program's curricular "track" in feminist theory during the eighties, my peers included feminists from Australia, Britain, Brazil, France, India, and Japan. Retrospectively, I see only too vividly how lightly I took this situation and at the time how little I intentionally took advantage of all this knowledge about the varieties of local and international feminisms. I remember ashamedly one such graduate student friend once remarking on how little the U.S. crowd asked about her country and her feminist history.

My graduate program has subsequently (I left in 1986) produced two "conference books" (actually journal issues) mapping out such concerns and overlapping with the fields of inquiry produced in Mohanty, Russo, and Torres's book: from a small conference in the spring of 1987, the special issue of *Inscriptions* on "Feminism and the Critique of Colonial Discourse," and from another mini-conference February 11-12, 1989, the next issue of *Inscriptions* on "Traveling Theories, *Traveling Theorists*."[36] The first I've already referred to at the beginning of this chapter; the second introduces itself thus: "The conference grew out of concrete dilemmas faced by graduate students working on their dissertations. . . . It soon became apparent that the problems were of more than local significance. As academic writers originating from, and looking toward, diverse places on the postcolonial map, many of us have found ourselves both empowered and hemmed in by the theories we depend on to frame and develop our research" (vi).

Originating from and looking toward maps of postcolonialisms situates traveling scholars in relation to this object "theory." Migrant scholars, metropolitan subjects, cosmopolitan feminists—there are a variety of overlapping ways to name some locations of these women who have shifted and changed women's studies over the last decade. The complexities of their various positionings are brought up by Rey Chow's essay in *Third World Women and the Politics of Feminism*.

First, this essay is complicatedly intertextual. It comes from a later, rather different conference, reflecting subsequent shifts in status, emphasis, and points of consumption over the eighties. That conference was held at Harvard University June 16-18, 1989, and it too led to a conference book, *Nationalisms and Sexualities*, echoing its conference title.[37] Chow's first footnote in *Third World Women* explains:

> During this time [shortly after June 4, 1989, the date of the so-called Tiananmen
> Square massacre] I was to deliver a paper at a conference called "Nationalisms
> and Sexualities" at Harvard University. I had planned to discuss work of the con-
> troversial modern Chinese writer Yu Dafu. Watching the events in China unfold
> in the U.S. media, I felt more and more that, at that moment in Chinese history, a
> talk devoted to "sexuality" was out of place. I therefore decided to speak about the
> current events. This essay is, in part, the talk I gave. (99)

This essay—"Violence in the Other Country: China as Crisis, Spectacle, and
Woman"—subsequently becomes part of Rey Chow's book *Woman and Chinese
Modernity: The Politics of Reading between West and East*.[38] In the preface to *Nationalisms and Sexualities* Rey Chow's name is listed (with thirty-six others) as one of
those who participated in the conference "but whose work could not be accommodated within the confines of the present volume" (ix). If nothing else, this emphasizes how many people spoke at the conference (this count would suggest at least
fifty-nine). *Third World Women* and *Nationalisms and Sexualities* are academic texts
but with both subtle and obvious differences. The first volume includes only work
by women, is situated very explicitly between "feminist theory and politics by third
world women" and would probably be valuable both as a class text and as a collection for research, and possibly even for political inspiration by some nonacademics.
In the second volume, almost half of the authors are men, and the book is located at
some juncture of gender studies, gay and lesbian theory and historiography, studies
of sexuality, and postcolonial critique. *Third World Women* could be described as at
the same juncture, but in fact the differences are striking: *Nationalisms and Sexualities* is far more at home in the academy and academic research, although in deeply
concerned politicized accountabilities; it is less likely, I would think, to be used as
either a class text or by non-academics. The names from the Harvard conference
reflect many rising and risen academic "stars." Chow's worry that a talk on "sexuality" might be out of place at this moment of political horror very much belongs
with some of the debates that took place at the "Common Differences" conference.
This weighing of priorities in immediate political struggles is more in keeping with
the politics of the Mohanty, Russo, and Torres book as it locates itself in relation to
nationalist struggles. *Nationalisms and Sexualities*, with persuasive sophistication,
has a less complicated, more wholly critical relation to the multiply (in each book)
problematized notion of "nationalism."

Second, in her essay, Chow describes her location as what some have called a
"metropolitan subject" in relation to some object "theory":

> I often meet sinologists and China historians, some male and some female, who
> ask me this question directly or indirectly: "Why are you using Western theory on
> Chinese literature?" . . . I am also asked from time to time, "Why am you using
> Western feminist theory on Chinese women?"
>   The contradictions about modern China as a site of the production of knowl-
> edge-as-surplus-value are revealingly demonstrated in these simple interroga-
> tions. . . . The above kind of interrogation slaps me in the face with the force of a

nativist moralism, precisely through a hierarchical dichotomy between West and East that enables my interrogators to disapprove of my "complicity" with the West. Such disapproval arises, of course, from a general context in which the criticism of the West has become mandatory. However, *where does this general critical imperative leave those ethnic peoples whose entry into culture is, precisely because of the history of Western imperialism, already "Westernized"?* For someone with my educational background, which is British colonial and American, the moralistic charge of my being "too Westernized" is devastating; it signals an attempt on the part of those who are specialists in "my" culture to *demolish the only premises on which I can speak.* (90–91) [Emphasis mine.]

I emphasize here the points in which Chow names the constitution of her subjectivity within the structures of power shifting between colonialism and decolonization. The two essays by Mohanty that introduce *Third World Women and the Politics of Feminism*—the introduction and the already influential "Under Western Eyes: Feminist Scholarship and Colonial Discourses" (originally published in the United States in 1984 and in Britain in 1988)—also engage in complexly layered forms of description and critique. "Under Western Eyes" is a devastating analysis of the colonializing discourse of "Western" feminist theory itself. Mohanty's careful and highly ordered deconstruction of the analytic moves and tools constructing "woman" and "women" in (especially but not exclusively) U.S. feminism and her insistence on "the political effects of analytic strategies" (69) are understood within the axiom set out in the introduction, that "the practice of scholarship is also a form of rule and resistance and constitutes an increasingly important arena of third world feminisms" (32). Mohanty also names her own implication within this form of rule and resistance (52), as does Chow above.

Whether it affected the time lag between the conference and the publication of the Mohanty, Russo, and Torres book is not stated, but in the preface the editors do comment that "in 1983 a leading feminist publisher told us (with kindly condescension) that there was no such field as 'third world feminisms.' . . . This collection maps a political and intellectual field which has gained increasing significance in the last decade" (x). Not only has the field been constructed over this time in the U.S. academy, but it has become commodified over this time, as that publisher now would probably be only too quick to notice. As I named them before, migrant scholars, metropolitan subjects, cosmopolitan feminists (and other permutative possibilities), have not only "contributed" to women's studies and feminist theory, but also understand themselves to literally embody issues of a world historical order that to those in hegemonic stasis appear to be discursive or abstract. (The quotation from Rey Chow is an example of this.) Their travels between several nations and nationalisms, their networks interconnecting a variety of feminisms, their influences within the U.S. academy are newly visible along such recent lines of commodification. Publication is one trail of such commodity formation within a feminist theory now in the process of reconfiguration inside the United States, and along other specific lines of movement, marked by language, international copyright agreements, possibilities of distribution, the movements of particular networks of cosmopolitan feminists, the interconnections among national academies, and differential modes of national productions of "feminist theory."

Not only are volumes of feminist theory ordered by country now in the process of being published—*British Feminist Theory, Italian Feminist Theory*, and so on, as in the Blackwell series—but also feminist theory books are being published intended for dual- or multinational consumptions. For example, Cynthia Enloe's *Bananas, Beaches and Bases* was published in 1989 by Pandora in Great Britain, while the first U.S. edition of *Bananas* was published in 1990 by the University of California Press. Not only are its publication locations dual (not an especially new phenomenon), but the content of the book is clearly and intentionally referential to more than one national audience, filled with popular icons and exemplary material from Canada, the United States, and Britain. Other works of feminist theory now in production reflect the special interests and particular knowledges of authors familiar with several national feminisms and their specific histories. For example, Donna Landry and Gerald MacLean's *Materialist Feminisms* (Blackwell, 1993), depends upon the knowledges the two have acquired in their travels and engagements between Britain and the United States; Landry is from the United States and MacLean from Britain and the two make their political communities transatlanticly. Even within the United States, such travelers have produced new insights for them/us into particularized productions of feminist theory. For example, Hester Eisenstein's recent *Gender Shock: Practicing Feminism on Two Continents* describes her experience leaving U.S. women's studies to practice and produce feminist theory as a "femocrat" in Australia.[39] "Transnational cultural studies" is the academic field in production by the journal *Public Culture*, out of the University of Chicago, and transnational feminisms and feminists new terms in current use and dispute; see, for example, *Scattered Hegemonies: Postmodernity and Transnational Feminist Practices*, edited by Caren Kaplan and Interpal Grewal, from the University of Minnesota Press.

Such new knowledges and new commodifications, new at least in the United States, reconfigure what can count as feminist theory. Traveling theorists are in the position of synthesizing wide ranges of academic and popular literatures and engaging in multiple political struggles, in which the radical incongruity between divergent intellectual and political objects, displayed seemingly under the same sign/s, are only too uncomfortably obvious. Such experiences have pushed these theorists to new expressions of "theory": see, for example, the essays by Lata Mani, "Multiple Mediations: Feminist Scholarship in the Age of Multinational Reception," and by Mary E. John, "Postcolonial Feminists in the Western Intellectual Field: Anthropologists *and* Native Informants?" both in "Traveling Theories, *Traveling Theorists.*"

As I said before, Chandra Mohanty's introduction to *Third World Women and the Politics of Feminism* organizes and synthesizes literatures (produced mostly between but not exclusively about India, the United States, and Britain and throughout the eighties), theorizing and deconstructing that unity "third world women." In the earlier essay, "Under Western Eyes," Mohanty analyzes several books and their publication by Zed Press ("London & New Jersey") as an exemplary site of the production of "Western feminist theory" (cohering in its political effects).[40] She criticizes analytic strategies used by some of the books, and uses others to exemplify local, specific forms of analysis. This is not a wholesale critique only, but rather also a complicated dissection of theoretical tools implicating "Western feminist theory" in colonializing practices structuring domination and suppressing the heterogeneity of women. In the later introduction, "Cartographies of Struggle," Mohanty deploys an object "theory" most useful in terms of its ability to disclose and produce "relationality."

Mohanty is more apt to use the term "theorizing" than to valorize the term "theory," which she uses rather sparingly. "Cartographies of Struggle" is made up of two sections: "Definitions" and "Contexts." The first section reexamines the problematizations of the term "third world women" and uses of feminism. Feminist theorists who might have thought that Mohanty's earlier critique of the analytic category "third world women" required the erasure of the term altogether from their linguistic repertoire, will find again and again Mohanty refusing to model analytic moves that attempt only renunciations of power. Rather, Mohanty repeatedly models disclosing and *ordering* the dense texture of relationality in its analyzed detail, aided by and developing new methodologies. Mohanty models accountability in the play of domination and resistance in knowledge production; rather than prescribe "theory," Mohanty exemplifies methods, even techniques, of "theorizing."

The bulk of the essay is taken up with "Contexts: History, the State, and Relations of Rule" and elaborates specific histories of "relations of rule," as Mohanty borrows the term from Dorothy Smith and transforms it. Mohanty examines five such contexts: "Colonialism, Class, Gender," "The State, Citizenship, and Racial Formation," "Multinational Production and Social Agency," "Anthropology and Third World Woman as 'Native,' " "Consciousness, Identity, Writing." The contexts fall into two clusters, and Mohanty describes them: "the first three chart political and historical junctures" and "the last two focus on discursive contexts" (39). It is the first three that are most densely synthetic and that convey almost self-contained mini-histories—for example, the context for the emergence of feminist movements in India or such explication of the history of immigration and naturalization in the United States that connects with current strategies for feminist struggles over immigration in Britain.

Each context charting political and historical junctures grapples with a slightly different use of and emphasis in processes of historicization: "Colonialism, Class, Gender" examines past contexts and interconnected struggles; "The State, Citizenship, and Racial Formation" shows the relations between several locations of current struggles by an exemplary historicization; and "Multinational Production and Social Agency" suggests a historicization of the present that makes problematic contemporary political strategies as they look to changes now in process and strategies for the future. Of the last two contexts, "Anthropology and Third World Woman as

'Native' " looks to knowledge-production as a site of struggle, and "Consciousness, Identity, Writing" demonstrates how to read and theorize the products of recent U.S. identity politics, including a mini-analysis of the work of Gloria Anzaldúa as a "theorization of the materiality and politics of the everyday struggles of Chicanas" (37).

Relationality is the key term for the object "theory" being deployed more than displayed in Mohanty's introductory essay and in the conference book as a whole, for Mohanty's essay implicitly organizes all the book materials. Consider the permutations on "relationality" drawn upon by Mohanty in her consolidation of the section "Why Feminism?":

> To sum up, third world women's writings on feminism have consistently focused on (1) the idea of the *simultaneity* of oppressions as fundamental to the experience of social and political marginality and the grounding of feminist politics in the histories of racism and imperialism; (2) the crucial role of a hegemonic state in *circumscribing* their/our daily lives and survival struggles; (3) the significance of memory and writing in the creation of *oppositional* agency; and (4) the differences, conflicts, and *contradictions internal* to third world women's organizations and communities. In addition, they have insisted on the complex interrelationships between feminist, antiracist, and nationalist struggles. In fact, *the challenge of third world feminisms to white, Western feminisms has been precisely this inescapable link between feminist and political liberation movements.* In fact, black, white, and other third world women have very different histories with respect to the particular inheritance of post–fifteenth-century Euro-American hegemony: the inheritance of slavery, enforced migration, plantation and indentured labor, colonialism, imperial conquest, and genocide. Thus, third world feminists have argued for the rewriting of history based on the *specific* locations and histories of struggle of people of color and postcolonial peoples, and on the day-to-day strategies of survival utilized by such peoples. (10) [Emphasis mine except for Mohanty's "specific."]

Simultaneity, circumscription, oppositional agency, internal contradictions, and specificity as well as this "inescapable link" *between* liberation movements: these mark out *terms and forms* of relationality, while the linking of liberation struggles sets one historical context for the *embeddedness* of relationality in this deployment of feminist "theory." Mohanty's consolidation of many discourses emphasizes the "interdependent relationship between theory, history, and struggle." (13)

Thinking back to Echols's analysis of radical feminism and the construction of its autonomy in a critique of the new left, clearly it is not at all the case that Third World women's movements are *un*critical of national liberation movements in comparative terms, or in their own historic specificity, or as mobilizing some male interests. However, as is clear from the diverse arguments presented in the essays of *Third World Women* from, say, the section "National Liberation and Sexual Politics" (which is by no means the only location of discussion about national liberation struggles in the book; this section focuses on Africa, Latin America, and the Middle East, particularly Iran), each feminism has its own specific historical connection "within and against" the political context of nationalisms.

The tone Mohanty conveys is theoretically revealing here. It is "descriptive" rather than prescriptive (while also not neutral) at a level that frames historical contingency *and* circumscription, political agency *and* immense scales of complex circumstances. This tone is very striking in Mohanty's brief history of the emergence of Indian feminisms out of "nationalist struggles against an imperial state, religious reform and 'modernization' of the Indian bourgeoisie, and the consolidation of an Indian middle class poised to take over as rulers. In fact, it is Indian middle-class men who are key players in the emergence of 'the woman question' within Indian nationalist struggles. . . . This particular configuration also throws up the question of the collusion of colonialist and nationalist discourses in constructions of Indian middle-class womanhood [and modes of surveillance]" (20). But Mohanty's analysis doesn't imply at any level "more" or "less feminist" structures in describing such origins, rather she comments: "After all, histories of feminism also document histories of domination and oppression. No noncontradictory or 'pure' feminism is possible."

It is this complex understanding of "rule and resistance" that connects Mohanty's analysis with Rey Chow's location as a metropolitan subject (and with the comodification of such subjectivities), the possibilities of her own feminist discourse (and its embeddedness in U.S. women's studies), her uses of so-called Western feminist theory (and its consumption and effects). It is the lack of such theoretical apparatus of the movements of rule and resistance that makes it difficult for Echols to consider the history of U.S. feminism after "radical feminism" as anything but degenerating.

Jane Gallop describes her book by its title *Around 1981 [Academic Feminist Literary Theory]* (so punctuated on the cover) as a history that radiates out from a center: that center is "Around 1981." What radiates out are several themes linking this significant moment, in the one turn, to theoretical debates in feminist literary studies and, on the other turn, to the patterns of history that Gallop puts into order through this moment "Around 1981." Both thematic and historical radiations center in meanings of feminist academic institutionalization, and Gallop's controlling narrative of this institutionalization is sober and optimistic and not simple. Radiating themes link academic institutionalization to (1) debates over poststructuralism, (2) debates over centering feminist literary practice in the study of women writers, and (3) white women's debates about their own racism. (Note the framing of the last; I paraphrase Gallop's words: "the acrimony and guilt around the question of race for and by white feminists." I've emphasized pattern here; Gallop surfaces affect by paralleling "the debate," "the argument," "the acrimony and guilt" [6]. The result is a recentering of white women.)

The patterns of chronology put into order through the moment "Around 1981" are most explicitly institutional and personal. Gallop sometimes suggests this is also a pivotal generational moment; I would partially agree by also overlayering more specifically an invested cohort, what Gallop names as personal but which operates in the spaces between a personal and an institutional: "Around 1981 I entered into contact with the mainstream of academic literary feminism in the United States.

That is where I come in" (1). It is not only Gallop for whom this personal trajectory matters. "This book reads anthologies of American academic feminist literary criticism published from 1972 to 1987. Reading over a decade and a half of feminist criticism, it keeps circling back to the fictive moment I call Around 1981" (10). "Writing and Sexual Difference," an anthology first published in 1981, is the material out of which, in her critique of it, also published in 1981, Gallop develops the method this current book depends upon. Gallop connects her moment around 1981—"[what] I experienced simply as an event in my individual trajectory"—to institutional moments—" 'Writing and Sexual Difference' locates itself as the intersection of feminist criticism and poststructuralist theory" and "represented a certain moment in American academic criticism" (1).

What is being constructed in Gallop's text is this object enclosed by brackets on the cover of the book—"[Academic Feminist Literary Theory]"; constructing this object with its center "Around 1981" in "Academic" requires some contesting for histories and chronologies. Gallop engages in such contests through symptomatic readings of this series of anthologies: "reading a plural text as a whole" (1).[41] Gallop is very aware of the shifting meanings of her own book within its specific "moments" and the book embodies several palpable plots, discussed in the introduction:

Plot 1: "Had I written the present book around 1985, it would have been centered on the point where I came in, on the encounter between French deconstructive theory and American feminist criticism."

Plot 2: "The main story [in the first chapter written specifically for this book in 1986] is about the theoretical definition and institutional establishment of feminist literary criticism. Although a different tale, this one too centers around 1981" (2).

Plot 3: "I now [1988] wanted the book to tell the story of the main stream of American academic feminist literary criticism.... This layout around a center disturbs the straightforward unfolding of the history, entwining the story of academic feminist criticism with the progress of the subject writing the history, herself necessarily limited by the moment(s) in which she writes. An equation with two variables: a history told by a subject in history" (2).

Plot 4: "Whereas in the early eighties the project focused on the theoretical debate, by the late eighties it was organized around the institutionalization of feminist literary criticism. By which I mean its acceptance as a legitimate part of literary studies. I locate that 'event' around 1981 and am interested in what led up to it and the subsequent effect it had on feminist criticism" (3).

Near the end of the book Gallop reframes the strains/strands of plot:

> If indeed I could bring those two terms together ["a feminist criticism both psychologically and historically informed"], then I could also bring together two different versions of my own project. One version dates from around 1984 and is centered in psychological categories, interpreting feminist critical relations in familial and psychoanalytic terms, in particular the mother-daughter relation. The other version dates from around 1987 and sees feminist critical positions in terms of institutional history.... I am beginning to realize that feminists need to stop

reading everything through the family romance. If we are going to understand our relation to the academic institution within which we think and teach and speak, we need to recognize its specific dynamics which are obscured in the recourse to familial metaphor. (238–39)

And finally:

From around 1975 to around 1983, the mainstream of academic feminist criticism focused on women's writing in the Euro-American high cultural tradition. This book tells the story of that period, from the preparations for it up to its dismantling. (240)

"This layout around a center" is visually and conceptually embodied in the table of contents, where the four large sections of the book begin with "Around 1981," then encounter "Sidetracks," after which comes "Going Back," finally pressing on to "Going on (In)"; thus the center is doubly figured: both spatial positioning of time in a spiral in which moving forward first requires going back, and also the play of sexual movements multiply figurable as masturbatory, lesbian or heterosexual or both, or neither and something else, or something not definable. The first two chapter titles of the section "Going on (In)" also continue and socialize these ambiguities or multiplicities; chapter 10 is called "Tongue Work" and chapter 11 "The Attraction of Matrimonial Metaphor." The section concludes with chapter 12, called "History Is Like Mother." Thus allusions to, at least, lesbianism, sanctioned heterosexuality, and pre-Oedipal sexuality. And the dedication of the book dramatizes and polysexually draws upon several layers of theoretical uses of such sexual metaphors (as does the rich referential texture of the entire book) from Luce Irigaray to Adrienne Rich as Gallop offers the book:

To my Students:
The bright, hot, hip (young) women who fire my thoughts, my loins, my prose. I write this to move, to please, to shake you.

In an academic historical climate in which sexual harassment is a potent issue, such pedagogical fantasies are daring, even if only fantasmatic (and Gallop's public heterosexuality offers some protection, even if such public personas are never unalterable or unassailable); at the same time, such pedagogical eros is deeply conventional and such figures strikingly stable historically, if usually alternately gendered. And the crypto-lesbian status of some major figures of poststructuralist feminist theory adds yet another spicy layer of meaning, allusion, and gossip.

What objects are deployed by Gallop under the sign "theory"?

Although the present book looks at literary criticism, I have subtitled it "Academic Feminist Literary *Theory*." In the anthologies I concentrate on the theoretical pieces. In the essays of practical criticism, I focus on theoretical positions and suppositions rather than on what they say about any specific text. My subject, the collective feminist critic, necessarily speaks theory since her voice is a composite of statements which recur in different specific readings. Because the symp-

toms are collective, they are themselves moments of theorizing, points where theory is attached to history, life, position. (8–9)

Going backward through this piece of text, I see four loci from which to consider
objects under the sign "theory": (1) "theorizing" is defined as "points where theory
is attached to history, life, position." What does "position" mean here? It resonates
with the "positionality" as political location used by Mohanty with its poststructuralist reverberations; it also echoes ordinary language uses, such as "position" as a
job, or "position" as in class position, sometimes glossed "position in life." Rather
than "power," Gallop invokes terms like "authority," "prestige," "privilege," "exclusion," "inclusion,"—and though there are "threats" and some "had to pay attention," with implications of coercion, the theoretical languages used to describe
domination (such as thoroughly inhabit Mohanty's text within the rubric of "historicizing," Mohanty's text which privileges "theorizing") are largely absent from
Gallop's text.

This absence is in part the result of Gallop's tactical location of "academic," the
site of this theorizing, as simultaneously the elite sign of ideological hegemony;
however, note the difference from Mohanty's designation of knowledge production
as a field of rule and resistance. Here, rather, it is psychological, theoretical languages appropriated, developed, and elaborated by Gallop herself which richly texture and explain "position." For example, when Gallop describes some specific
forms of power structuring the field of relations possible to women within an academic field in her description of Joanna Russ's critique of Ursula LeGuin, she says:
"It may be useful to think of Russ's troubled note to LeGuin—displaying a combi-
nation of admiration, guilt, and aggression—as speaking a certain kind of woman
to woman relation: the view of a more established woman by a woman with ambi-
tions in the same field. We might call this the little sister's discourse on the big sister" (85). Not only "familial metaphor" but also affect itself figures and displays
power relations.

"Speaking" (as above) opens out theoretical languages of enunciation, such as
when—in chapter 8, "An Idea Presented before Its Time"—Gallop describes the
differential reception of the work of two authors distinguished by their relative professional locations in an academic hierarchy: "The difference is not intrinsic to the
concepts but refers to the relative authority of their enunciation, to history and
speaking position" (117). In sum, theorizing is not so much the making of theory
itself, but rather the making of relations between theory, history, life, and "position,"
for which one can also often read "power." Theory is prior to theorizing, not its
product.

(2) "My subject, the *collective* feminist critic, *necessarily speaks theory* since her
voice is a composite of statements which recur in different specific readings. Because
the symptoms are *collective*, they are themselves moments of theorizing." [Emphasis
mine.] I said before that Gallop was constructing the object "academic feminist literary theory." It is by way of this "collective feminist critic" that this object is con-

structed; it is theory because such a collective subject "necessarily speaks theory," "since her voice is a composite of statements," "because the symptoms are collective."

> I have joked that what I seek is some sort of "collective unconscious." I do not mean something shared across time and cultures by all human psyches. I mean "collective" in the political sense of a specific group of individuals joined by shared interests and located together, whether explicitly or implicitly, in a field of conflicting interests. Academic feminist critics might have a collective unconsciousness not because women or even feminists or even academic feminists inherently have similar psyches, but because we speak within the same cultural enterprise and thus share its historical contradictions. If it is a contradiction to be an academic feminist literary critic in America in the late twentieth century, then that contradiction will manifest itself in our writing. And if certain symptoms recur in a number of feminist critics, these textual symptoms may point to some sort of inner conflict, shared but not sufficiently recognized. (8)

Feminist critics embody as inner conflict historical contradictions. Manifested in feminist critical writing, such contradictions/conflicts can be read there as recurring symptoms. It is the collective feminist critic (which may include but is not equivalent to Gallop herself) who is reflecting as inner conflict the historical contradictions of a shared cultural enterprise. The political is *inside* the theoretical (and thus, at least in some manifestations, inside the literary). Gallop's method shapes what is relevant in the political in her indication of a hegemonic unity and in its deconstruction: "[These are] my procedures in the present book. Typically, I identify a central, hegemonic voice in the anthology, usually the editor(s)'s, which would organize all the voices into a unity and then I locate points of resistance within the volume to that unification. I place my weight behind those internal differences as a wedge against the centrist drive. Such a reading, which might be termed a deconstruction, consists precisely in seeking 'cross-currents' and 'discontinuities' " (165). But, of course, it is Gallop who has read the symptoms and thus created and invoked—not just recognized and analyzed—this collective subject, which includes but is not exhausted by Gallop herself.

(3) "In the anthologies I concentrate on the theoretical pieces. In the essays of practical criticism, I focus on theoretical positions and suppositions rather than on what they say about any specific text." Here Gallop's uses of "theoretical" are plainly inclusive. Above, in the formation of the collective subject, theory is the set of unifying abstractions. Here, theoretical pieces are distinguished from "practical criticism" which speaks of a "specific text." The theoretical and the nontheoretical are unproblematically different, or, at least, their distinctions are not tactically problematized. It is in chapter 2—"The Problem of Definition"—that Gallop examines arguments about inclusive/exclusive definitions. She uses Bonnie Zimmerman's "What Has Never Been: An Overview of Lesbian Feminist Literary Criticism" (1981) as one "wedge against the centrist drive" of the anthology *The New*

Feminist Criticism to examine by analogy what Gallop calls "this dilemma of definition in feminist criticism, the choice between being coherent but exclusive or vague but inclusive." Zimmerman deliberately problematizes definitions of "lesbian" and "lesbian writing"; Gallop describes her work:

> Rather than choose sides, Zimmerman's "Overview" makes it possible to think through the relation between the two positions. Exclusive definition is not only a "suspect strategy," but a *suspicious* strategy, "overly defensive" as befits a young criticism, orphan in the theoretical wilderness. Zimmerman's "double vision" can appreciate the need for such a strategy, without relinquishing the sense that it is also finally "limited," as definition and as theory. . . . This problem of the boundaries of a field cannot be just a question of choice between a larger all-inclusive field and a smaller exclusive subfield. . . . Zimmerman's lucid analysis illustrates the extent to which this problem cannot be transcended. Analyzing the pitfalls of both sides, she considers the argument not only unavoidable but central to lesbian critical theory. (26–27)

(4) "Although the present book looks at literary criticism, I have subtitled it "Academic Literary Feminist *Theory*." Although Gallop here has emphasized the word "theory," I suggest that the newest elements of her object-in-construction are not this piece of it "theory" but rather that piece "academic" by way of "literary." These are the most contestable elements of Gallop's construction of this object of knowledge, and it is to their defense that Gallop summons reconstructions of history and chronology. Indeed, theory is precisely the element that Gallop most takes for granted, most undefensively, possessively (and sometimes vaguely) uses inclusively. Only toward the end of the book does "theory" come to have a defensive edge, and that edge is more often reported on in Gallop's reconstructed history of feminist criticism than enacted by Gallop herself.

In that final chapter 12—"History Is Like Mother"—Gallop describes heightened investments in "history" by feminist literary critics and the hegemonic voice of Jane Marcus in the anthology *Feminist Issues in Literary Scholarship* (1987). Gallop narrates: "Earlier in the history of literary studies, criticism and scholarship had been polemically opposed alternatives. By the time feminist 'criticism' enters the scene, the terms can be used synonymously to refer to the literary academic's production. Although scholarship and criticism are no longer at odds, by the 1980s a new opposition polarizes literary studies. Marcus opposes 'scholarship' to 'theory' " (207).

Here we can begin to take up the issue of the epistemological costs of this object "[Academic Feminist Literary Theory]," which involve the complicated intersections between cohort implication in the piece "academic" and Gallop's own theoretical tool bag drawn upon for the piece "literary." This tool bag is consolidated in Gallop's description of her method as "symptomatic" reading, and one range of its powers are ruminated upon in Gallop's own self- and literary theoretical-critique: "I am beginning to realize that feminists need to stop reading everything through the family romance. If we are going to understand our relation to the academic institution within which we think and teach and speak, we need to recognize its specific dynamics which are obscured in the recourse to familial metaphor." Of course, not all feminists do read through the family romance, but Jane Gallop has, brilliantly. And, as her choice of anthologies demonstrates, there are *various* kinds of feminists who also read through the family romance, or who use the same kinds of theoretical tools (for similar but not the very same purposes) that Gallop herself uses to read through family romance. As Gallop locates herself at the leading edge of the academic forms that finally permit academic feminist institutionalization in literary studies, those forms that in that process she sees become hegemonic, first in literary studies and then in feminist literary studies, so Gallop's own methods of reading are understood by herself as current hegemonic feminist literary practice. This is both true and not true. Hegemonic, of course, does not mean practiced by all; it refers to that powerful center that requires all other forms to define themselves in terms of it. And "hegemony" may, contradictorily, be local and relative, confined within various "fields": institutions, disciplines, historical moments, cohorts; just how hegemonic a hegemony actually is may indicate where the very edges of those "fields" lie, one method by which Gallop locates historical moments.

It is the response to this palpable hegemony that motivates Gallop's description of Jane Marcus in "History Is Like Mother" and that occasions Gallop's ruminations on the powers of "familial metaphor" in historical and institutional analysis. "History" is that problem that may say something about just *how* hegemonic that new and powerful *intersection* between a particular academic feminist cohort and several related sets of theoretical tools may be. As Gallop's plots for her book suggest, her own trajectory in the book itself runs *from* "the theoretical debate" *to* "the institutionalization of feminist literary criticism," alternately called "a history told by a subject in history." Knowing this particular "ending" of the story reframes Gallop's description of what Marcus has staged as an opposition between "scholarship," shadowed by "history," and a putatively ahistorical "theory": " 'Theory is not immune to historical forces.' [Thus Gallop quotes Marcus; Gallop continues:] If Marcus needs to assert something so obvious, it is because she fears that theory is, precisely, passing as transhistorical" (208).

One cost of Gallop's method of reading this series of anthologies symptomatically is in this unitary construction of this historical collective subject the feminist literary critic. She/the collective feminist critic embodies "hegemony" and its deconstructions, her voice speaks "theory" and political conflict becomes internal contradiction. Processes and conflicts are all describable only in developmental terms, as they are stunningly described in chapter 2—"The Problem of Definition." There Gallop works to explicate what I call epistemological moments in the construction of an object of knowledge, in this case Gallop describes the construction of both "lesbian criticism and theory" and "feminist criticism" in vivid, lively, theoretical terms. Notice how Gallop elaborates time and process here, how history becomes developmental:

Zimmerman suggests that a "*developing* lesbian criticism and theory may need limited and precise definitions."[42] Definitions do not function in the abstract; they find their place in history. A "developing" criticism, a young theory, a new field, needs and generates precise, rigid, limited definitions. A young criticism is vulnerable, needs shelter and boundaries for survival and defense. (32) [Emphasis Gallop's.]

Like Zimmerman, Robinson recognizes that a developing criticism needs limited definitions. In her account, however, there is a serious threat to development if the exclusive phase lasts too long. In order to be secure enough to grow, a young criticism needs firm limits, but if sheltered too long, it will stiltify and never reach maturity. The problem all too quickly becomes how do we know when it is no longer early but already too late. (34)

The lesson to be learned from Baym's account of the history of American literary theory is that *the very same theoretical position* can swerve from defensively exclusive to vague and over-inclusive. (34)

It is time that may be at stake here: different moments in the political history of a criticism. (32)

Gallop's metaphors generating an apparatus for considering these epistemological moments-in-construction are vividly developmental: "A young criticism is vulnerable, needs shelter and boundaries for survival and defense." "In order to be secure enough to grow, a young criticism needs firm limits, but if sheltered too long, it will stiltify and never reach maturity." But imaging the object of knowledge as a child frames conflict and contestation as either internal or external, complex overlayerings threaten this image's bodily integrity, and change in the object is namable only as a developmental unity. Affect elicited by this child inhibits and skews discussion of and interests in contestations, even as it figures and prioritizes *some* relations of power.

Gallop doesn't use this apparatus of epistemological construction in her description of the oppositions staged by Marcus between scholarship and theory. It is possible to imagine using this apparatus to describe "theory" in construction, or maybe a theory, in this chapter, but this chapter is also the site from which Gallop's self-critique about the limits of familial metaphor emerges, and this object of knowledge as little child calls out so vividly for reader/writer parents that the contestations that this chapter are about would be dramatically rewritten. "Theory" in this chapter, from the mouths of others than Gallop, involves many more occasions for (implicitly) exclusive definitions and understandings. This chapter hints in a few isolated metaphors at the political interests engaged in debate rather than internal or logical oppositions, and delicately points out others' use of languages of power, which are allowed to vulgarly display themselves:

This collection has been taken as an attack on theory, but I see it more precisely, here in Marcus's specification, as *a resistance to an alliance with theory* that would isolate criticism from scholarship. And what is rather insistently at stake, according to Marcus's formulation, is "history." (208) [Emphasis mine.]

[Gallop says:] What in the text appears as a breach of etiquette, in the footnotes gets politically colored as exploitation: [Gallop quotes Marcus:] "This minimalism in annotation has the political effect of isolating the critic or theorist from scholars and from the history of scholarship. If present practice in footnoting is a legacy of *nineteenth-century capitalist* recognition of the ownership of ideas, the minimalism of theorists, as opposed to scholars, represents a new economy of critical exchange in which the work of scholars is fair game (*like exploitation of third world countries*) and the Big White Men only acknowledge each other." (footnote from Marcus: quoted in Gallop 207–208) [Emphasis mine.]

"A resistance to an alliance with theory," for me, prompts questions about which cohorts of feminists are making alliances with which others. Such coalition politics within literary studies are not generally understandable within the terms that center *Around 1981*. Hegemony, its coming, its dismantling take up all such political space. What one might understand as mini-ecologies within the academy, their relative moments and relations to rule and resistance, differentials in Gordon's funding and status, which might very well refigure "History Is Like Mother," those absences are some prices paid for "[Academic Feminist Literary Theory]." Gallop writes beautifully about the entrance of her cohort into "the mainstream of American feminist literary criticism" and the encircling theoretical themes that radiate out from that center. What her method doesn't allow her to analyze are the palpable entrances and movements of other cohorts as they too encounter, or cruise through, this feminist stream or as they manipulate it through their alliances and shifting identities. What Gallop calls "an ongoing history of divided loyalties" (89) can be refashioned as the never-quite-the-same repetitions of reencountered meaning at varying historical sites of entry for new cohorts of feminists entering this stream as they come *from* shifting locations. New academies embody for themselves the central "history," encountering and reconfiguring feminisms with their own "histories." Just as Gallop, quite rightly, points out that "in writing this history of feminist literary criticism, I am at times reminded that there is *no single history* of some homogeneous national body of feminist readers" (80; my emphasis), neither is there a single "academic."

What especially isn't brought out by "History Is Like Mother," despite its title naming the discipline of history (nor is it brought out elsewhere in the book), is anything about the politics of interdisciplinarity in feminist theory or about the ranges of influence that feminist theory in disciplines other and/or adjacent to literary studies have upon "academic feminist literary theory," except the uses of and references to psychoanalytic tools thoroughly embedded in the "literary" as "reading." The dependence on the piece "literary" of "academic feminist literary theory" affects what historical possibilities are palpable for the pieces "academic," "feminist," and "theory." At this point, what looks like an inclusive meaning of "theory" becomes more clearly exclusive. Within the hegemonies of literary studies Gallop's location is undefensive. With*out* the hegemonies of literary studies, albeit still within ranges of academic feminisms, Gallop's construction is defended. "Academic" becomes equivalent to "literary" as each becomes the site of the other's feminist hegemony. Ironically, women's studies is thus not connected with "academic feminist literary theory," nor is its institutionalization even suggested, let alone connected, in these narrowly drawn fields of academic literary feminism. Those brackets around the subtitle on the cover become meaningful as the enabling constraints of this object in construction.

What I admire most about this book is its frank attempt to create "a history told by a subject in history"; within this rubric it's clear that all objects of knowledge production must cost. I'm particularly interested in Gallop's placing this subject in history into the writing technologies in which this history is created. Typically, Gallop surfaces affect in order to explicate power and time; she calls these constraints on production "the pain of history":

> I want to stress the pain of history for those of us trying to produce knowledge. Even if we have no illusions or beliefs in the enduring, we want our understandings to last at least until they can be written, published, and read. This book, which took too long to write, not only passes through two different theoretical formations but around 1989 begins to feel the pressure of a third and grows increasingly anxious as I push to get it done and out before its power of strategic intervention is lost, before it enters a configuration different than the one for/in which it was written. (4)

> The present book stops around 1987. And, in fact, most of the 1987 anthology was already published by 1985. Thus the present book does not take us up to "the present," certainly not to your present of reading (whenever that might occur), but not even to my present of writing (around 1991). (240)

Notice how it is the book that grows anxious as Gallop labors to give it birth. These are the flows of history and theory I talked about eddying around Echols while she constructs "radical feminism." In her afterword, Gallop notes feminist criticism's participation in recent reconfigurations from literary to cultural studies. This book uses methods that anticipate cultural studies, but the consolidation of its object of knowledge heavily weights it back in a literary only too painfully previous.

Somehow "Around 1981," as Jane Gallop understands it, her own feminist cohort becomes implicated in the institutionalization of "academic feminist literary theory" (in which understanding each piece of this object now becomes exclusively meaningful). Around 1981, Gallop's cohort discovers, for them, another ongoing stream of U.S. feminist literary criticism, and in Gallop's circling/encircling narrative this event is not just coincident with an emerging academic institutionalization of feminist literary theory, but fundamentally its motor.

> As "French Feminism" installed itself in the American literary academy, it arrived as a short list of names—Cixous, Irigaray, Kristeva—separated off from any larger body or movement or struggle of women. Separated off, they quickly began to function as token feminists par excellence, in the American literary academy.

By 1981 or so, French-style literary theory had become the most prestigious, the "highest" discourse in American literary studies. That is "the wilderness of theory" where Elaine Showalter locates us in 1981. And that is why the American feminist critic had to contend with "French Feminism," had to pay disproportionate attention to three or four women writing in the mid-1970's in Paris. Literary theory seminars in American universities which had never included any women much less feminist authors suddenly were reading Kristeva or Irigaray or Cixous.

In the American literary academy "French feminism" became the token feminism: "in order better to exclude" the body of feminist critics. Those of us American feminist academics who were clever enough or lucky enough to be associated with "French feminism" were rewarded and accepted as literary theorists: "encouraged to see [ourselves] as different from most other [feminist critics], as exceptionally talented and deserving; and to separate [ourselves] from the wider [feminist] condition." If I use the first person plural here, it is precisely and pointedly to interrogate the career that goes by the name Jane Gallop. (47)

But an analysis of the institutionalization of academic feminist literary theory that could take into account the formation of women's studies, the dynamic interdisciplinaries embodied in feminist theory as they inform literary theory, and the embeddedness of feminist literary studies within those political movements that constitute not only an "outside" of the academy but also intersect with continually shifting forms of alliance among feminists *within* mini-ecologies of the academy, might not have to overvalue either this particular cohort, or load it with "acrimony and guilt."

As I said before, what I admire most about Gallop's *Around 1981* is her successful framing of this history in two variables, a history by a subject in history; my remarks can be taken as explications of exactly how well she frames this history and this subject as "necessarily limited by the moment(s) in which she writes" (1), explications subject to my understanding also necessarily limited by my own historical moments and investments. A subject in history is both individual and collective; but how to understand what collective means is a nodal point where Gallop and I differ methodologically and conceptually. We both examine the process of construction over time of particular theoretical objects, although with very different descriptive apparatus. Like Gallop, I, too, have offered readings of several texts, and I, too, have understood these texts to be complexly both individual and collective and to embody "fields of struggle" (77). Gallop's use of "collective" requires the reading of historical contradiction symptomatically, as inner conflict within individuals and within a larger "collective" (unconscious); the anthology, as an "organized chorus" (8), is the site of Gallop's explication of the political and the historical as they are shaped by movements of power. My method is to contextualize books as objects produced within fields of struggle and to try, often by playing off other books, to say something about the conditions of production—especially those political and epistemological—in which these books become objects. Each methodology has been shaped by literary practices and by different ranges of poststructuralist theory. My use of "theory" as the product of mutually implicated practices of theory-building, alliance shifting and political identity production, requires me to consider multiple shapings of collectivity; for example, to consider cohort, political identity, mini-ecology as marked examples of non-parallel collectivities of varying ranges.

Gallop's "theory" is prior to theorizing, and it encompasses the political in a complex dance of what's inside and what's outside that resonates with Gallop's fascinating explication of the epigraph from Barbara Johnson's *The Critical Difference* as deployed both by Johnson and by Mary Jacobus in "Writing and Sexual Difference." (See Gallop's chapter 1) Gallop calls this complex dance an enactment of internal difference. She says: "I have become more interested in the blindnesses that I share rather than those I feel superior to" (9). I imagine both Gallop and myself to be working within, and working out, different pieces of a large but overlappingly shared project of mapping out the locations of "theory" (I name it in my own terms). While engaged in constructing my object "theory," I've played off of the work of Echols, Collins, Mohanty, Gallop (and others). With Echols and Gallop I reflect on what Gallop calls "the pain of history," which I also see in terms of the epistemological investments one has in one's object-under-construction at different moments in the process of its materialization. For example, Echols's concerns with separating out radical feminism and cultural feminism, the passion that fired her project, end up framed "painfully" within a political history of degeneration, as her own historical separation from radical feminism becomes clearer and clearer in the course of its consolidation. My framing of how my work is historically located and epistemologically pricey and my display of the tools I use trying to sketch out my investments in this object "theory," are indirectly the subject of each of the following chapters of this book.

U.S. feminist theory also needs to be situated in terms of its conditions of production inside the specific locations that mark "the U.S."—political, institutional. I see myself connected in this project with Collins and Mohanty, although we take up different pieces of it, all of us using very different tools and often addressing different audiences. In bits and pieces over the work of many people are consolidating two very important strategies that encompass this situation of U.S. feminism but extend beyond it. One would compare U.S. feminism with other nationally specific forms of feminism; another would place U.S. feminism as one of many on some map of many internationally intertwining feminisms. Hester Eisenstein's *Gender Shock* could be seen as an example of the first and Joyce Gelb's *Feminism and Politics: A Comparative Perspective* an example of the second; both are by feminist scholars from the United States.[43] What I'm trying to do in relation to this large, joint, multilayered and multi-produced project, is to reframe theoretical objects that pass and travel as generic, to ask questions like those I mentioned at the beginning: What investments are embedded in these objects? Under what signs are they displayed? Which signs display multiple objects? How can we substitute an understanding of local, marked theory for specious generics? Which theoretical objects travel globally, and what meanings do they accrue in their travels? Which people travel globally and what theoretical objects do they take with them?

In this chapter, I've looked at the recently consolidated and strategically un-problematized objects of Echols and Collins (radical feminism and Black feminist thought) and the "fragile" (breakable) alliances they embody and were produced by. I've also looked at the construction over time of the objects deliberately problema-tized by Mohanty and Gallop (Third World feminisms and academic feminist liter-ary theory) and the retrospections involved. In the next chapter I will demonstrate more tools to detail the conditions in which U.S. feminist theory is produced in or-der, on the one hand, to consider political-theoretical agencies in the U.S. academy, and on the other hand, to consider theoretical debates as sites for making and un-making political alliances.

2

Writing Conversations
in Feminist Theory
Investments in Producing Identities
and Struggling with Time

To be in the margin is to be part of the whole but outside the main body. As black Americans living in a small Kentucky town, the railroad tracks were a daily reminder of our marginality. Across those tracks were paved streets, stores we could not enter, restaurants we could not eat in, and people we could not look directly in the face. Across those tracks was a world we could work in as maids, as janitors, as prostitutes, as long as it was in a service capacity. We could enter that world but we could not live there. We had always to return to the margin, to cross the tracks, to shacks and abandoned houses on the edge of town.

There were laws to ensure our return. To return was to risk being punished. Living as we did—on the edge—we developed a particular way of seeing reality. We looked both from the outside in and from the inside out. We focused our attention on the center as well as on the margin. We understood both. This mode of seeing reminded us of the existence of a whole universe, a main body made up of both margin and center. Our survival depended on an ongoing public awareness of the separation between margin and center and an ongoing private acknowledgement that we were a necessary, vital part of that whole.

bell hooks, *Feminist Theory: from margin to center* (1984)[1]

U.S. third world feminism, however, functions just outside the rationality of the four-phase hegemonic structure we have just identified. [That is, liberal, Marxist, radical/cultural, socialist feminisms and the generative axioms "women are the same as men," "women are different from men," "women are superior," "women are a racially divided class."] Its recognition will require of hegemonic feminism a paradigm shift which is capable of rescuing its theoretical and practical expressions from their exclusionary and racist forms. I am going to introduce this shift in paradigm by proposing a new kind of taxonomy which I believe prepares the ground for a new theory and method of oppositional consciousness. [The new ideological forms described are: "equal rights," "revolutionary," "supremacist," "separatist," and mobilizing them all "differential."] The recognition of this new taxonomy should also bring into view a new set of alterities and another way of understanding "otherness" in general, for it demands that oppositional actors claim new grounds of generating identity, ethics, and political activity.

Chela Sandoval, "U.S. Third World Feminism" (1991)[2]

IN THIS CHAPTER I intend to elaborate upon some "material circumstances" of the production of U.S. feminist theory, especially within the classroom, as a written and published product of the U.S. academy and as inspired by several generations of women's liberation movements. Both published and unpublished theorists rarely include such circumstances of production in their accounts of feminist theory. In the preceding chapter however, I did highlight bits of such inclusions as they appeared in the work of Echols, Collins, Mohanty, and Gallop. Practically speaking, the circumstances of publication are only too well known to those engaged in this form of "feminist theory" and ironically in practice are taken for granted. Other feminists— students, political activists, theorists who have not published their work, theorists who do not engage in written theory—may not take into account these particular circumstances of this form of production. Similarly, the productions of "theory" in the classroom are likely only to be recognized when they become published feminist theory (and thus distributed in a different network), for the classroom as a site for distribution overshadows such production.

I will demonstrate or discuss several tools that make this kind of detailing possible. One is reemphasized in the title of this chapter: the "conversations" in "Writing Conversations in Feminist Theory." I mean to distinguish "conversations" from "debates" as political contour from theoretical contents. Conversations are units of political agency in action in theoretical discourse. They often overlap several debates, or may be found layered over each other within a single debate. Conversations may overlap more than written theorizations—oratory, group production, private oralities, public actions—or they may be reflected in varieties or versions of informal writing or circulating manuscripts. The delineation of conversations will tie together several strands of my argument toward the end of the chapter. Another tool I will explicate is the apparatus of marked and unmarked categories, similar to what Collins calls "the matrix of domination." Marked and unmarked categories describe asymmetric power relations and specious generics; they forefront shifting power relations among both group political identities and within the political identities/subjectivities of individuals as they vary strategically and historically. This discussion will initiate my detailing in this chapter. I will continue to demonstrate throughout my argument my use of the object "(feminist) theory" as the mutually implicated actions theory-building, alliance-shifting, and political identity-production, especially as I continue giving examples of strategies for contesting histories and theoretical objects. In describing the conditions of production of published feminist theory, I also will examine (as detailing tools) issues of timing, revision, and pedagogical reception. As I pointed out in chapter 1, Paula Treichler's essay on feminist theory, from which I borrow one of that chapter's epigraphs, tries to hold in tension both "academic theoretical writing" and "feminist political theorizing," with the classroom as one privileged location. In this chapter I begin by visiting that site for the production, distribution, and reception of feminist theory.

Time moves differently for different forms of theorizing. I'm going to use as touchstones notions of classroom time, circulation time, and publication time. Those eddying flows of feminist theory around one's objects in construction can move at different rates, in different structures. I'm about to simulate classroom synthesis of some feminist theoretical materials. This is some of the fundamental material I deliver in all my classes; it's been developed over about ten years, and has been influenced by my own pedagogical training during part of this period. This material has a varied life in the courses I teach, from very introductory undergraduate courses that are both introductions to women's studies and part of the general education curriculum of my university, to advanced undergraduate courses meant to allow students to synthesize a varied education, to introductory graduate courses in feminist theory. All my teaching now is carried out within a women's studies program. Sometimes this material is lightly and briefly touched on in a kind of top-down lecture format. Sometimes it's drawn out over several lectures and classroom exercises with lots of student interaction. Sometimes it emerges more fully in a course in which I intended only a brief discussion because students become very engaged. Other times it peters out in a course in which I intended fuller discussion because the students just don't seem to be touched by it at all. In some courses the synthesized content takes center stage. In other courses, the genealogy of authors and a tree of bibliographies is emphasized, as one version of a history of feminist theory.

In this synthesis, I'm engaged in constructing an apparatus for communicating the shifting meanings of political identities. This apparatus is an extension of the linguistic notion of markedness and emerges from identity politics. My point in this construction is to communicate to my students something of what I understand about "oppositional consciousness," Chela Sandoval's own construction and synthesis. Over the eighties I have found Sandoval's material a historically and theoretically powerful synthesis across social and political theory, poststructuralist apparatus, and those transnational political alliances to which Sandoval is indebted. I started teaching this material before Sandoval had done much in the way of publication, so originally my understandings were largely drawn from oral presentations she had given on this material in the early eighties and necessarily still include many of my own appropriations and elaborations. I pull out this material now, on the one hand, for the same reason I introduce it in my courses, because it fundamentally underlies my own thinking and methods. But here, in the context of this chapter, I offer first its contents as my own interested synthesis against the backdrop of which my later comments and criticisms of Nancy Hartsock and Alison Jaggar are projected and second, its contours as an example of "classroom time." When I first started teaching this material it felt very new to me, very much on "the cutting edge," as they say. Now it feels very fundamental to me, the ground that needs to be cleared in order to go on to build any "new" stuff, or the backdrop against which to evaluate current feminist work. Its content hasn't changed nearly as much as the classroom techniques for communicating it have. Its parts expand and contract, reflecting my own feelings in the classroom, the time constraints of the course, and the reactions from the students and how I read and respond to them. This expansion and contraction of pieces of material in response to student engagement and the teacher's historical sense of how "new" or how "fundamental" material is, makes up "classroom time." Classroom time also includes stabilities imparted by pedagogical polishing, that is, points at which "old" material has a kind of favored—because "foundational"—status, even as "new" and current readings are traded off against such "old" materials. ("Old" and "new" are very relative here, shifting with the pace of new scholarship in disciplines, interdisciplines, and subfields and, in women's studies, with new political developments.) Classroom time valorizes both conservative impulses to hold onto favorite material, but also impulses to share and engage with current feminist work as newly understood by the teacher, often within this favorite framework. Classroom time is likely to reflect one's own cohort(s)' interests, and one's training and networks of influence.

In one guise or another I've been formally teaching feminist theory since 1982, first as a graduate student. Over this last decade I've developed several tools for teaching feminist theory to introductory students. From the very beginning I try to build into any of the women's studies courses I teach (or courses with some feminist content I taught as a graduate student) this apparatus of marked and unmarked categories I mentioned above. In 1982, this started quite simply with asking students to refrain in their papers from using the generic masculine, that is, what Wendy Martyna calls "he/man" language—the use of "he" for both he and she, or "man" for humans.[3] Indeed, I had just begun my graduate teaching career by completing a stint as a teaching assistant in Wendy Martyna's social psychology course on language. In 1982 many students were quite incensed at being asked to come up with their own linguistic strategy for avoiding the generic masculine, and to dispute this suggestion they not infrequently brought to class the Bible and various dictionaries or style books as authorities for such generics. This was at a smallish and politically fairly progressive campus of the University of California. Today I teach feminist theory at a very large campus of the University of Maryland; it is extremely heterogeneous, especially politically. But in 1992 no one brings in the Bible or the dictionary to dispute any suggestions to avoid the generic masculine. In fact, I hardly ever make the suggestion, for students rarely use it; almost never in speech and pretty infrequently in writing. But then, neither does *The Washington Post*, nor do their high school class texts use it, nor are most of their college texts from publishers whose style sheets still contain it. Only one decade later the generic masculine is much more easily contested. It is also true that I discuss the generic masculine as one of several examples of marked and unmarked categories near the beginning of the course, which undoubtedly directs students' expectations. But still, nowadays this example has less and less oppositional force. I used to begin with it as a familiar contest that students had positions on; nowadays I begin elsewhere. However, now it also functions as an example of exactly this kind of social change.

So, I once began with an analysis of Wendy Martyna's findings in the late seventies on the linguistic production and reception of the generic masculine, at first to bolster my own authority to ask students to respond to this specious generic. Now, before I turn to that material, I first work with my students to examine the central metaphor/reality elaborated in bell hooks's preface to *Feminist Theory: from margin to center*: her analysis of the segregated town, a descriptive piece of which I've used as the first epigraph to this chapter. In class I begin there in order to end this initial series of lectures (and also finally the course itself) with a discussion of Chela Sandoval's notion of oppositional consciousness and my own contention that feminist taxonomies work as little machines that produce political identities. I use the second epigraph here to reflect this conceptual movement.

hooks's narrative is graphic. We draw the graphic in class: a rectangle of the town, divided down one side by the railroad tracks into one square and a thinner rectangle. Arrows describe the movements of the Black people working in the white part of town, crossing the railroad tracks and returning. "As black Americans living in a small Kentucky town, the railroad tracks were a daily reminder of our marginality. Across those tracks were paved streets, stores we could not enter, restaurants we could not eat in, and people we could not look directly in the face. Across those tracks was a world we could work in as maids, as janitors, as prostitutes, as long as it was in a service capacity. We could enter that world but we could not live there. We had always to return to the margin, to cross the tracks, to shacks and abandoned houses on the edge of town." I remember as a young white girl in another segregated town paying for tickets to sit in the balcony of the local movie theater and being shamed in front of my little brother, "But child, those seats are for the Negroes!" My shame and confusion was for not understanding these rules of segregation, although I was growing up an Army brat in a supposedly desegregated military similarly divided by rank but under rules into which I was already socialized. Today I live near Washington, D.C., in a metropolitan region complexly segregated by race and class. This is the reference point for my students today, who know this current system of segregation in their own daily lives but in many divergent forms, while their childhood experiences differ historically from my own and from bell hooks's. They offer examples of their understandings of these systems and make analogies with other forms of segregation, from class consolidated school systems to ethnic neighborhoods reflecting both communities and prejudices to the strategies of immigrant businesses and their implications in racial tensions to systems in other countries, such as the changing rules of apartheid in South Africa; they repeat wisdom and clichés from families and churches and media and schools. All this analysis of everyday life sharpens the political realities of the vivid metaphor of hooks's narrative. "There were laws to ensure our return. . . . Our survival depended on an ongoing public awareness of the separation between margin and center and an ongoing private acknowledgement that we were a necessary, vital part of that whole." Her conclusions about her Black townspeople's understanding of the whole town, both sides, are intuitively appreciated by students. Like Collins, hooks is developing a style of feminist standpoint theory here.

So, it is against this backdrop of metaphors of location and multiplicities and complexities of segregations that I explicitly talk about marked and unmarked categories, the terms and apparatus. Wendy Martyna's work usefully brings in these terms from linguistic locations looking to another set of asymmetries. Although hooks's analysis specifies Black/white oppositions of power, her analytic apparatus of center and margin immediately lends itself to describing various systems of oppression, even complex interconnections among oppressions, her implicit correction of a (white) feminist standpoint theory. Its primary metaphor is spatial location. Martyna's work specifies a male/female opposition. In the past I felt comfortable beginning with this seemingly "single" dualism, even when I knew I wanted to communicate more complexity. Now I find bell hooks's preface intentionally aligns students' intuitions toward shifting multiplicities and cues them to extend their analysis of Martyna's work beyond a too easily constructed male/female opposition as a totalizing universe of power. Part of the point of this whole exercise is to encourage students to experience their own intuitions as both counter-ideological and ideological, to encourage students to practice both mining their intuitions and valuing counter-intuitive investigations.

Disciplinarily rigorous, Martyna's research concerns found their source and inspiration in the women's movement of the early seventies, in the multiple linguistic jokes and interventions of that early period, and in one of the interdisciplinary locations—communication studies—in the U.S. academy early affected by and affecting feminist theory. Some of these political locations undoubtedly make Martyna's work especially attractive to me, when I recognize us as belonging to overlapping networks. Martyna's study was meant to empirically support the early contentions of U.S. feminists that "language matters," especially that women's psychological/material lives are affected by sexist language. Language change with a concomitant change in women's psychological/material lives is the political action Martyna envisions as the result of her academic research. Focusing on the generic masculine, Martyna asked in her research whether "man" really is generic. Is it actually used as the generic term for humans, or are other alternatives used? Is it understood as generic or as specific? Martyna reported from her data that generic terms other than "he" and "man" were used by informants in her empirical study almost one third of the time, and more often by women than by men. Also more men mentally imaged males when using the generic masculine, while women often had no image at all. The implication I've drawn from these results over this decade is that women are more likely to be struggling for male/female inclusive generics, either actually using the masculine as generic or using alternative generics, while men intuitively image themselves and thus have less need to struggle linguistically to generalize beyond "man." Women do but men don't have to ask, "Am I included?"

In an extension of the linguistic categories, this asymmetry of particular and general use can be described as marked and unmarked.[4] For example, when I interpret the Martyna study I draw upon the notion that "man" is unmarked, that is, conceptually characterized not by difference but by similarity. The marked category— in this case "woman"—in contrast is "other," exactly what the word marked means.[5] What we have here is a conceptual distinction between category and element. As signifier for human, man functions as the category in which woman is an element. Presumably there is a similar marked element in the category also, the element man. But the signifier man refers both to this element man and this category man. The signifier woman refers only to the element woman. Man as signifier exists on two levels of abstraction simultaneously: both category and element, or both unmarked and marked. It's this simultaneity of abstraction that produces a particular confusion. That the marked category and the unmarked category exist on two different levels of abstraction can become a problem in both thinking and writing. Wonderful (and now apocryphal) examples noted by feminists in the seventies exemplify a kind of logical error in which the word "man" at the beginning of a paragraph (or sentence) signifies humans and by the end of the paragraph signifies men in particular. The author has never noticed the switch in category, in level of abstraction.[6] I use the following two examples to initiate extended discussion in my classes:

> (1) As for man, he is no different from the rest. His back aches, he ruptures easily, his women have difficulties in childbirth . . .

> (2) Man can do several things which the animal cannot do. . . . Eventually, his vital interests are not only life, food, access to females, etc., but also values, symbols, institutions . . . [7]

In discussion I direct students to notice the consequences of this switch from category to element. They proceed to point out how women become possessions in the first sentence, or how in the second women are unreflectingly aligned with animals and seemingly locked out of the signs of culture, becoming "sex" itself. We play around with other ways of framing these sentences: How could the generic masculine be appropriately used, how could alternative linguistic structures be used, which they like most and why.

Martyna's work suggests that men have the experience of being signified by a term that can mean both the marked and the unmarked category. Thus, in relation to linguistic gender, they have the privilege of not being obliged, in writing or thinking, to make a distinction between category or element, unmarked or marked, similarity or difference. A corollary to hooks's story might parallel this analysis, suggesting that the white people not focused on in her story can be under the delusion that their part of the segregated town is "the town," while the Black people's daily experience stressed in the story is of the whole town, as they work and live in all its locations and understand particularly the extent of its edges and boundaries and their own centrality to its workings. In both interpretations, such "knowledges" are both conscious and unconscious, multiply layered together with other stories, some contradicting this knowledge and some supporting it. Collins's claim that Afrocentric institutions support such knowledge (what Nancy Hartsock calls "a specific view from below") for Black women while white women's institutions deny it, suggests the complexity of the layers of ideology and counter-ideology experienced subjectively.

In my experience, at this point of introducing marked and unmarked categories

via hooks's story and Martyna's study, many students come up with two interpretations of this material. First, they conflate marked categories with "being labeled."
Alternately and/or on top of that, they understand "being marked" as a visualiza-
tion rather than an alternate conceptual term, associating it especially with skin
color. These are not surprising associations, given the examples I've offered them so
far. So, I bring in the notion of standpoint theory here, actually to expand the repertoire of associations, to emphasize epistemological claims, and to discuss feminist
uses of the term "privilege." I use Nancy Hartsock's definition of a standpoint from
Money, Sex, and Power:

> A standpoint . . . carries the contention that there are some perspectives on soci-
> ety from which, however well-intentioned one may be, the real relations of humans
> with each other and the world are not visible.[8]

Resonating with hooks, in Hartsock's description, the physical metaphor of a place
to stand, a spatial location from which one can see only a limited range of the world,
has an inverse relation to the possession of privilege. (Subordinating Hartsock to
hooks here is another deliberately counter chronological move.) I've found that
what my students consider especially shocking and have most difficulty with actually using in their own thinking is Hartsock's clear contention here that all viewpoints are not, in some relativistic fashion, equally partial-visioned (the contention
my students find intuitively appealing), but that some have the potential of revealing more of the world than others. It makes sense within the concrete story that
hooks tells, but stated abstractly students feel more skeptical. In class I emphasize
this point, ask students to reflect on their own reservations and on experiences they
think either support or counter this claim, and ask them to spend time outside class
considering its implications and analyzing it in terms of daily life. Sometimes I take
this also as an opportunity to introduce Hartsock's use of the term "labor" as she
takes it from the early Marx. For Hartsock, the term standpoint originally depends
upon an analysis of relations between the proletariat and the bourgeoisie in which
the sensuous and daily physicality of labor entails this truer understanding of the
material world than do the highly mediated systems of exchange in which bourgeois
interests flower. Thus the proletarian standpoint is actually constrained to be wider-
visioned than the bourgeois view, the latter's blindness directly related to the possession of social privilege.[9] In an extended sense a standpoint is only available from
the marked category.

   If students are going to confirm or counter Hartsock's contention that a standpoint offers a deeper, wider view of people with each other and people with the
world, at least provisionally they have to locate themselves in relation to a standpoint. Locating themselves in terms of marked and unmarked categories promises
to *help* name a standpoint, but also complicates the whole notion of *a* standpoint,
for students discover themselves at the intersection of multiple possible standpoints.
(It also begs the question of what Hartsock calls the *achievement* of a standpoint. I'll
return to the notion of achievement in my extended discussion of Hartsock later in

this chapter.) We refer in class to a whole series of asymmetric relations of power pointed out in women's studies, some dualist, some not. For example, besides the marked/unmarked pairs Black/white and female/male as suggested by hooks's story and Martyna's study are homosexual/heterosexual, disabled/temporarily able-bodied. Relations with more than two terms suggest more complex movements of power and history: Jewish, Moslem, Hindu, Buddhist, (Catholic)/(Protestant) Christian might work for the United States in the late twentieth century in dominant ideology, but might not name the relations of power in specific locations in the United States, let alone in other places in the world, and at other times in history. Suddenly the relations Black/white, female/male, homosexual/heterosexual, disabled/temporarily able-bodied look different and more historical as well. Black/white, for example, could be redrawn by the relation people of color/white; what advantages would there be in such reframing? Homosexual/heterosexual might be redrawn as lesbian, gay, bisexual/heterosexual. How does one locate power and generics among relations youth, old/young adults? Power relations may figure more complexly than specious generics can map: working class, poor/middle class, rich could name several marked categories with different shifts suggesting the dominance of the middle class ideologically as an understood generic class in the United States today, but with the rich reaping new rewards under Reagan-Bush capitalism in the eighties and nineties, not only the dualism suggested by proletariat/bourgeoisie. Individuals get named by complex multiples: the white, middle-class lesbian teacher from the United States who grew up in an Islamic country, for example. Students name themselves in various mixtures of marked and unmarked categories, unsure about how many to pile on, what to include, what to prioritize. In speaking of her similarly conceptualized "matrix of domination," Collins points out: "Adhering to this inclusive model provides the conceptual stance needed for each individual to see that she or he is *both* a member of multiple dominant groups *and* a member of multiple subordinate groups" (230).

Inevitably this attempt to name actual people in the class in these kinds of terms and coming up with possible marked and unmarked categories to examine and to give names to is contentious. Students argue over whether to use the term "disabled" or "physically challenged" and give testimony to the meanings of these terms in their own lives. The meanings of redrawing Black/white to people of color/white or Third World/First World raises political objections among differently sophisticated political students. Some students object to all this "labeling" and just want to be people. At this point, suspicions about the non-relativism of Hartsock's notion of standpoint may erupt in passionate declarations of everyone's own personal knowledge being right for each individual. The politics of naming, as groups and as individuals, breaks out. The politics of the names themselves often overshadows the epistemological claims also being made. At this point I bring in material from an early essay by Chela Sandoval; that is, I do so if the class hasn't already disbanded for this day in the midst of contention over who is trusted or distrusted to name themselves or name others and for what reasons.

The point Sandoval embodies, illustrates, narrativizes, and continually reiterates in her 1982 essay "Women Respond to Racism: A Report on the National Women's Studies Association Conference, Storrs, Connecticut" is the fragile and at times illusory character of the group "women of color."[10] It is with much concern and debate that even a name, "women of color," is chosen by the particular women doing consciousness-raising in the group Sandoval describes. Differences this name threatened to hide include, for example, culture, ethnicity, national associations, religion, skin color, race, language, class, and sexual differences. Sandoval begins by examining a taxonomy often assumed in feminist circles, especially in the late seventies. Imagine a set of four boxes, two piled on top of each other. The first box on the top left is labeled "White Men" and the second on the top right "White Women." The second level's first box, bottom left, is labeled "Men of Color," and the second, bottom right, "Women of Color." Now this imaginary figure we've just mentally drawn was open to much debate in the late seventies; it was derisively termed a hierarchy of oppression or a taxonomy of victimization. The struggles for positions in it, victim or oppressor, and for which groups to include in it, has been contested among feminists for close to two decades. White feminists especially were concerned about "ranking" oppressions. However, in the work of Chela Sandoval, the figure and the taxonomy it represents are put to very different purposes. This figure is reconstructed, first, as a model of the construction of a "self" by the power domination over an "other": white men over white women and women and men of color, white women over people of color, and men of color over women, while, as Sandoval says, women of color "become survivors in a dynamic which places them as the final 'other' in a complex of power moves." "Women of color" becomes "the crucial category against which all the other categories are provided their particular meanings and privileges"[11] (22).

While as the ultimate marked category this position is one women of color are forced to occupy, its possibility as a fragile and strategic resonance between marked and unmarked categories (that is, the unity of the group women of color, the construction of this political object), although unstable, contains a liberatory possibility. It provides those who occupy it with "visions, intuitions, and values which work to charge the definitions of 'liberation' and 'feminism' with new and different meanings" (23). As such a liberatory position, "women of color" occupies a "standpoint," as Hartsock uses the term. However, Sandoval's challenge to the metonymic reduction of humans to particular groups requires a subtle readjustment in the idea of a standpoint. The standpoint that is wider-visioned is the position "women of color." The privilege of constructing a "self" against an "other" is the source of a blindness to difference, yet the self-consciousness about the fragile resonance between marked and unmarked categories within and encompassing the group women of color is the source of new knowledge. (Not at all then like the slip between category and element in the specious generic, reflecting the privilege of not having to ask, "Am I included?" What is especially important are the necessities for continually reconstructing this "unity.")

The assumption of the unmarked category allows women of color to "tactically use this kind of 'unity' to temporarily force power relations into new positions" (26) but must be continually reconstructed from subtle coalitions among the marked as power relations change. Note the word "temporarily." In 1990, Sandoval encapsulates this point by saying, "The meanings of our sisterhood will change. If society's powers are ever mobile and in flux, as they are, then our oppositional moves must not be ideologically limited to one, single, frozen, 'correct' response" (66). There cannot be a single, stable standpoint, then, from which one's vision is more inclusive. Certainty about the location of such a single, stable standpoint is not possible or desirable in history—that is, in the flux of contextual event. It is rather the reso- nance between a "standpoint" and "standpoints" in coalition that is the source of liberatory possibility. Thus, Sandoval's appropriated model is actually not a static taxonomy at all but a shifting, many-dimensional field continually reconstructing itself. "What U.S. third world feminists are calling for is a new subjectivity, a politi- cal revision that denies any *one* perspective as the only answer, but instead posits a shifting tactical and strategic subjectivity that has the capacity to re-center depend- ing upon the forms of oppression to be confronted" (67). The dynamism of this model suggests that "privilege" is multilayered, and that there is some necessary connection between the assumption of privilege and the empowerment of the op- pressed. It makes explicit what Hartsock's doubled examples of the proletariat and the bourgeoisie, and of women and men, might imply—that there are multiple stra- tegic standpoints and the singling out of one is a powerful ideological and strategic move. Hartsock's use of the word "feminist" (in "feminist standpoint," rather than, say, "women's standpoint") is such a move, as is Sandoval's "women of color." The points I want to underscore here in Sandoval's appropriation of the taxonomy of oppressor/victim are: first, her emphasis on these as constructed and mobile catego- ries, constructed by a strategy of selfhood not innocent and even determined by dominations both gross and subtle, and second, her emphasis on the liberatory po- tential of "women of color" as a constructed position, assumable as a position of possibility and of new knowledge, but ever responsible to its members for its privi- lege of unity.[12]

Classroom presentations and exercises are one form in which literatures are synthesized. The synthesis I've just given offers evidence of the epistemological, po- litical, and cohort-interested filters I've used to process and delimit a wide literature. Gone are the early days of women's studies in which feminist literature was so pal- pably finite as to be entirely readable, in which students and teachers were on more equal footing because such literature was new to everyone, no matter how intellec- tually sophisticated. I was a student in women's studies during some of that time, and it was a heady feeling as a student to know *the* literature at least as well if not better than one's teacher. (As literatures proliferate it's possible for some students to know parts of this expanding literature better than their teachers. It keeps us on our toes.) Interdisciplinary work was a more general enterprise as well, since when feminist materials were scarce one read in disciplinary literatures outside one's expertise, and everyone was a novice at women's studies, but also a contributor. Feminist theory in the United States still retains some residues of this period, in that its expertise can sometimes still be held to be located in feminist longevity rather than, say, degree certification, and women's studies as a field is still fairly kind to those who find themselves "retooling" or newly invigorated in its intellectual and political environs. Women's studies *can* facilitate both interdisciplinary work and also movement from one disciplinary location to another, or even more likely, from one narrow subfield to a range of subfields.

The second epigraph to this chapter refers to "the four-phase hegemonic structure," which I would claim has often operated as one device to process feminist literatures. In 1991, Sandoval refers to teleological taxonomies, which I see as machines for producing political identities. But they also can operate, as can other pigeon-holing systems, to process large feminist literatures. As feminist literatures proliferate, so are such processing devices increasingly necessary. They're especially useful for new cohorts and individuals entering into feminist debates and conversations. This may include students. Sandoval's alternate taxonomy produces her object "oppositional consciousness": "I am going to introduce this shift in paradigm by proposing a new kind of taxonomy which I believe prepares the ground for a new theory and method of oppositional consciousness." My classroom synthesis has a similar interested teleology. The four-part taxonomy Sandoval analyzes has one form in a canon of feminisms, that is, the list of liberal, (traditional Marxist), radical, and socialist feminisms. (Sandoval considers this taxonomy side-by-side with the generative axioms "women are the same as men," "woman are different from men," "women are superior," "women are a racially divided class.") I call this a canon of feminisms, Sandoval calls this four-part structure hegemonic feminism. As hegemonic feminism it situates itself such that all feminisms must define themselves in relation to it. Sandoval both does and doesn't self-define thus, is both inside and outside this hegemonic structure in her analysis of its operation and in her offer of a "new kind of taxonomy." In my own feminist theory classes I've also tried alternate modes of delineating feminist theory to students; while at times I've been successful in getting students to consider how taxonomies work, I also have met with resistance to alternate framings by both students and colleagues for whom this particular taxonomy provides a highly valued history and rationale to feminist theory.

In classroom time it's difficult to present objects of knowledge as constructed, even though the classroom is one location of their construction. A pedagogical attitude tends to emphasize authority and stability rather than contingency and contestation, despite the sometimes contentious atmosphere in a women's studies classroom (maybe even because of it). I'm all too aware that in my classroom synthesis, however much I try to communicate epistemological construction in the material about taxonomies as machines for producing political identities, or describe an oppositional consciousness of strategic mobile subjectivities, the circumstances of communication themselves make all this material appear as a general, consensual bedrock. I even exploit this appearance to counter ideological intuitions. Over time, too, the material more and more becomes or approximates such a bedrock. And even presenting it as such produces the effect on myself of making it feel more fundamental in my own thinking. A good syllabus shifts and moves and changes, but parts can feel better and better over time as one learns how to teach the material, as one learns how to predict the reactions students will have. Teaching anthologies and textbooks also create stabilities and (somewhat constrained) consensus, as well as operate as devices for filtering literatures. (As copyright restrictions over photocopying tighten, teaching materials will be even more constrained and constraining.) It is in this light I want to examine briefly as a device for processing feminist literatures this four-part structure Sandoval calls hegemonic feminism, within the pedagogical distributions and receptions that stabilize it. I do this to give one account of its synthetic power and also to reposition its often axiomatic location. I intend afterward to connect this section of my argument to other notions "circulation time" and "publication time" and to think again about what Gallop calls "the pain of history."

Remember Echols's construction of the object "radical feminism." She is elaborating, contesting, but remaining within the hegemony of this canon of feminisms. Frankly, there isn't a lot of room for moving outside it. One site for examining this taxonomy is in the 1978 women's studies textbook *Feminist Frameworks: Alternative Theoretical Accounts of the Relations between Women and Men*, ed. Alison M. Jaggar and Paula Rothenberg Struhl, a synthesis of women's liberation materials from 1967 to 1976.[13] (It also includes some other earlier background materials, such as bits of Freud, John Stuart Mill, Engels, Bettelheim.) I want to contrast this textbook with two others: one I've mentioned in the preceding chapter, Betty and Theodore Roszak's *Masculine/Feminine: Readings in Sexual Mythology and the Liberation of Women* from 1969, and from 1992 *Feminist Philosophies: Problems, Theories, and Applications*, ed. Janet A. Kourany, James P. Sterba, and Rosemarie Tong.[14] So from 1969, 1978, and 1992 these "textbooks" operate as devices to produce, distribute and consume "feminist theory." Neither the terms "textbooks" nor "feminist theory" have a single meaning across this time frame, rather, they are differently inflected at these distinct moments.

The 1969 text is a campus text, but not only—maybe not even primarily—a textbook. "If there is a justification for an anthology like this, it lies in the fact that, off the college campuses and outside small, intense circles of metropolitan militancy, the home truths of women's liberation continue to seem alien, quaint, and absurd" (viii; also quoted on the back cover). Approximately half the book contains writings from the women's liberation movement. The first half of the book is divided into three sections: "The Man Problem" (selections from Nietzsche, Strindberg, Freud, Graves, Tiger), "Some Male Allies" (Shaw, Ellis, Myrdal, Sampson, Roszak), and "Toward Liberation: Between the Old Feminism and the New" (Horney, Sayers, Herschberger, Hacker, Beauvoir). The second half is in two sections: "The New Militancy" (Mitchell, Rossi, Dixon, Lydon, Robinson, Jones and Brown, Rubin, Morgan) and "Rattling the Invisible Chains: A Collection of Women's Liberation Manifestoes." "Finally, there is a collection of manifestoes which may serve as collective self-portraits of women in search of their liberation" (xii). These include Bernstein, Morton, Seese, and Wood's "Sister, Brothers, Lovers ... Listen ... ," "S.D.S. National Resolution on Women," "The WITCH Manifesto," Solanas's "The SCUM Manifesto," Women's Liberation Collective's "Toward a Women's Revolutionary Manifesto," "Redstockings Manifesto," Joreen's "The BITCH Manifesto," San Francisco Redstockings' "Our Politics Begin with Our Feelings," and "No 'Chicks,' 'Broads,' or 'Niggers' for Old Mole." The text is not only an editorial collaboration between a woman and a man (presumably married partners), but also orders its history with earlier generations of female and male feminists, while also showcasing and celebrating new militancy with some of the most radical statements of women's liberation. Its framework is academic, its editorial tone reasoned, balanced, liberal. Its foreword begins, "He is playing masculine. She is playing feminine." Its afterword, titled "The Human Continuum," responds to this script: "Out of a common oppression women can break the stereotypes of masculine-feminine and enter once more into the freedom of the human continuum. Women's liberation will thus inevitably bring with it, as a concomitant, men's liberation" (303). While such careful balances between women and men are enacted, the book also paints a fairly sympathetic picture of the new left and also sympathetically explains the feminist rejection of male radicalism, contextualizing each feminist manifesto in appreciative terms. (However, there are politically critical editorial comments, such as those preceding the SDS resolution: "The language of the resolution is an unfortunate example of the pompous jargon employed in S.D.S. literature since it has taken a strong Marxist-Leninist line" [254].) As a teleology, this text functions to produce "the new militancy" and "the human continuum" both, with a latent "feminist theory."

Against that is a very explicitly constructed "feminist theory" in 1978. This is Jaggar and Rothenberg Struhl's book. My fantasy is that this book is the published version of a much-photocopied packet of class materials (as is, for example, Anzaldúa's *Making Face, Making Soul* with additions and revisions, from which Sandoval's 1990 essay is taken). "Feminist Theory" is defined against "Feminist Practice" in the introduction to this textbook, published by a textbook publisher and including such pedagogical apparatus as "suggestions for further reading" at the end of each large section. The three large sections are: "Part I: The Problem/The Need for Women's and Men's Liberation," "Part II: Alternative Feminist Frameworks/The Roots of Oppression," and "Part III: Practice: The Implications of the Theories," which is divided into further sections, "Filling in the Frameworks: Work," "Filling in the Frameworks: Family," "Filling in the Frameworks: Sexuality." The frameworks—which further divide up parts II and III—are: conservatism, liberalism, traditional Marxism, radical feminism, and socialist feminism. "We have selected five theories or frameworks, only four of which would ordinarily be described as feminist," producing as political identities: conservatives (not feminists), liberal feminists, traditional Marxist feminists, radical feminists, and socialist feminists (xii). "What this characterization does ... is illustrate the way in which feminist theory building can be viewed as a dialogue, each theory constructed in order to remedy apparent deficiencies in earlier accounts. Our order of exposition reflects this historical development [actually, only very roughly]. This is not to say, of course, that the last theory, socialist feminism, is accepted as any kind of orthodoxy in the women's movement (although we do see increasing acceptance of it and although we ourselves do believe that some version of socialist feminism offers the best hope of providing an adequate conceptual framework for women's liberation)" (xiii). Notice the similarities with Echols's account of radical feminism—both the idea of theory building and also the building of theory in remedying deficiencies. But here, predating Echols's work, the object under construction is "socialist feminism."

Against both these texts is 1992's *Feminist Philosophies*. This is also explicitly a textbook, published by Prentice Hall, visually textbook "sized," printed in double columned space-conserving text. The preface begins: "This anthology is designed to be a basic text for a first course in feminist philosophy or a first course in women's studies" (ix). It is divided into two sections, the first of which is "Being a Woman: Problems of Gender Inequality," which is further divided into sections (after the first each containing several readings), "Introduction," "Sex-role Socialization," "Sexuality," "Reproduction," "Self-Images," "The World of Work," "The Domestic Scene," "Cultural Invisibility." The second section is "Feminist Theories and Applications: Explaining the Present and Changing the Future," divided into some now-familiar categories and some new categories: "Liberal Feminism," "Radical Feminism," "Psychoanalytic Feminism," "Marxist/Socialist Feminism," "Postmodern Feminism," and "Methodological Postscripts" (and a final "Suggested Reading"). Of this list of theories the editors say, "To be sure, these labels are imperfect. Often they distort the precise meaning behind a feminist thinker's ideas and words. Nevertheless, they are helpful, each of them suggesting a partial and provisional answer to women's oppressed, repressed, and/or suppressed 'condition' and what, if anything, can and ought to be done about it" (16). "Postmodern feminism" is not the telos of this machine producing political identities and processing literatures. Rather it is in "Methodological Postscripts" that the editors suggest a "type of feminist theory that . . . has not been written yet," envisioned but not instantiated by the two final essays, Maria Lugones and Elizabeth Spelman's "Have We Got a Theory for You! Feminist Theory, Cultural Imperialism, and the Demand for 'The Woman's Voice' " and bell hooks's "Sisterhood: Political Solidarity between Women."

Where Jaggar and Rothenberg Struhl look to socialist feminism for the most "adequate" framework, but an adequacy that is not "some clearly defined end state and is viewed instead as a continual process" (xii), Kourany, Sterba, and Tong say, "because these descriptive accounts and these theories are partial and provisional in nature, it is vital that we neither accept or reject them at face value" (1). All three texts reproduce materials primarily by white women (and some white men), although all three have, at most, a handful of readings either by women of color, usually black women, or about race by white women. The Roszaks include material about race that makes the analogy between Black people and women (in general?), producing "women" as a newly politicized category, as well as including the work of Robinson and her Mt. Vernon groups. Jaggar and Rothenberg Struhl include demographic material from 1973 comparing median income, unemployment rates, and educational levels for white women and men and Black women and men, as well as a couple of articles by Black women in "Part I: The Problem." While Kourany, Sterba, and Tong conclude their anthology with work (not yet a "theory") by a Latina, a white woman, and a Black woman, the rest of the anthology consists primarily of readings by white women.[15] Both *Feminist Frameworks* and *Feminist Philosophies* are produced for a women's studies market, the first primarily a women's studies course text and the second for two markets, both women's studies and philosophy. (In 1978 there was less—perceived or real—market value in a text geared to an introductory feminist course specifically in a philosophy department. Philosophy was not one of the disciplines most dramatically affected early on by feminist work and theory, despite the pioneering work of philosophers such as Jaggar. Notice that this has changed over the last decade.)

Feminist Frameworks and *Feminist Philosophies* each have what might be called companion volumes of feminist theory by one of the editors. Jaggar's *Feminist Politics and Human Nature* (1983) came out after *Feminist Frameworks* (1978) and is its theoretical, encyclopedic, disciplinarily rigorous elaboration. Tong's *Feminist Thought: A Comprehensive Introduction* (1989) came out before *Feminist Philosophies* (1992) and canonizes not only the list of feminisms produced by Jaggar (and others, of course) and proliferates them, but also codifies and canonizes specific critiques, some internal to feminism, some external.[16] Examples are: "A Communitarian Critique of Marxist Feminism" and "A Socialist Feminist Critique of Marxist Feminism" or "The Feminist Case for and against Dual Parenting" and "The Feminist Case for and against Woman's Morality." These companion volumes suggest something about the interrelationships between classroom apparatus and disciplinarily recognized research accomplishment—that is, interrelationships between such sites for the production, distribution, and reception of feminist theory as the classroom and publication.

The two most recent textbooks describe their projects in epistemologically fluid terms: Jaggar and Rothenberg speak of theoretical adequacy as a "continual process"; Kourany, Sterba, and Tong mention the "partial and provisional" nature of theories. But the classroom practices of canonization, of processing literatures, of fundamentalizing materials all practically work to stabilize such processes, to stabilize the partial and provisional. Now I want to look even more closely at stabilizations over the course of something other than classroom timing, what I'll call "circulation time" and "publication time." This is a kind of preface to my final discussion of conversations in feminist theory reflecting shifting feminist political alliances. In this next part of my argument, I'll examine the notion of "a standpoint" as a bit of theoretical work in flux and subject to changing feminist political pressures. I'll do this by focusing very narrowly on distinctions in the notion of a standpoint by political theorist Nancy Hartsock and philosopher Alison Jaggar—how these distinctions operate to construct for Hartsock the objects "the feminist stand-point" and "materialist feminism" and how for Jaggar they operate to construct the objects "the women's standpoint" and "socialist feminism." In this context I'll also point to issues of circulation and publication time by briefly examining changes in the manuscript and published versions of a pivotal essay by Hartsock.

Hartsock and Jaggar, side by side, represent two contiguous moments in U.S. feminism as seen in their conceptions of standpoint—"the feminist standpoint" and "the women's standpoint"—in their respective books *Money, Sex, and Power: Toward a Feminist Historical Materialism* and *Feminist Politics and Human Nature.*[17] The copyright dates of the two books, both 1983, obscure this "momentary" historical difference. Hartsock's first formulation of a feminist historical materialism predates the powerful issues raised in the work of women of color to which Jaggar is more directly responding. The range of time here is very slight: two or three years are significant periods given the pace of development in feminist theory. Two or three years is the time a single book may require for publication. The final essay of Hart-sock's book circulated for several years before the publication of the book; indeed, Jaggar's book is indebted to it. "Circulation time" and "publication time" are con-toured a bit differently here.

In 1991, Hartsock prepared a paper for delivery at the annual meeting of the International Political Science Association in Buenos Aires titled "The Feminist Standpoint Revisited." In this paper she responded to critiques of her notion of a feminist standpoint, especially concerned to counter charges of essentialism. In the last few years, Hartsock has vigorously engaged in a political critique of postmod-ernism, and this 1991 paper continues this engagement. And finally, this paper re-vises Hartsock's single version of *a* standpoint, influenced by the theory of women of color—among them Patricia Hill Collins—and postcolonial theory, taking heart from Fredric Jameson's reframing of feminist standpoint theory as a viable "princi-pled relativism" and revisioning her understanding of a materialist feminism in terms of the "situated knowledges" spoken of by Donna Haraway.[18]

When I gave my classroom synthesis of marked and unmarked categories, standpoint theory, and oppositional consciousness, I emphasized, as I have and will throughout this book, mobile elements of the construction of objects of knowledge and the tactical, strategic elements of the construction of political identities. In this emphasis I follow Chela Sandoval. From the retrospect of my synthesis, and now too, from the retrospect of work like Collins's as well as Sandoval's, and even from the retrospect of Hartsock's own "The Feminist Standpoint Revisited," one's attention is drawn to the solidity and relative immobility of Hartsock's historical conception of "the feminist standpoint" over this decade. Examining Hartsock's 1983 chapter "The Feminist Standpoint: Toward a Specifically Feminist Historical Materialism" (from *Money, Sex, and Power*) reveals basic difficulties with conceptualizing the feminist standpoint as a constructed and mobile position. Using class and gender as the nodes of her analysis, Hartsock strategically links as analogues proletariat/bour-geoisie and women/men when she introduces the idea of a standpoint. Within an analysis of the institutionalized sexual division of labor—in which women's work is inextricably tied to "the bodily aspect of existence" (233)—the feminist standpoint is seen to continue and even deepen the "descent into materiality" (231) structuring and constraining the paradigmatic proletarian standpoint's broader view of reality. However, by tying this "descent into materiality" so closely to bodily experience, in fact by exemplifying it in the challenges to body boundaries unique to women— epitomized by the experiences of pregnancy, lactation, and menstruation—I've long considered that Hartsock jeopardizes the status of the constructive aspect of the category "feminist" in "feminist standpoint." This constructive aspect is most clearly seen and intended in Hartsock's description of achievement and struggle. What's at stake here is the complex and dialectical tension and synthesis between the social and natural that informs the utopian strain of Hartsock's vision of labor and constructs what counts as "material." Hartsock's intentions are clear: this is not biologism; she is not interested in making an argument that locks men and women into immobile biological locations. Notice instead how she oppositionally reframes the word "sex" in "sexual division of labor" as that very undecidable point of distinction/conflation between the social and the natural:

> I discuss the "sexual division of labor" rather than the "gender division of labor" to stress my desire not to separate the effects of "nature and nurture," or biology and culture, and my belief that the division of labor between women and men cannot be reduced to simply social dimensions. . . . Thus the fact that women and not men bear children is not (yet) a social choice, but that women and not men rear children in a society structured by compulsory heterosexuality and male dominance is clearly a societal choice. . . . There is some biological, bodily component to human existence. But its size and substantive content will remain unknown until at least the certainly changeable aspects of the sexual division of labor are known. (233)

Hartsock has no intention of making a simple biologist argument, so politically defeatist and dangerous and which would actually subvert the powerful analogy to Marxist categories of bourgeoisie and proletariat that inform Hartsock's notion of a standpoint. Yet the location in the body of both the proletarian and the woman is crucial to Hartsock's notion of the "material."

Hartsock does offer as constructions the dichotomy "abstract masculinity" and "the feminist standpoint," and the explanations she gives of their material foundations in the construction of the self parallels Sandoval's (much less delineated and explored) contention that the boxes in her model are "selves" defined against "others." The basis of Hartsock's dichotomy are the great dualisms of Western political theory; the ones she pivotally operates are abstract/concrete, mind/body, culture/nature, ideal/real, and stasis/change (241); rather ironically she implicitly mobilizes dualistic/continuous as another dichotomy (242). In her very criticism of these dualisms she assimilates them to "male" and "female," to which "abstract masculinity" and "the feminist standpoint" become problematically welded, for the feminist standpoint finds its center in its "material" basis in women's reproduction, where "women's bodies, unlike men's, can be themselves instruments of production" (243). Thus Hartsock's feminist standpoint, in the midst of its very project to explain them, manages to reinscribe some of the unmarked categories of the powerful "self" of humanism, in a seemingly innocent stance of dissociation by polar opposition. Hartsock's explanation of the dialectical relationship between these dualisms is based in her construction of the complex tension between the natural and social— that is, "the material"—and is constructed by analogy with the relation between appearance and essence, in which the essence is the reverse of and includes, but goes beyond, the appearance. Her explanation thus reverses the hierarchical order of these dualisms, with the result that the traditionally despised element is now substituted for the other as its material truth. At moments this logic of reversal undermines even the privileged tension between the natural and social in the material, instead replacing the social with the natural. Actually, this reversal even may unintentionally romanticize women's relations to nature, as, for example, when Hartsock declares: "Women's experience in reproduction represents a unity with nature that goes beyond the proletarian experience of interchange with nature" (237). Hartsock criticizes dualisms for their location in abstract masculinity; however, her own strategy of reversal, privileging an opposite as innocent truth, also reconstructs a "twoness" that suspends the very multiplicity she intends to evoke. For example, her criticisms of abstraction disable the examination of multiple levels of abstraction, or varieties of the concrete. "I use the terms abstract and concrete in a sense much influenced by Marx. 'Abstraction' refers not only to the practice of searching for universal generalities but also carries derogatory connotations of idealism and partiality. By 'concrete,' I refer to respect for complexity and multidimensional causality, and mean to suggest as well a materialism and completeness"[19] (250). This putative multiplicity of the "concrete" is reinscribed in the dualism abstract/concrete, and Hartsock never goes beyond its "completeness" to make this multiplicity clearer or to mobilize it. Hartsock's strategic singling out of the feminist standpoint has the consequence of disallowing a tension between the marked and unmarked statuses of "women" much as the slip in abstraction between man and men does in so-called he/man language. Thus this singling out ironically makes it difficult to conceptualize the feminist standpoint as constructed and mobile. That Hartsock fully *intends* the feminist standpoint to be socially and epistemologically constructed, as the term "feminist" embodies, is clarified in her discussions of achievement both in 1983 and in 1991.

Alison Jaggar relies heavily upon Hartsock's work, both in her discussion of a standpoint and in her criticism of abstract individualism.[20] Jaggar is very concerned to underscore with Hartsock that this "women's standpoint" must be discovered through what Jaggar calls a collective political and scientific struggle. The insights from the distinctive social experience of women are *tested* in political struggle and *developed* into a systematic representation of reality. Both Jaggar and Hartsock use the notion of "achievement" to talk about the struggles that those sharing a standpoint must engage in as historical and liberatory agents. However, the subtle tones of the relationship between the standpoint and achievement reveal fundamental differences between their understandings of standpoint. This difference can be seen especially clearly in their choice of designations: "feminist" (Hartsock's) and "women's" (Jaggar's). (Despite my examination of the consequences of theoretical moves by Hartsock here, I often find my own sympathies lie more closely with her project than with Jaggar's.) For Hartsock the standpoint is the future, as yet unknowable, liberatory position, which still may be prefigured now by our current understanding of what a deeper materialism must be. That it lies in the future makes it unknowably single. For Jaggar the standpoint is the current testing and development that opens up to the future liberatory struggle. For Jaggar "women's" signals these starting points subject to liberatory transformation, that is, achievement; for Hartsock "feminist" signals the achieved status, which "picks out and amplifies the liberatory possibilities contained in [women's] experience" (232); those points of possibility can be recognized even now because we know that they follow the logic of the descent into materiality experienced by the worker.

The centrality of Hartsock's investments in a feminist materialism uneasily permits her conception of the "material" to slip into and out of an equation with the "universal." It's not that Hartsock intends such a universalization, but rather that Hartsock shares this problem with the feminist object relations theorists upon whom she relies so heavily for her description of the effects of the sexual division of labor. Her important concerns with the standpoint as a position of truer knowledge make it almost impossible for this slip into the "universal" not to occur, another legacy of dualistic thought: the structures of psychic development, the biological (even though here oppositionally understood as this complex tension between and synthesis of the social and the natural), and the true are all imagined as universal.

Compare Jaggar's different (and dependent) formulation of "standpoint"; first Hartsock:

> A standpoint ... carries the contention that there are some perspectives on society from which, however well-intentioned one may be, the real relations of humans with each other and with the natural world are not visible. (117)

then Jaggar:

> According to the socialist feminist conception, a standpoint is a position in society from which certain features come into prominence and from which others are obscured. Although a standpoint makes certain features of reality visible, however, it does not necessarily reveal them clearly nor in their essential interconnections with each other. (282)

Hartsock's definition of a standpoint includes features that heighten its radically unrelativized character and depend upon the inverse and inclusive character of materiality that is revealed by it.[21] Jaggar's version of a standpoint is more strikingly relativized than Hartsock's, and it is by shifting the emphasis in achievement as the contemporary struggle and connecting the standpoint with "women" rather than with "feminism," that Jaggar reconstructs the standpoint. While both labor to explain pre-liberatory consciousness, each has a different investment—Hartsock concerned with the appearance inverting, perverting and telling only part of the story that a focus on materialism reveals, and Jaggar concerned with explaining how it is that all women don't see the liberatory truths that feminism embodies. Jaggar's investments are in current feminist political struggles while Hartsock's are more broadly intellectual and abstract. The effect of Jaggar's focus in political struggle—contemporary feminist conversations—adjusts Hartsock's investments in the "material," making the "women's standpoint" more mobile in Jaggar's formulation. (In chapter 6 I talk more about the mobility of what counts as the material, which I also claim is an aspect of what is meant by the term "postmodern.")

Finally, at the end of an encyclopedic book, Jaggar resituates questions about the unity of a standpoint of women from concerns about who such a unity describes to concerns about who currently develops this systematic representation of reality. Description and development are necessarily simultaneous activities that reflect the interests (rather than the intentions) of the groups that engage in them. Jaggar ends *Feminist Politics and Human Nature* by asking about the "standpoint of women": "Do all women really occupy the same standpoint? And if they do not, which women occupy the standpoint that is most advantageous?" (385). It is this point that Collins's book picks up on. Jaggar's difference from Hartsock makes her uncomfortable enough to ask these questions. The very privileging of the group "women" as an unmarked category here in Jaggar's comment begins itself to deconstruct, making the group oppositionally subject (if not entirely accountable) to the kinds of responsibilities Sandoval both assumes and discusses in her analysis of "women of color." One may begin to hear the fragile resonances between "standpoint" and "standpoints" that I mentioned earlier. Hartsock's interests in the power of the dualistic model men/women, analogous to the Marxist model, allow the marked status of the group "women" against the unmarked group "men" to overshadow the simultaneously possible conceptualization of "women" as an unmarked category. Thus, Hartsock feels less pressure to make this unmarked "women" accountable to its marked elements, as the overwhelming salience of markedness makes this reduction to "women themselves" seem politically most urgent and powerful (although Hartsock does move between "women themselves" and "all women's lives in Western class societies" as she signals her intention to make women a historical category). As Hartsock says,

> In addressing the institutionalized sexual division of labor, I propose to lay aside the important differences among women and instead to search for central commonalities across race and class boundaries. I take some justification from the fruitfulness of Marx's similar strategy in constructing a simplified, two-class, two-man model in which everything was exchanged at its value. . . . My effort here takes a similar form, in an attempt to move toward a theory of the extraction and appropriation of women's activity and women themselves. Still, I adopt this strategy with some reluctance, since it contains the danger of making invisible the experience of lesbians or women of color. At the same time, I recognize that the ef-

fort to uncover a feminist standpoint assumes that there are some things common to all women's lives in Western class societies. (233–34)

In order to search out the commonalities that construct the object "Woman" as one in which we can all share (all women in Western class societies, if delimited still a tall order), Hartsock makes this powerful reduction—the simple display, the immediate understanding, and the urgent mobilization of what is epistemologically at stake in the feminist standpoint. In this attempt at empowerment her strategy is similar to Sandoval's construction of the unity of women of color. Hartsock privileges as representatives of the "differences" among women the groups "women of color" and "lesbians." Yet her search for commonality is exactly not the strategy followed by Sandoval and her consciousness-raising group for making this construction of the unmarked category responsible to its members, nor is her consideration of "difference" as invested and nuanced. Hartsock's footnote on these representative differences refers to the work of women of color and lesbians on the dangers of the denial of difference, but contrary to her usual documentary practice she does this without a summary of what these dangers are, and without placing herself in relation to the arguments contained in these conversations. Hartsock's particular understanding of achievement determines her heuristic here. As does the descent into materialism, commonality itself cues us to which possibilities inherent in women's experience may ultimately develop the feminist standpoint. After all, without such cues, how else would you know a liberatory possibility if you saw one? "The liberatory possibilities present in women's experience must be, in a sense, read out and developed. Thus, a feminist standpoint may be present on the basis of the commonalities within women's experience, but it is neither self-evident nor obvious" (246).

The differences between Hartsock and Jaggar on the notion of standpoint are differences that reflect the rapidity of change in feminist conversations. I now turn to look at practices that constrain both this rapid change and the form of these conversations, especially the practice of publication and the use of informal social networks. As I pointed out earlier, Hartsock and Jaggar represent two contiguous moments in U.S. feminism. The quotation from Hartsock's book on the commonalities of women just discussed exemplifies the difficult position Hartsock occupies in her efforts to be accountable to important new thinking that impinges on her in the time just before publication (What Gallop called "the pain of history," a widening incongruity between the political stakes in the feminist theory about to be consolidated in publication and its already shifted theoretical environment of reception). Jaggar's work occupies the very next succeeding moment, as she attempts some structural response to the shifts in identity politics that newly center women of color and require theoretical innovation. In Jaggar's argument this influence is already mediated by the words of Dorothy Smith and Sandra Harding, neither of them women of color. Genre also matters here. Jaggar's unexamined and disciplinarily narrow conception of "theory" causes her to discount work by women of color written in "descriptive" rather than theoretical genres.[22] However, she is clearly influenced by the conversations in which these materials participate, and in fact it is often insight from these materials that influences the theorists (such as Smith and Harding above), who then present them in acceptable "theoretical" forms. For Jaggar such acceptability requires making explicit epistemological claims.

Hartsock's efforts to be accountable to the conversations of and about women of color are seen in the layerings of revision in her writings on a feminist historical materialism. I've been working from three versions of Hartsock's work on standpoint. Until now I've referred most to her book *Money, Sex, and Power: Toward a Feminist Historical Materialism*, which was published in the same year—1983—as another long-anticipated book, a volume of collected essays, *Discovering Reality: Feminist Perspectives on Epistemology, Metaphysics, Methodology, and the Philosophy of Science* (Sandra Harding and Merrill B. Hintikka, eds.), which includes an earlier essay by Hartsock, "The Feminist Standpoint: Developing the Ground for a Specifically Feminist Historical Materialism." (That is, portions of it were written earlier than the revisions of *Money, Sex, and Power;* portions of it are unique to its publication version.)[23] Earlier still (most likely 1979) is the circulating manuscript "Can There Be a Specifically Feminist Historical Materialism?" which Hartsock mentions in her preface to *Money, Sex, and Power* as grounding chapters 5 and 10 and the appendixes of that volume. In fact, the manuscript is, in many cases, identical word-for-word with large portions of chapters 5, 6, 10, and a piece of 11 as well. Similarly, the manuscript also fundamentally overlaps with the Harding and Hintikka essay: part II of the manuscript essentially becomes the essay. In other words, very little fundamentally changed in Hartsock's argument on the feminist standpoint, even in the very wording of the argument, in the years between the circulating manuscript of 1979 and the publications in 1983 of both *Money, Sex, and Power* and the essay "The Feminist Standpoint" in Harding and Hintikka.

The telling exception to this generality is the caveat on the commonalities of women that I quoted earlier. In 1979 it read only,

> I will ignore the important differences among women across cultures and across race and class boundaries. I take some justification from Marx's similar strategy in constructing a simplified, two-class, two-man model in which everything is exchanged at its value. (manuscript, 26)

Hartsock's 1983 versions demonstrate that she abandoned the idea that the "commonalities" among women could be drawn across cultures, instead restricting her characterization to Western class societies.[24] Nor in 1979 had Hartsock invoked the term "commonalities" in distinction to differences, as "difference" did not yet have the metonymic power as magical touchstone of a collection of feminist conversations that it came to have over the eighties.[25] "Difference" does carry this weight in the concluding chapters of Jaggar's book (and she, too, invokes the term "common-alities" in parallel), as it does in the final version of *Money, Sex, and Power*. However, even in Hartsock's book, difference is adequately coded for her as the groups "women of color" and "lesbians," while for Jaggar the term is already more nu-anced.[26] The materials Hartsock cites as carrying on the conversation on the danger of the invisibility of differences among women were published 1979, 1980, and 1981 and perhaps reflect a hurried processing of these literatures.[27]

Hartsock's concerns in the construction of the feminist standpoint are already solidified in 1979, even as her manuscript was circulated in her social network. Her difficulties with theoretical mobility in reaction to newly emerging conversations about difference are structurally similar to her difficulties with theoretical mobility in her formulation of standpoint. Comments and suggestions she received changed nuances but not the larger structures of her thinking or expression. But this circu-lation clearly influenced Jaggar in her description of the category of "standpoint theorists," of whom Hartsock is one. Hartsock and Jaggar refer to each other in ac-knowledgments in their books, Hartsock even more prominently in both manuscript and essay. However, Hartsock never cites Jaggar, while Jaggar indeed cites Hart-sock—in personal communication, in a variety of published materials, and in refer-ence to manuscript versions of current writing not yet published (for example, she cites the Harding and Hintikka essay still forthcoming as in typescript). Dependent upon and indebted to Hartsock, Jaggar is also puzzled and challenged by Hartsock's work and person: Hartsock poses a theoretical problem for Jaggar as well as a re-source, as I will detail shortly. As Hartsock's stakes in her work are in the construc-tion of a materialism accountable to and constitutive of feminism, so Jaggar's stakes are in the construction of a taxonomy of feminisms that justifies a particular politi-cal program and identity, namely socialist feminism. "This book is intended as a substantive contribution to feminist theory, insofar as it argues for the superiority of one conception of women's liberation over all the others. That one is socialist feminism" (8). (For more discussion of a feminist history of such taxonomic analy-sis, see chapter 4.)

For all of Jaggar's final appeals to the discourse on "difference" as a political resource, difference is the epistemological and evaluative problem with which she begins her book. The whole of Jaggar's book is intended to reduce diversity, to or-ganize, tame, and conquer it. Jaggar seeks "a sound methodology to provide the ba-sis for a theory and a practice that will liberate women. Consequently, I seek to re-duce rather than proliferate theories" (10). This one theory and practice is socialist feminism. Reduction is accomplished by organizing feminist theories into mutually exclusive, fundamentally incompatible genera.

> In order to do this [reduction], of course, I must decide which differences count as 'fundamental,' and I find it most useful to identify fundamental differences by ref-erence to four distinctive conceptions of human nature. These conceptions, I shall show, are correlated with distinctive analyses of women's oppression and distinc-tive visions of women's liberation. (10)

Compare also:

> The reconstruction of feminist theories as ideal types minimizes the similarities
> between them and sharpens the differences. My ultimate aim is certainly not to
> deepen divisions among feminists; rather, it is to help resolve them. I think this
> can be done best, however, by an in-depth examination of our differences that
> clarifies exactly what is at stake. The way is then prepared for a resolution of those
> differences, a resolution that can provide a sound basis for future political work
> and for further theoretical development. (13)

Notice that for Jaggar the way to resolve differences among feminists is to construct
a single political position that is the "most adequate" theoretically (9).

Jaggar's four-part taxonomy produces as positions liberal feminism, a liminal
Marxism, radical feminism, and socialist feminism; these positions structure both
Jaggar's book and argument. As I've suggested before, Jaggar's taxonomy is actually
a "machine" for generating "socialist feminism."[28] In particular, Jaggar uses "radical feminism" as the straw position from which the distinction between naive and
achieved standpoints can be drawn, assigning to socialist feminism, via Marxism,
the self-conscious understanding of the implications of achievement. Hartsock's
work and person problematize Jaggar's taxonomy. Claims that "the women's standpoint" as an epistemological device (my term) demonstrates the theoretical sophistication of socialist feminism ground Jaggar's argument for the superiority of socialist feminism as a theory of women's liberation, and in Jaggar's final chapter this
standpoint apparatus even comes to stand for socialist feminism.[29] Hartsock and her
work are fundamental then to Jaggar's construction of what socialist feminism is.
Jaggar also ties "the standpoint of women" to a group of women she describes as
"working to develop this insight, although they do not all use the terminology of
women's standpoint or even mean quite the same thing by it when they do. [Remem-
ber, this is in 1983.] These theorists include Elizabeth Fee, Jane Flax, Sandra Harding, Nancy Hartsock, Evelyn Fox Keller, and Dorothy Smith" (370). Four of these
six women have powerful investments in feminist object relations theory (Hartsock
I've already mentioned in this regard). All are women who make claims about feminism's contributions to epistemology. The connections between standpoint theory,
the sexual division of labor, and psychoanalytic materials are suggested as Jaggar
says:

> Socialist feminist theorists argue that a consideration of the distinctive differ-
> ences between the experience and work of women and the experience and work
> of men, both as infants and as adults, sheds light on certain distinctive differences
> in the way that each sex tends to conceptualize reality. (375)

So strong are both these powerful investments in object relations and Jaggar's equation of socialist feminism with these standpoint theorists that Jaggar finds herself
required to make the disclaimer that:

> socialist feminist epistemology does not stand or fall with feminist psychoanalysis.
> ... It is quite compatible with socialist feminism for the gender-structured adult

experience of women and men to be more influential than their infant experience in shaping their world view. (376)[30]

Despite the fundamental grounding Hartsock's work (and the work of the others Jaggar names "standpoint theorists") gives the identity "socialist feminism," Jaggar is also forced to admit that Hartsock's presuppositions make the distinction between radical feminism and socialist feminism problematic. "The basic structure of the world, as Hartsock claims that it appears from the standpoint of women, bears a strong resemblance to the world as described by radical feminism. Indeed, my characterization of several of the theorists mentioned above as socialist rather than radical feminist is perhaps presumptuous and may not be in accord with their own definition of themselves"[31] (376). Indeed, probably any individual's work is problematic in relation to Jaggar's taxonomy. The taxonomy doesn't work to sort individuals, it operates to construct socialist feminism. Jaggar claims that her taxonomy is simultaneously diachronic and synchronic, but what she means by "developed chronologically" (12) in describing her four positions is that they are teleologically related to each other; liberal feminism is answered logically by radical feminism which is answered logically by socialist feminism.

Jaggar's lack of historical context for any of her characterizations works to stabilize her ideal categories. As a result, any reader interested in constructing such a historical or even chronological sense of her materials using her citation apparatus will find it difficult if not impossible.[32] Her citation apparatus does strikingly reveal something else, however. It demonstrates the rapidity of feminist thinking, which I mentioned earlier as the reality of Hartsock's publication position. In the single footnote in which Jaggar details the work of the standpoint theorists upon which she is relying, of the thirteen articles referenced, six are not yet published at the time of their citation.[33] In the whole of Jaggar's final chapter on feminist theory, more than 20 percent of the citations of feminist materials refer to work not yet published. The fast-paced character of feminist theory is both obscured by and constrained in publication time. Time constraints especially require that engagement with feminist conversations is crucially determined by participation in social networks that ensure access to unpublished materials. As conversations shift (as they are continually doing) privileging these social networks has the consequence of excluding materials as well as including them. The odd, cursory quality to Hartsock's reference to the discourse on difference in *Money, Sex, and Power* can be partially attributed to this kind of exclusion as well as to the problems writers find in finishing a specific argument in the face of rapid change. It is not surprising that neither Hartsock nor Jaggar had access to Chela Sandoval's work, for example; nor did Sandoval's career trajectory and cohort connections permit her to engage in the same conversations with Jaggar and Hartsock in 1983. At the time of the writing of either Hartsock's or Jaggar's book, Sandoval was a graduate student completely unpublished. However, in 1992 Sandoval does figure briefly in Hartsock's citation apparatus in a list of names of a heterogeneous group of scholars arguing for "a specific view from below": "See for example, work by Patricia Hill Collins on a Black feminist standpoint, Marilyn Frye, Teresa de Lauretis, Molefi Asante, Sandra Harding, Che Sandoval, and Donna Haraway" (23).

Access to publication becomes crucial, as I said, to participation in and in distribution of particular feminist conversations. This is one important reason for the formation of new publication avenues, for example, Kitchen Table: Women of Color Press. Sandoval's essay "Women Respond to Racism" was originally published in photocopy form (from Sandoval's own computer processed pages) by The Center for Third World Organizing in Oakland, California. This names one network of distribution. Sandoval's published material in *Signs* (naming another network of distribution) was not actually an article but a reply to a review of social science literature. Sandoval is not an expert in the literature on the social sciences, but a Third World woman asked to comment as such. Sandoval's work as a theorist on the identities, politics, and conceptualizing of "women of color" informs the critical reply she offers, but the conflation of her work and her personal and political identity here is powerful in her reaction to the institutionalized racism that also structures the publication institutions she connects with. She strategically uses the mobile and constructed character of "women of color" in her political actions here. She turns her position as commentator into one of developer of feminist theory. Earlier I spoke of Jaggar's attention to *who* develops feminist liberatory possibilities in a new representation of reality, and this attention is echoed by Sandoval's rejection of "the common ground" the unmarked character of women is supposed to provide. "If we are not going to attempt to find a common ground for our community building . . . then we are free to explore a different kind of community building" ("Racism," 27). Notice that "difference" is not structurally paired with "commonalities" here; instead a mobility of interests and intentions are necessary. As Jaggar says that "the woman's standpoint" is not a representation immediately available to women—or only available to women, if counter-intuitive to men—so Sandoval's field of power relations, or, as she terms it, "oppositional consciousness," offers the possibility that the position of liberatory insight, as constructed and mobile category "women of color," will develop a new representation of reality in profound coalition.

I've just described the accountabilities to new literatures enacted by Hartsock and Jaggar just before 1983 publication. Such accountabilities become pressing for different feminist cohorts at different moments, as chronological time intersects with publication time and circulation time. Gallop recounts an analogous moment of such accountability, as a white woman responding to the conversations on difference, in a different chronology and in a different cohort. This deliberately staged conversation is taken from the book *Conflicts in Feminism;* it was originally taped in 1989 and then extensively edited for inclusion in this 1990 book.[34] The participants—Jane Gallop, Marianne Hirsch, and Nancy Miller—are described in the editors' introductory note as members of the same cohort as distinguished by field ("edging out of French"), career trajectory (dates of Ph.D.—"mid-1970s"—and tenure—"early 1980s") and by a mini-history of the rise and consolidation of poststructuralism and feminism. Unsurprisingly this mini-history recapitulates the one Gallop gives in *Around 1981*, and the conversation itself keeps recentering around Gallop's book, not yet published, but in its finishing stages. Gallop's anecdote is launched by Hirsch's question, "How inclusive are you in this history?" Gallop responds:

> I'm doing Pryse and Spillers's *Conjuring*.[35] Race only posed itself as an urgent issue to me in the last couple of years. Obviously there has been a larger shift in the valent feminist discourses in which I participated. I didn't feel the necessity of discussing race until I had moved myself out of a French poststructural orbit and began talking about American feminist literary criticism. . . . (363)

Gallop then tells her story about what motivated the inclusion of *Conjuring* (1985) in *Around 1981;* she says she read from her book at the University of Virginia in February 1989:

> I had hoped Deborah McDowell would come to my talk: she was there, she was the one person in the audience that I was really hoping to please. Someone in the audience asked me if I was writing about a black anthology. I answered no and tried to justify it, but my justifications rang false in my ears. Some weeks later a friend of mine showed me a letter from McDowell which mentioned my talk and said that I was just doing the same old thing, citing that I was not talking about any books edited by black women. I obsessed over McDowell's comment until I decided to add a chapter on Pryse and Spillers's *Conjuring*. I had already vowed not to add any more chapters out of fear that I would never finish the book. As powerful as my fear of not finishing is, it was not as strong as my wish for McDowell's approval. For McDowell, whom I do not know, read black feminist critic. (363)

Notice that the kind of political pressure that motivates the changes in the work of Hartsock and Jaggar peaks at a different chronological moment for Gallop, around 1987, as her field shifts (both for Gallop and for her cohort, the conversation suggests). Also notice how she understands this political pressure (typically underscored by Gallop in affective terms suggesting power shifts) against pressures of publication timing. The histories such cohorts tell must be differently inflected and invented as we compare the disparity between the pressures felt around 1983 with Hartsock and Jaggar with the pressure described by Gallop here around 1987.

Sandoval and Collins are theorists whose lines of affiliation delineate even more divergent investments. Both appear to have responded to Jaggar, and in significantly different ways. In Sandoval's 1991 essay, a piece of her critique of "The Great Hegemonic Model" names Jaggar's work explicitly and critically. Patricia Hill Collins's book, published in 1990 when she was associate professor of African-American studies at the University of Cincinnati, implicitly embodies a response to Jaggar's 1983 book that builds upon that pedagogical anthology, published in 1978 when she was associate professor of philosophy at the University of Cincinnati. In her 1983 book *Feminist Politics and Human Nature*, Jaggar makes the following claim (thus exemplifying "hegemonic feminism" as Sandoval uses the term):

Black feminism has not been omitted from the book, but it has not been treated as a separate theory because black feminists utilize a variety of theoretical approaches. . . . Given the variety in the theoretical orientation of black feminism, I think it more useful to examine their contributions in the context of the four categories of feminism I identify than to present those contributions as reflective of a single black feminist perspective.

A relatively small body of written work is available by feminists of color other than black feminists, and what is available is mainly at the level of description. . . . So far . . . relatively few attempts exist by non-black feminists of color to develop a distinctive and comprehensive theory of women's liberation. . . .[36]

Collins's development and description of a Black women's standpoint and of Black feminist thought could be understood as a dramatic 1990 counter example that shatters this organization of knowledge. Collins does mention the work of other (white) standpoint theorists, naming Hartsock, Jaggar, and Dorothy Smith, while also naming Sandra Harding as critiquing standpoint epistemologies and Donna Haraway as reformulating them. Collins locates Haraway's work on situated knowledges as approximating her own use of standpoint theory.

Notice exactly how "a Black women's standpoint" and "Black feminist thought" as objects of knowlege confound Jaggar's consolidation of her taxonomy above. One of Collins's definitions of a Black women's standpoint runs: [A Black women's standpoint names] "the special angle of vision that Black women bring to the knowledge production process" (21). A Black women's standpoint is the starting point for Black feminist thought that interprets and clarifies the realities the standpoint reveals. All Black women are included in a Black women's standpoint. One doesn't have to be a feminist. Black feminist thought builds upon a Black women's standpoint. Black feminist thought thus cannot be added to Jaggar's taxonomy as a new node, as it embodies a particular entailed relationship to a Black women's standpoint that the other nodes of Jaggar's taxonomy do not analogously embody in relation to a "women's standpoint." Its very construction belies Jaggar's claim that it can be accommodated through dispersion among her named taxonomic nodes, for Collins clearly feels that a description of its unity is currently called for and is also under attack. Jaggar's production of "a women's standpoint" is reckoned inadequate, indeed discarded as Collins makes no attempt to interconnect such "a women's standpoint" with "A Black women's standpoint." And a definitive relation is established between a Black women's standpoint and the multiplicity of Black feminist thought, conspicuously without even the kind of taxonomy Jaggar offers, let alone without this particular taxonomy. Unlike Tong's revision of the taxonomy, which retains its hegemony while dramatically altering it, Collins refuses the very terms the taxonomy rests upon, while retaining but profounding altering the notion of a standpoint. Notice how her object "thought" in some of its conspicuous indeterminacies enables her refusal of Jaggar's assumed locations for "a separate theory" by Black women. (I think here too of Echols's assumed locations for an "autonomous" Black women's movement.)

Consider Jaggar's phrase "a distinctive and comprehensive theory of women's liberation" and her characterization of the available written work of feminists of color as "at the level of description" ("what is available," that is, circulating, in her networks, disciplines, and distributions of influence). Genre and disciplinary filters here privileging only very particular kinds of written materials justify the dismissal of "what is available" from her project. Some materials "available" might have been, say, *Common Differences* (1981), *This Bridge Called My Back* (1981), or earlier *conditions five: the black women's issue* (1979). Citations to such materials are missing from Jaggar. Both *This Bridge Called My Back* and *conditions five* are largely collections of literary materials, although their editors see the collections as having theoretical implications and as possible texts for classes in feminist theory. This perspective is not at all shared by Jaggar, who would classify this material as radical feminist, saying, "Radical feminism has shown us that women have a distinctively valuable perspective on the world; it has not fully comprehended that an adequate expression of the standpoint of women must be a theoretical and scientific achievement as well as a political and artistic one" (381); this perspective is thus "at the level of description." Jaggar isn't accountable for the fact that the categories for inclusion skew, at the very least, the race and class composition of their writers/theorists, except to lament with Sandra Harding that "we theory-makers are our own subject/objects but not a very historically representative part of 'women' " (386). Literary genres were the ones in which the "thought" (by Collins deliberately indeterminately slipping between ideas and "theory") of women of color was most available to white women and many women of color, too, through new avenues of publication in the late seventies and early eighties. For example, Kitchen Table: Women of Color Press, the first small press dealing specifically with women of color as a group (a "unity"), began by publishing only literature. (See chapter 3 for more discussion of productions of theory in the overlapping conversations at the site of the apparatus for the production of feminist culture.) Its first three anthologies—*Bridge* (1981), *Home Girls* (1983), and *Cuentos: Stories by Latinas* (1983)—have since been used by women's studies and ethnic studies courses in universities.[37] In Jaggar and Harding's lament here, "theory" and "theory-makers" are disciplinarily determined objects. Collins refuses these objects as well in her construction and consolidation of "Black feminist thought."

Collins's constructions "a Black women's standpoint" and "Black feminist thought" precisely enable the inclusion of communities theorizing into the processes of "thought" (and the reifications of "theory"), while retaining the key notion of achievement so, if differently, essential to the notions of standpoint developed by Hartsock and Jaggar. She does this through the "core themes" at the heart of her book. These core themes are dense syntheses of both experiences and ideas, that is, the materials from a Black women's standpoint and the materials of "thought" in its widest ranges, including the work of Black women intellectuals outside the academy, as well as the academic scholarship of feminist and Afrocentric theorists. The core themes exemplify especially Collins's phrase "the interdependence of thought and action," which defines for Collins that liberatory struggle in the development of the standpoint differently emphasized by Hartsock and Jaggar. In the interdependence of thought and action, Collins names three levels of interdependence, from concrete experiences to a self-defined standpoint to acts of resistance. Each core theme touches upon these levels, although each theme also is distinctively shaped. The core themes are: "Work, Family, and Black Women's Oppression," "Mammies, Matriarchs, and Other Controling Images," "The Power of Self-Definition," "Black Women and Motherhood," "Rethinking Black Women's Activism," "The Sexual Politics of Black Womanhood," and "Sexual Politics and Black Women's Relationships."

Finally, in her description of the matrix of domination, Collins explicitly describes multiple standpoints. (This is one of the few times in the text that Collins extends beyond the group "Black women" to other people of color.)

> Those ideas that are validated as true by African-American women, African-American men, Latina lesbians, Asian-American women, Puerto Rican men, and other groups with distinctive standpoints, with each group using the epistemological approaches growing from its unique standpoint, thus become the most "objective" truths. Each group speaks from its own standpoint and shares its own partial, situated knowledge. But because each group perceives its own truth as partial, its knowlege is unfinished. Each group becomes better able to consider other groups' standpoints without relinquishing the uniqueness of its own standpoint or suppressing other groups' partial perspectives. . . . Partiality and not universality is the condition of being heard; individuals and groups forwarding knowledge claims without owning their position are deemed less credible than those who do. (236)

Collins's idea of multiple standpoints, enabled here in its characterization as "partial, situated knowledge" by Donna Haraway's essay "Situated Knowledges: The Science Question in Feminism and the Privilege of Partial Perspective," informs the revision that Hartsock performs in 1991.[38] Collins's refusals and reformulations are appropriately understood within that axiom set out by Chandra Mohanty (discussed in chapter 1) that "the practice of scholarship is also a form of rule and resistance and constitutes an increasingly important arena of third world feminisms" (32) and in relation to the cautionary examination by Mohanty of "the political effects of analytic strategies" (69).[39]

As I said before, the notion of a standpoint is a bit of theoretical work in flux. I enact this pressure and change in my own classroom synthesis, and I flag it in this chapter's historical analysis. Like classroom time, circulation time and publication time are likely to reflect one's own cohort(s)' interests and one's training and networks of influence. In her "The Feminist Standpoint Revisited," Hartsock also enacts this pressure and change. She calls a standpoint "a technical theoretical device which can allow for the creation of better (more objective, more liberatory) accounts of the world" (18). I'm concerned about how one patches together theoretical apparatus and what happens when you turn it on. My earlier discussion of Hartsock details some of the political effects I see happening when Hartsock turns on her particular analytic device, and I distinguished these effects from Hartsock's intentions. In her revision, though, Hartsock is deeply invested in her intentions, and the reason for this is that reiterating them redraws the conversations she is mobilizing in the construction of her technical theoretical device. Reiterating them also allows her to dispute the literary processing devices through which her work has been filtered and the political identities to which she has been assimilated. Hartsock reiterates her intentions in response to criticisms of her work on the feminist standpoint (as *she* names and understands them) that

> (1) her "case is based on biology and reinscribes the split between nature and culture";
> (2) she is an essentialist, both making cross-cultural claims and "putting forward a notion of a unitary subject";
> (3) she is "arguing that masculine personality is the source of women's problems"; and
> (4) she is engaging in a politically dangerous "gender oppositional strategy" (this criticism from both the left and the right) (13).[40]

Stated in these terms, I personally would agree that she is not guilty of any of these "charges," although I have already noted unintended effects of her valiant reframings of nature/culture distinctions and her early, but excised, claim to cross-cultural commonality. I think the literature processing check-off terms that Hartsock's version of these criticisms suggests are: biologism (charge 1), essentialism, universalism, humanism (all charge 2), and radical feminism (charges 3 and 4). The first four implicate Hartsock's myriad recraftings of what counts as the material. The third and fourth are allusions to her development of the notion of abstract masculinity. Note that ascription to a political identity can count as a "charge." (The term "charge" encodes both Hartsock's own misunderstood tone and something of the complicated responses feminists have to being critical and being criticized. I'll discuss this further in a moment.) Hartsock understands these check-off terms to inaccurately process her work. She attributes this inaccuracy to feminist ignorance of Marxist theory. For this reason in "The Feminist Standpoint Revisited," she often responds by having Marx, rather than herself, answer her critics.

Hartsock's reformulations of her feminist standpoint are in 1991 located as one "specific view from below" (23) in response to the one criticism (not named above) that Hartsock allows.

> But there are problems with my argument, in particular that it worked to subsume the "marked" categories of feminists under the unmarked and therefore white feminist, and lesbian under the category of straight just as women can be subsumed under the category "man." That is, in following Marx's procedure of reducing the world to a two-class, two-man model, I ended up with a problem similar to his own—ie., unable to see in his case important axes of domination, even while recognizing their operation. . . . So while I too took note of some race and class

differences in terms of the sexual division of labor, I too made no theoretical space
which would have accorded them proper significance. (22–23)

Thus, Hartsock now speaks of "multiple subjectivities" that challenge any notion of
a unitary subject. She also abstracts several fundamentals shared among views from
below: multiplicity (somewhat more elaborated in this version rather than taken for
granted as before under the rubric "concrete"), "being locatable in time and space
and particular cultures," specific embodiments, and "operating as standpoints" in
the plural. I still find Sandoval's understanding of the shifting, tactical, and mobile
character of subjectivities to be missing from Hartsock's revision, and I still find myself using it as a touchstone in my own descriptions and understandings of the productions of marked and unmarked categories. However, I also understand this
particular sense of mobility to be part of the meaning of the term "postmodern,"
and Hartsock still sees standpoint theory as an alternative to the postmodernism of,
especially, Foucault and Rorty. Such "mobility," as Hartsock herself currently values
it, is still located within notions of achievement; historical and political struggle
would include historical shifts and political tactics. My suspicion is that Hartsock's
continuing critiques of postmodernism actually mark an ongoing engagement with
it, suggested by the kinds of theoretical changes and new indebtednesses she displays: to the postcolonial theorists, the women of color such as Collins, and the—unacknowledged—postmodernisms of Jameson, Haraway, and Sandoval.

I just said that Hartsock emphasizes her intentions in order to highlight the
particular conversations she is mobilizing, to dispute the literary processing she receives, and to refuse the political identities to which she's been assimilated. I said at
the very beginning of this chapter that thinking in terms of conversations emphasizes political contour over ranges of theoretical contents (debates). Conversations
overlap several debates or are layered over each other within particular debates;
they overlap more than written theory—including public speech and action, private
oralities, group products and processes—or varieties and versions of informal writing or circulating manuscripts. I'm using the term conversation as a unit of political
agency in action in theoretical discourse. For example, during the sexuality debates
several *conversations* were layered in process:

- One disputed the production of the political identity "radical feminist," correcting and consolidating a new set of meanings by splitting it apart from another
political identity "cultural feminist."
- Another redrew the maps of what counted as "revolutionary sexuality" by
oppositionally displaying radical forms and newly contextualized historicizations of
(especially socialist feminist) heterosexuality and reactionary forms of lesbian
feminism.
- Another criticized the anti-pornography movement, theoretically and tactically.
- Another overlapped a socialist feminist critique of a variety of feminist
forms of entrepreneurial capitalism and worker exploitation.

- Another overlapped wide-ranging discussions of racially or culturally specific forms of sexuality and sexisms as they interconnect experientially and possibly theoretically.
- Another overlapped with calls for separations among theories of gender, theories of sexisms, theories of sexuality and sex hatreds.
- Another valorized lesbian, s/m, and public and multiply partnered sex.
- Another overlapped a celebration of sex in a new historicization of the current climate of sex hatred. Some political-theoretical actors engaging in one conversation were confused with and by those in other conversations, resulting in one form of "talking past one another." Some mixed several different conversations into particular packages that were not shared by others' entirely different mixed packages of conversations, each confusingly counting as "the sexuality debates." Some conversations were carried on informally in groups rather than represented in written "theory," others were "reported on" in journalist productions, still others were enacted (for example, as ZAP actions).

Finally, conversations embodied and effected shifting political *alliances*.

- In one shift, white, heterosexual, socialist feminists aligned with lesbian, s/m activists against "cultural feminists" and the anti-pornography movement.
- In another shift, working-class lesbians aligned with lesbians of color to discuss and reframe culturally specific sexual meanings.
- Remade "radical feminists" self-consciously aligned with socialist feminists rather than with "cultural feminists."
- Some lesbians, especially s/m lesbians, made new alliances with gay men, especially man/boy lovers.
- New space was made within radical sex activism for work on AIDS; new space was made within AIDS activism for radical sex theory and action.

I use this relatively well-known and only summarized set of configurations about the sexuality debates here (1) to exemplify the *patterning* of what I mean by feminist conversations; (2) to interconnect with and recapitulate some of my arguments about the production of feminist identities, especially the rehistoricization of "radical feminism" and the taxonomic production of older and more current forms of "socialist feminism"; (3) to exemplify another form in which literatures (maybe better "writing technologies"; more about that in the next chapter) can be (and are here) processed; and (4) to describe what I mean by theoretical-political agencies.

In their written-up conversation from *Conflicts in Feminism*, Gallop, Hirsch, and Miller talk about current forms of "trashing feminists." I understand the term "trashing" from the earlier time periods that Echols writes about and in which she describes trashing in *Daring to Be Bad*. I recall trashing as the volatile and often emotionally violent circumstances in which especially charismatic individuals were challenged by other individuals or groups for this charismatic power. To be "trashed" generally meant to be silenced, disempowered. But I remember this term as used for both small-scale trashing, say in a single meeting, as well as for large-scale trashing, say of figures valorized by the media. For some this silencing was permanent or permanently disabling. For others this was only part of the rather recriminatory movements of power one struggled with and perhaps even manipulated. In that sense I've both experienced being trashed and trashing. For the cohort Gallop, Hirsch, and Miller represent, the meanings of this historically specific action have been extended as one form of a broadly understood problem and ambivalence about "feminist criticism." For this group "feminist criticism" has a triple meaning: first, the disciplinarily specific activity and academic genre; second, the broadly understood academic notions of "critique"; and finally, the generic meanings of finding fault. Echoes from the past Echols describes that may also inform this term for a variety of cohorts are from the activity called "criticism–self-criticism," which feminists took from Maoist valorization of the Cultural Revolution and which inform meanings of "consciousness-raising." I still remember when the last portion of a women's studies class was understood to require everyone to engage in "criticism-self-criticism." I'm happy not to continue this practice in my courses, although when done well such discussion about group process and individual action can build in and upon new intellectual and political accountabilities. Some feminist political groups still practice versions of such self-criticism.

What Gallop, Hirsch, and Miller refer to by trashing are: (1) dismissive forms of what I call processing literatures—dismissive with varying ranges of rancor and result; (2) gatekeeping; (3) political "othering"—as in, it's your group that my position is formed against; and (4) a generalized tone of contempt in critique. Gallop and Hirsch dispute just to what degree and how such dismissive critiques affect one's career. Gallop, on the one hand, contends that feminists such as Showalter, Gilligan, and Chodorow—subject to some wide-ranging critiques of their work—have lost little in terms of power, career trajectory, or broad cultural influence. Hirsch, on the other hand, contends that such dismissive criticisms affect both work and career and further wants to speculate about historical changes that might exacerbate trashing currently. Gallop claims: "Feminists have been attacking feminists from the beginning. I think it's a myth that there was a moment feminists didn't attack feminists" (365). In response, Hirsch speculates:

> I think it's a generational thing and I think that that generation has somehow not been able to raise a generation that builds on what came before. You're saying that maybe it was there in the beginning, but I guess I don't believe it was the same. In the seventies we were hungry for every new book and its discoveries. And, of course, there were disagreements and there was criticism. I think it again has very much to do with the issue of power and who is in power and how many of us there is room for in the academy. (365-66)

Perhaps Hirsch's location in the academy "in the seventies" protected her from the kind of trashing Echols describes. And I'm not at all clear about who is being named as "that generation" (Gilligan's cohort? the cohort(s) of her critics?) or how it is located in relation to any generation Hirsch might be part of. After all, this is an edited transcription of a conversation and as such is difficult to pin down in written terms. But still, Hirsch is insisting that this question not be easily dismissed and that it be seen in current historical context.

It was Hirsch who first introduced the term and the topic at the beginning of the conversation, recounting a story about "the only feminist speaker" in a particular academic context whose "paper was built on what appeared to me and others as the *trashing* of other feminists' work. The paper summarized, erroneously, and dismissed, as naive, a range of complex and influential feminist theoretical work *for an audience that took these summaries to be 'useful.'* All that lead up to the 'correct' answer which was Freud" (350). [Emphasis mine.] Although she doesn't say who this was at this point in the conversation, clearly Gallop and Miller know (and the footnote identifies) this person was Toril Moi. Moi and her very influential summary of feminist literary theory, *Sexual/Textual Politics*, function throughout the rest of the conversation to emblematize "trashing," especially in that form I call processing literatures.[41] Miller encapsulates her reaction: "The issue—and it's bound to become more acute with the arrival on the scene of a whole generation of younger feminists trained by us(!)—is the performance of a critique without the edge of violence that creeps into the tone. Maybe violence is too strong—without the contempt for other work that seems to come with the territory" (363). Gallop ties together these issues and the meanings of her history in *Around 1981*, comparing it to *Sexual/Textual Politics* and characterizing these projects as "a struggle over whose version of history is going to be told to the next generation." (She specifies feminist graduate students.) She continues:

> I clearly am trying to write that history. Oddly enough, although maybe it makes me just the same, one of things I see myself trying to undo is the effect of books like *Sexual/Textual Politics* and the amount of influence that they've had for graduate students as a version of seventies feminist criticism. I see myself literally and directly trying to write, not the reverse of these books, but some other mode of looking at history as well as trying to demystify what I see as a reigning myth. I see this misconception of the seventies, for example, and all these received notions about French feminists and American feminists. It drives me up the wall and has actually given me something specific that I want to undo. Presumably we would then have something like quoting Gallop which would not be any better than quoting Moi or quoting Todd. I hope I am not doing the same thing, saying somebody is bad, somebody is good: this is the line, this is what they are. But rather insisting that these people be read in order to understand what they are saying. Moi's work represents to me what I hope I am not doing but also what I am writing to counter. But I'm not sure I'm not doing the same thing in perhaps some fancier way. (362–63)

My use of Hartsock, Jaggar, Collins, Sandoval and Gallop, Hirsch and Miller makes them representative of larger conversations that they have consolidated in these published locations. All of them (and myself) are influenced by conversations in their many forms, which are then refashioned into these published reifications. Including conversations within the economy of publication often entails tokenization, even essentialization, as a form of consolidation. My consolidations produce stagings in which a single figure speaks an entire unpublished, multilayered group production or takes the opportunity to distribute individual work among new audiences, distinguished by oral and written networks. Like Gallop, I too am trying to work out "some other mode of looking at history" and engaging in demystification. I'm trying to tell my own interested story to feminist cohorts who don't share it. I don't apologize for the interestedness of my characterizations—perhaps, unlike Gallop, I even *like* this contending for histories—but I do understand that my characterizations are interested. What I'm also trying to do is hand around some tools for the kind of detailing that permits contentions for histories that permits positioning me, too. I can only partially position myself, just as Gallop can only partially position herself, but I think some of my tools are generally usable for positioning of such political-theoretical agencies.

3

The Politics of the Oral and the Written
"Poem," "Story," and "Song" as
Writing Technologies in the Apparatus
for the Production of Feminist Culture

IN THIS CHAPTER I do two things: first, I contest for the term "cultural feminism," constructing an alternative object intended to destabilize an equation with the anti-pornography movement and to refuse a location as the political "other" of Echols's revised "radical feminism." I do not do this by answering Echols or other critics of cultural feminism and thus remaining in the epistemological paradigms she's constructed, borrowed, and exemplifies, allowing their hegemony, but rather by mapping an altogether alternative terrain. I call my alternative object "the apparatus for the production of feminist culture." In my rehistoricization, this apparatus is the site for the feminist proliferations of new political identities in the seventies, eighties, and nineties through such "writing technologies" as "poem," "story," and "song." Deliberately "writing" is extended here in meaning beyond inked words on paper, borrowing from deconstruction the added and complicated investments in understanding the ideologies under which writing has been divided from other generations of cultural meaning, and also cannot be so divided. My intention is both to call writing's history into political relief in the movements of power—stories in which feminism has great investments, as I shall soon describe—but also to do so without simultaneously romanticizing "orality." Rather, oral and alternate "writing technologies" (cultural technologies for producing meaning in a very broad sense) also have political histories and chart material movements of power and at the same time are complexly commingled with written "writing technologies." The "oral" and the "written" are not conceived of here as mutually exclusive terrains, each with distinct epistemologies and ideologies, but rather "writing technologies" are historically variant, commingle in material and ideological proliferations. So, the second thing I do in this chapter is to introduce my work on feminism and writing technologies, as it extends from my description of the implications of "poem," "story," and "song" as writing technologies in the movements constructing and proliferating feminist identities.

Since my object "(feminist) theory" messily brings together the mutually implicated actions theory building, alliance shifting, and political identity production, such a construction of this object "the apparatus for the production of feminist culture" and its positioning in relation to making political identities within my understanding is deeply "theoretical." That is, the contents of such discussion and description are theoretical, but especially the very construction of this apparatus as it builds theory, now shifts alliances, and renames and itself proliferates political identities enacts the political-theoretical agencies I've described before. The idea of conversations overlapping and overlayering theoretical debates that I used as a narrative thread through the last chapter is mobilized here as well. The range of overlap in conversations that are not recorded in writing or primarily in writing gets more play in this chapter, as "poem," "story," and "song" all complexly intermingle across the oral and the written and highlight many more forms for the production, distribution, and reception of feminist theory, even still within the U.S. academy. So I want to begin with an emblematic example of this production, distribution, and reception of feminist theory within the apparatus for the production of feminist culture, an example describing a deeply pivotal historical moment and metaphor bringing together, on the one hand, that "transnational political alliance" Sandoval describes as the context for the making of U.S. Third World feminisms and, on the other, the so-called white women's movement. I want to detail the complex layerings of action, event, oratory, writing, political intervention and theory building that can be named Bernice Johnson Reagon's "Coalition Politics: Turning the Century."[1]

The "struggle," political and intellectual, that accountability to the elements of the unmarked category requires is the subject of Reagon's 1983 essay "Coalition Politics: Turning the Century." This struggle for accountability is expressed in Sandoval's prediction that "the meanings of our sisterhood will change."[2] With its origins in oratory, Reagon's essay focuses dramatically on how this struggle *feels* and on the shifting contours of just who is involved in it. "There is no hiding place. There is nowhere you can go and only be with people who are like you. It's over. Give it up" (357). "No hiding place" echoes like a phrase in a verse of "women's music" and this is not coincidental, for Reagon is a lead singer in the musical group Sweet Honey in the Rock.[3] The front cover disc jacket of Sweet Honey's *Good News* appropriates the term "culture" from the discourse of cultural nationalism in its international left context (quoting Amilcar Cabral of Guinea-Bissau) and applies it to the antiracist element of "cultural feminism" exemplified in the volume of women's music that *Good News* is.[4] The cover names "differences" whose voices Sweet Honey serves: "people, who by reason of color, national origin, age, sex, and economic status, are denied a hearing in the courts of the powerful." It is as a volume of so-called women's music that *Good News* enjoys one avenue of distribution.

Behind Reagon's evocative words one can hear Mary Watkins's song "No Hidin' Place," which Watkins performed on the album *Lesbian Concentrate: A Lesbianthology of Songs and Poems*.[5] Lesbians of color occupy a generative theoretical-political location as agents mobilizing multiple identities, those multiple identities that are later named in Collins's matrix of domination and which build upon and extend the political location of "the lesbian" in feminist avant garde politics in the late seventies. This extension is first and pivotally deployed in the apparatus for the production of feminist culture. The album *Lesbian Concentrate* was part of the lesbian and gay response to the homophobic Brigg's initiative in California and to Anita Bryant's 1977 anti-gay "Save Our Children" national campaign; the record jacket jokingly pictures in "high-Pop" style a "lesbian concentrate" orange juice can. The inner jacket material includes not just the customary lyrics, but also serves as a lesbian resource guide including: a polemical discussion of lesbianism, lesbian oppression, and social change (written by Ginny Berson and Robin Brooks for the women of Olivia Records); a description of Olivia Records; material on the Lesbian Mothers' National Defense Fund—toward which part of the proceeds of the record go—and on a film about lesbian mothers, with a contact address and a poem (by Maureen Brown); a listing of records of interest to lesbians—those by Olivia, those distributed by Olivia, and those by other women-run recording projects; a list of women's publishing houses with books of interest to lesbians; and a national directory of lesbian community organizations. It is this kind of institutional generation that I characterize as one strong element in the term "the apparatus for the production of feminist culture." Berson and Brooks's text lists a series of such institutions: publishing houses, record companies, health centers, credit unions, magazines and newspapers, concert production companies, rape crisis centers, land trusts, women's and lesbians' centers, films and film production companies, restaurants, radio shows, food co-ops, consciousness-raising groups, support groups, bookstores, printing presses.

The uses of the phrase "no hiding place" move from Watkins's lesbian "coming out" love song to Reagon's national call to political accountability for the very community defined by the intertangled knowledge of such music and such coming out. Reagon's essay, based on an earlier speech, explicitly challenges one unspoken basis permitting such a "women's community," that is, racism and cultural (feminist and/ or lesbian) separatism. Both Watkins and Reagon are Black feminists with stakes and histories in antiracist work, cultural nationalisms, feminism, lesbianism, and productions of feminist culture. Reagon's speech was directed to the women who attended the West Coast Women's Music Festival at Yosemite in 1981. Thus, it dates from the same moment in the U.S. women's movements, and on both coasts, that Sandoval's participation in the N. W. S. A. meeting in Storrs, Connecticut, does. Both Reagon's and Sandoval's essays are also rewritings and reconsiderations of these "simultaneous" events published two years later. Both 1983 essays destabilize the unmarked category "women" assumed and exemplified by the "simultaneous" 1983 essays of Hartsock and Jaggar. They especially participate in the transformation of "women" as the object of feminist theoretical description, constructed by the interests and intentions of U.S. feminists in the academy, to "women" as the tenuous "unity" or "coalition"—described by Sandoval and Reagon—a theoretical construction traveling, cruising within and without that U.S. academy, and altering those feminist mappings of the "political." The kinds of exclusions implicit in Jaggar's definition of "theory" and theoretical adequacy and comprehensiveness are redressed by work like Reagon's and Sandoval's. Both write in oracular voices, even religious in their tones and promises (one of Reagon's albums is titled *Good News* out of her civil rights and gospel legacies, while Sandoval's work is touched by the elements of "spirituality" that also characterize so-called women's culture). Sandoval is an academic; Reagon is also found in academic locations—for example, giving a speech at the Modern Language Association in Washington, D.C., in 1984, as the theoretical reception of "Coalition Politics" begins to snowball. Reagon received her Ph.D. in oral history from Howard University and has been director of the Program in Black American Culture at the Smithsonian's National Museum of American History.

Reagon uses the metaphors of "home" and "streets," "food," and "safety" and "survival" to elaborate the powers and dangers that the destabilization of "women" poses to U.S. women's movements.[6] "Most of the time you feel threatened to the core and if you don't, you're not really doing no coalescing" (356). "Coalition work is not work done in your home. Coalition work has to be done in the streets. . . . You don't get a lot of food in a coalition. . . . You can't stay there all the time" (359). The destabilization of "women" also rocks the idea of "women's culture"; any cultural nationalism is a kind of "home" with great and limited possibilities. "The women's movement has perpetuated a myth that there is some common experience that comes just cause you're women. And they're throwing all these festivals and this music and these concerts happen. . . . [The myth] comes from taking a word like "women" and using it as a code. . . . It's not safe! It should be a coalition!" (360).

The focus on the constantly redrawn lines of both similarity and difference that responsibility to the elements of the unmarked category requires also requires that "culture" have both its marked and unmarked resonances, too:

> You can't know everything when you start to coalesce with these people who sorta look like you in just one aspect but really they belong to another group. That is really the nature of women. It does not matter at all that biologically we have being women in common. We have been organized to have our primary cultural signals come from some other factors than that we are women. We are not from our base acculturated to be women people, capable of crossing our first people boundaries—Black, White, Indian, etc." (361)

Reagon's "first people boundaries" are those defined by privilege and oppression—she rejects any "biological sex" as any proper ground for political identity. The tension between necessary and contingent identity here radically reverses Hartsock's understandings in the sexual division of labor of the necessary and contingent and is more congruent with the mobile field of power relations of oppositional consciousness. The tension and slippage between different resonances of the word "culture"—from an almost ethnographic construction of ethnic identity to, on the one hand, songs and the performing arts and, on the other, education and sensibility—

this slippage becomes a resource for the political work that Reagon does and also for the politics of cultural feminism. Reagon's work for the Smithsonian, her degree in oral history, and her long history of political organizing also embody this tension and these sliding redefinitions. So, in respect for Reagon's merging of many aspects of the apparatus for the production of feminist culture, I'll begin my examination of this apparatus with the writing technology "song." Reagon's location at the intersection of U.S. Third World feminisms and the so-called white women's movement is at this very apparatus site, at a pivotal moment. In this moment, from many sides and sites the identity "lesbian" is rewritten and extended—first by "lesbians of color"—and thus the subsequent proliferations of feminist political identities in their multiplicities are opened up.

"Song" and its many layers of political agencies and political communities are dramatized in two extraordinary essays, one by Reagon—"The Power of Communal Song"—and one by Holly Near—"Smile beneath Your Tears: Women's Song and Resistance in Uruguay."[7] Reagon and Near emblematize divergent feminist origins in the civil rights movements and the new left's antiwar activism. Each woman names her political investments in her characterization of "song." The two essays mingle and disentangle, produce multiple commonalities and differences, and situate U.S. women's movements on a broad historical and international stage. Each essay depends upon the phonocentrisms of voice and exploits the ideological power of voice as body, origin, material priority (an ideology which I analyze as it is mobilized oppositionally).

Reagon and Near center their discussion of song in its physicality. Voice and power coincide here. Voice as presence and power is created in this phonocentrism by the manipulation of interiority and exteriority. The place that embodies the story of song in its physicality for Reagon is the church. There, Reagon narrates:

> The church fell apart. People were shouting everywhere. . . . They talked about the singing and the power. I had felt it. . . . It was a very physical, spiritual, and emotional experience. Everything about you was affected. Your whole body felt raised up. . . . (172)

For Reagon the voice shatters the boundaries between the interior and the exterior: "But we weren't screaming; we were just exploding. There is a way that singing in a group transforms the human being you are" (172). For Near the scene of the power of song is not the church but the prison. Song and music there are powerful instruments to be used for both repression and resistance. Near's essay is about torture. In the prison, music and song have a dual nature; music is used to repress the physical in torture, where "there are no names. There is no night or day. Loud music is played to drown out the screams . . . music! . . . twisted into a brutal psychological weapon" (78). But song shatters this terrible absence/presence:

> We are told Chicha sang all the time. Against the orders of the guard, she would sing. She sang to identify herself. She sang to break down the psychological war-

fare as well as to sustain her courage during torture. She sang to make contact with other prisoners. She sang to fight alienation and insanity. (78)

The terrible unboundedness of the pain that does not end, the prison without names, the lack of separation between day and night, the destruction of the distinctions of meaningful sound, the terrible privacy of no communication with other prisoners, and the generality of fear—all are splintered by song. Song is also defined by codes, by secret meanings with hidden powers. Reagon says that Black congregational style singing puts the singer in touch with the computer bank collective memory of Black people.

> You see, Black congregational-style singing has a *memory bank* that goes beyond your life span. It hooks you into the *collected memory of your people.* You feel an experience, wounds and burdens, you may have sworn you would never bear again. There are certain sounds you can make with your voice that, *like a computer*, will bring up these *collective memories.* There are Black people and Black singers who stay away from those triggers with a passion because these *songs and sounds echo underneath the skin.*" (174) [Emphasis mine.]

This physical immersion in memory is renewed and politicized in the interpretation of songs. Reagon's debt to Bessie Jones was to learn "about songs that we'd been singing all our lives and . . . what they meant . . . old songs would turn new in our hands. Most of the time they had political and struggle definitions" (174). For Near, the codes of songs hide from the powers of oppression the noncompliance of the oppressed and simultaneously organize and mobilize resistance. Reagon's codes speak of historical resistance, and Near's speak to current people's movements, especially in the Americas. Reagon's codes are now broken and open, and Near's are functional in their secrecy, indirection, hermeticism, subversion.

Telling a personal/collective movement history of the three singing groups she created and in which she participated is Reagon's strategy for invoking the power of song. While this essay ("The Power of Communal Song") is a written one, it describes a past that largely is still only accessible in personal experience and memory, through oral accounts. Reagon's Smithsonian work collected such oral accounts and the material culture of the political movements of the sixties and seventies. The three singing groups she organizes her political history around are the Freedom Singers, the Harambee Singers, and Sweet Honey in the Rock, and they are distinguished by the movements that ground them, the strategies of cultural work each movement creates and depends upon, and the type of song each singing group deploys.

The Freedom Singers was a group of Black singers, women and men, who mobilized support, especially financial support, for the Student Nonviolent Coordinating Committee (SNCC).[8] "We tried to get people to feel, through song, their support of Civil Rights Movement issues" (173). The group attempted to reach audiences not already included in the struggle, especially middle-class Blacks and whites: "The songs allowed them to join the community of fighters in a way that humanized and personalized their support efforts as the crucial dollars and tele-grams could not" (174). The Freedom Singers accomplished this mobilization through a repertoire of congregational style singing. Reagon talks about two types of Black traditional songs—call-and-response and slow songs. Call-and-response songs are "boundless," limited only by the group as a force of sound; slow songs surface "hidden, untapped feelings," making a mournful wail of soft sound, "very, very heavy" (173). These two types of song are described as especially powerful for the mixed audiences of Black middle-class and white people, creating community in the physicality of sound and bringing to the surface memories of Black commu-nity sometimes ambivalently left behind.

In the later sixties, Reagon sang with a group of women calling themselves the Harambee Singers.[9] They defined themselves as a Black nationalist, Pan-Africanist group, which did not sing to white people and which did not record their music "be-cause of the CIA (maybe today they have the only recordings of this group)" (174). Their audiences were "Black studies departments in colleges, national Black con-ventions, community programs, and the independent schools which were springing up all over the country at that time" (174). The Harambee Singers were cultural workers for a Black nation. Their work was self-consciously "art," and they worked for a vision of song as a highly valued art form among the community they served, one that would be financially supported by that community. Their repertoire was mostly rehearsed singing, unaccompanied. Reagon characterizes this rehearsed and arranged singing as a blend of African-influenced songs with Western forms, includ-ing quartet and gospel choral songs, rhythm and blues, and jazz. This repertoire re-flected a self-consciously created Black nation/culture with its own cultural history and uniquely synthesized music.

In the early seventies, the group Sweet Honey in the Rock was formed, first as a group of eight men and women and shortly after as a group of four women. The first audiences for Sweet Honey were those coming to the D. C. Black Repertory Theater, a conference on the blues at Howard University, the Smithsonian's Festival of American Folklife, and the Toronto and Chicago folk festivals. After about four years, the group made connections—through Holly Near and Amy Horowitz—with the network of "women's culture." "It was a shock to go from Washington, D.C., where we sang for Black people, churches, schools, theaters, folk festivals, and politi-cal rallies to the radical, separatist, white women–dominated, lesbian, cultural net-work in California" (178). Reagon sees the bridging of these communities as the kind of risky coalition work Sweet Honey does, making it "the most courageous performing group in this country today because of our success in maintaining a po-litical and social stance that placed us both within and, at times, beyond our base community" (178)—this coalition work has lead to its national constituency.

Such bridging has placed Sweet Honey in the middle of struggles around racism and homophobia. "It has been both a frightening and interesting process to watch people's reactions when we offer so much of what they need but also offer aid and comfort to something they detest" (178). What characterizes Sweet Honey is not its membership (which has shifted continually over the years) but its "unique repertoire and sound." Sweet Honey sings both traditional and contemporary music; the contemporary is explicitly political and "split between topical issues, people building, and personal individual statements," often written by group members (178). Each of these singing groups offers a distinct vision of political community, and each group's repertoire—its construction of "song"—reflects its strategy for effecting social change.

Song is multiple and strategic in Reagon's use in her essay. The varying interests of each singing group are describable in terms of the shifts among the tones and meanings of the word "culture," distinguishing three registers: culture in the "anthropological" sense (that is, describing a distinct way of life, often located in the past as a "whole"); culture as in the "arts" (that is, enumerating the art forms of "civilization" and the cultivation of subjectivities required for their appreciation); and culture in the utopian sense (that is, the current creation of new community, sometimes envisioned as a return to an origin and/or the cultivation of new art forms and subjectivities). Reagon's description of her own singing group history draws upon the power of these registers of culture, as indeed do the political movements her history is embedded within. The Freedom Singers primarily use an "anthropological culture," in which song draws upon that "memory bank" of the past to create community at the same time that it moves beyond such edges to connect cultures in the plural. The Harambee Singers primarily use an "art culture" to value a notion of nationhood defined by its own art forms, in which art practice has a particular task. Sweet Honey in the Rock uses both an "anthropological culture" in its association with folk traditions and an "art culture" subordinated to social purpose. All three groups participate in a "utopian culture" as the vision of multicultural change.

Near's use of song is less specific and varied than Reagon's, less contextually and strategically determined. Song is a form that in power and coding ties many cultures together. One way to read Near's essay ("Smile beneath Your Tears: Women's Song and Resistance in Uruguay") is as a meditation on "what is a song?" and "what can't be said in a song?" Of course, the occasion for this meditation is work to end torture. The problem the essay is structured around is how to write a song about torture. But song itself is something larger than this occasion and broader than the very specific cultures as sites of repression that Near tells about.

As Near talks about different instances of song, at first it appears that the form itself somehow can't accommodate this terrible existence of torture, that the very power of song, its generation of images and its splintering of boundaries in its forceful interiority, mean that to speak of torture *in* a song is to abuse the powers song possesses. However, thinking through the existence of torture is also thinking through the existence of songs here. The coded nature of song is emphasized—for example, the *cantos nuevos* in Uruguay that must pass the censor and still inspire people to struggle against political imprisonment. This becomes the answer to Near's dilemma, which she describes:

> I have tried to write a song about torture . . . for ten years I have tried. I can speak of it and then follow the story with a song, but I cannot put the words to song. I cannot put *those* words to song. It is also that I do not want to give you the nightmares I have. I do not want to put horrendous images into tender minds. And yet, if it is being inflicted on people, we must know about it so that we have the freedom to stop it. And so I write a song that calls for your courage. . . . "(79)

In the song she ends up writing, Near tries both to represent the terrors of torture and the possibilities of resistance, constructing a kind of coded message herself, playing on both absences and presences, things said and things not said, following the example of the other codes she mentions.[10]

Take my hand
Or I may have to leave the room
Please end your story soon
It's not like me to run away
But I don't think that I can stay
To hear your story

Knowing your name
Ties my heart around each tortured cry
And you didn't die
Let me keep looking deep in your eyes
So I have no chance to break the ties
Though the cage is locked the spirit flies
The prison song escapes—the truth defies

Chorus:
Oh come smile with us
It helps to make the days seem less
like years
Oh come smile with us
Smile beneath your tears

Don't turn away
There are things in life my heart must know
Though feelings tell me go hurry go
Words that startle my waking dreams
But if you have lived it then it seems that I
must hear it
Feeling your hand resting on my shoulder
to ease the pain
To ease my shame

Have we forgotten or is it just too hard
to feel
Protecting tenderness with steel
And with the rarest kind of smile
You help me heal

At first it seems that Near needs to bend the forms and contents of what we think of as songs in order to write about torture, and yet the song she does write doesn't change what counts as a song, while it does powerfully use song to move people to action. By using the subversive codes of strategic presence and absence, meanings written between words, Near uses already politicized song forms in a type of cultural intervention.

As I said before, this proliferation of mixed identities emerges at the site for the production of feminist culture and in rewritten meanings of "the lesbian." Briefly, let me look at another but related writing technology "the poem" and its seventies conflations with "the lesbian" in the apparatus for the production of feminist culture and in the person of Emily Dickinson. The notion of "identification," which activates the extension of identities but is also politically limited by its self-referentiality is problematized in feminist investments in Emily Dickinson. In the academy, a variety of agents and interests contest for Emily Dickinson and for what counts as a poem. Including and overlapping those agents and interests within and without the academy are reviewers and critics, readers and consumers, students and teachers, anthologists, feminists, poets, and activists. In the 1970's and '80's academy what is at stake are contests for the literary canon and assumptions of literary value that the construction "Emily Dickinson" both challenges and embodies.

The popular celebration of Emily Dickinson in the centenary year of her birth, 1930, together with academic consolidations of "the poem" as the privileged emblem of literature itself, fixed Dickinson as *the* woman poet of "the literary tradition." As an exemplary figure of the feminist seventies she was also fixed in the field of female identification valorized in "women's tradition." Some feminists saw Dickinson as the great transgressor; here is Louise Bernikow in the 1974 introduction to *The World Split Open: Four Centuries of Women Poets in England and America, 1552–1950*:

> In an earlier time Dickinson would have been burned as a witch, for she spoke in tongues and she spoke against authority. She is not only the poet of consciousness, the register of that mysterious interaction between the inner self and the world of nature, but the poet who has set herself against religious orthodoxy, the social order, and the poetic standards of her time. She assumes control, in the poems, of her own vocabulary, rhymes, meter, line length. She usurps control of the world, too, in those poems, making herself its ruler, its arbiter, at times its god.[11]

Other feminists find Dickinson a troubling pillar of the white male canon, as June Jordan suggests in her 1980 preface to her book of poems *Passion,* an essay titled "For the Sake of a People's Poetry: Walt Whitman and the Rest of Us."

My brothers and sisters of this New World, we remember that, as Whitman said,

I do not trouble my spirit to vindicate itself or be
    understood,
I see that the elementary laws never apologize.

                    "Song of Myself"

We do not apologize because we are not Emily Dickinson, Ezra Pound, T. S. Eliot, Wallace Stevens, Robert Lowell, or Elizabeth Bishop. If we are nothing to them, to those who love them, they are nothing to us![12]

Jordan's preference for Walt Whitman as exemplar over Emily Dickinson in turn troubles feminist poet Jan Clausen, who in 1982 struggles with commitments to and subversions of the literary canon, and refuses some processing devices of political correctness, while she herself mobilizes others:

What is the meaning of my secret relief at learning that a poet I like and respect has dared to be influenced by Tennyson? What about my astonishment at June Jordan's celebration of Whitman's influence on American literature (a *Black feminist* poet recommending a *white male nineteenth-century* one?)—followed by pleasure at the thought that I'd been given "permission" to reread *Leaves of Grass*? What does it mean to label *any* writer incorrect or off limits (as June Jordan does Emily Dickinson in that same essay)?[13]

Different as these comments on Emily Dickinson are, they all enhance her ideological centrality—a mix of both dominant literary and oppositional feminist centrality—and they all share a belief in poetry as an instrument of cultural intervention. To quote Jan Clausen again from this 1982 essay "A Movement of Poets: Thoughts on Poetry and Feminism":

any serious investigation of the development of contemporary feminism must take into account the catalytic role of poets and poetry; that there is some sense in which it can be said that poets have made possible the movement.

   It might even be claimed, at the risk of some exaggeration, that poets *are* the movement. Certainly poets are some of feminism's most influential activists, theorists, and spokeswomen; at the same time, poetry has become a favorite means of self-expression, consciousness-raising, and communication among large numbers of women not publicly known as poets. (5)

Clausen here allows "poem" to stand metonymically, as a part to the whole, for political action and "poet" to stand for the political identity "feminist." This is one strategic practice that constructs the feminist object "the poem."

   One of the poet-theorists who "*are* the movement" to whom Clausen is obviously referring is Adrienne Rich, and Rich's relationship with Dickinson is a powerful and exemplary one. As a sixteen-year-old undergraduate Rich imitated Dickinson's syntax and style in her notebooks, commencing what Betsy Erkkila has called "Rich's private apprenticeship to Dickinson."[14] Rich read Dickinson from Johnson's variorum in the late fifties and made explicit connections with her in

Snapshots of a Daughter-In-Law (1963), *Necessities of Life* (1966), and *A Wild Patience Has Taken Me This Far* (1981).[15] A revisioning of Dickinson from poet victimized by domestic womanhood to single-minded truthsayer choosing the terms of her life—the second lovingly elaborated upon in Rich's 1975 "Vesuvius at Home: The Power of Emily Dickinson"—is seen first in glimpses from the poems "Snapshots of a Daughter-in-Law" (1958–1960) and "I am in Danger—Sir—" (1964). Rich's personal identifications with Dickinson are dramatic ones, the artist struggling with wifehood and the poet practicing "necessary economies."[16] The puzzling power of identification is suggested as Rich asks,

> "Half-cracked" to Higginson, living,
> afterward famous in garbled versions,
> your hoard of dazzling scraps a battlefield,
> now your old snood
>
> mothballed at Harvard
> and you in your variorum monument
> equivocal to the end—
> who are you?

Rich's identification with Dickinson is most complete in the essay I mentioned, "Vesuvius at Home," from her book *On Lies, Secrets, and Silence* (1979), appearing immediately after the book of poems *The Dream of a Common Language* (1978).[17] In a preface to the essay, Rich calls for "a lesbian-feminist reading of [Dickinson's] poetry and her life," following a tradition of lesbian identifications of Dickinson's mysterious lover begun in 1951 by Rebecca Patterson and continued by Lillian Faderman in 1977 and 1981 and influenced by the 1975 work of Carroll Smith-Rosenberg (debates raised within this tradition productively continue today).[18] But Rich finally wishes to respect Dickinson in her "otherness" from herself, and repudiates identification in part III of her poem "The Spirit of Place" (1980): "this is my third and last address to you," able to express the limits of identification only with silence.[19]

Whether Rich intends it oppositionally or not, the lesbian narrative and her own "Vesuvius at Home," evocative and exciting as it is, do not disrupt the conventional narrative of Dickinson's life, elaborated in the twenties and thirties by Martha Dickinson Bianchi. Rich's attempts to limit identification with Dickinson may very well show how well she understands the self-consuming ideological power of this narrative, but her reaction also mirrors the narrative in her own renunciatory response and thus is only partially successful in its attempts to limit identification. One can match the beginnings of this lesbian story, Patterson's *The Riddle of Emily Dickinson* (1951), predating both the variorum and current U.S. feminism, with William Shurr's rather antifeminist *The Marriage of Emily Dickinson* (1983). Based on the 1981 facsimile edition, Shurr reads the fascicles as a lyric sequence telling a story of Dickinson's pregnancy by her mysterious male lover and abortion or miscarriage.[20] Both stories, seemingly very different, still retell the narrative of shameful/powerful love and renunciation. The structure of this narrative of Dickinson's life remains productive. From the seventies through the early eighties feminists such as Faderman, Rich, Smith-Rosenberg, Sandra Gilbert, and Susan Gubar (*The Norton Anthology of Literature by Women*, 1985) and Suzanne Juhasz (*Feminist Critics Read Emily Dickinson*, 1983) still contend for the sex of Dickinson's lover.[21] During this period in which Dickinson's person conflates the poet and the lesbian in feminist popular and academic discourse, the stakes are the exemplary nature of Dickinson's life and the valorization of female identification in "the woman's tradition." The multiple meanings made valuable by identification allow for the feminist contest for Dickinson, the contest for "poetry" as political action and for "poet" as political identity. "Lesbianism" as a powerful touchstone acts to permit identification for some and limit it for others. Perhaps surprisingly, this identification is not divided along lines of who does or does not self-identify as a lesbian. Instead it is constrained by the simultaneous existence in feminism of many "lesbianisms" to which all feminists have some access. The contests for Dickinson's sexuality, which build upon rather than disrupt the sexualized narrative of Dickinson's life, are part of the publication history that produces both poetry and author.

But the feminist object "the poem" also embodies this shift from the privileged feminist identity "lesbian" to mixed and proliferated identities. This object "the poem" destabilizes across the distinctions between the "oral" and the "written," where "poem," "story," and "song" promiscuously intermingle, but also pauses momentarily to consolidate racial, ethnic, and sexual "literacies." A 1980 literature textbook details this momentary consolidation: *The Third Woman: Minority Women Writers of the United States* by Dexter Fisher produces a feminist canon of racial/ethnic literature by creating for each political identity it draws upon *a unique story of literacy*.[22] The shifting boundaries of the oral and the written are mobilized by Fisher as a literary political resource, broadly synthetic, intellectually captivating, emotionally compelling. For each of the four kinds of "third woman"—American Indian, Black, Chicana, and Asian American—she also synthetically creates a canon of expressive genres and a specific history of oppression. In the phrase "a unique story of literacy," by literacy I mean a culturally specific and technically sophisticated use of language for expressive purposes. In other words, the term literacy I'm deploying here emphasizes the specific technologies of language developed by a particular culture (or subculture).[23] Reading and writing are two powerful technologies of language, but they are not the only ones, as Dexter Fisher's introductions demonstrate. This use of the word literacy is a political one. It means to intervene into the history of the term in such a way as to subvert the class associations the term has always carried and to take advantage of the wide range of stories told about the elusive and politically charged boundaries between the oral and the written.[24] In the phrase "a unique story of literacy," by story I mean to suggest the ideological narratives that construct particular political positions for those the stories are about, those who tell them, and those who hear them. This use of the term story comes from my description of feminism and writing technologies, and I'll give further examples of this use toward the end of the chapter. These stories are profoundly "identifying" in the sense that they produce identities that are strategic and ephemeral while simultaneously appearing natural and stable. Yet this is *not* the broadly constructed feminist object "story" that with "poem" and "song" I count as writing technologies in the apparatus for the production of feminist culture.[25]

To set the scene for the construction of a canon of identities in Fisher's book, first I want to examine four texts that historicize stories of canonization and pedagogy in the U.S. academy from the sixties to the eighties. I lay out these artifactual books in an array, putting them together first as pairs and then reordering and re-contrasting them, next drawing some large distinctions, and finally particularly inspecting Fisher's textbook in much more detail. The first pedagogical artifact is a book long out of print, copyright 1970, first published by Random House (Pantheon) in 1972 and then in paper by Vintage in 1973. I locate this book as a guidepost to feminist worries about academic professionalism and political accountability, already talked about at length and in various permutations in Gallop's *Around 1981*. Because Gallop's historical dates reflect retrospective anthology collection of critical writings, I notice that her dating process understandably tends to emphasize publication time, when what I emphasize here are earlier conversations, in which publications may figure. Titled *The Politics of Literature: Dissenting Essays on the Teaching of English*, from its dedication—"For George Jackson"—to the prescriptive quotation from Mao that concludes the introduction, this artifact bears many marks of its origins in the sixties (which some say lasted—in some places more than others—until about 1974). The introduction, written by editors Louis Kampf and Paul Lauter, describes powerfully and seriously the academic arena of struggle, where the political events of 1968 are not in Paris or Chicago, but in New York at the convention of the Modern Language Association (MLA). I pair this artifact with its 1983 sister, published by The Feminist Press and also edited by Paul Lauter, *Reconstructing American Literature, Courses, Syllabi, Issues*. The concerns with canonicity and pedagogy (which are both implicit and explicit in *Politics*) and the radicalization which is made equivalent to flowering feminist self-consciousness (suggested by the notes on contributors at the end of *Politics*)—both these concerns and this radicalization become obvious and pivotal in *Reconstructing*. The focus on working-class literature, which is strategic for the construction of a socialism of literature in *Politics*, in *Reconstructing* is multilayered with race, gender, region, and ethnicity, inside a history of colonialism and immigration—and this multilayered focus allows at least a feminism of literature. *Reconstructing* is an offshoot of the Yale Institute on Reconstructing American Literature held in June 1982. Lauter refers in his *Feminist Studies* article to the Feminist Press project on reconstructing American literature; this project includes a multivolumed anthology of American literature.[26]

So this first pair of artifacts concentrates attention on professionalism and accountability; the second pair highlights strategies, both academic and political. Both volumes in this second pair have strong ties to the MLA, the first through its editor, the second by publication and research funding. First is the book I've just introduced and will continue to explore later, *The Third Woman*, edited by Dexter Fisher (prominently authorized on the title page as "Director of English Programs, Modern Language Association") and copyright 1980 by Houghton Mifflin in Boston. This book is forthrightly pedagogical: it is intended as a textbook (xxvii) and as a major-press anthology, mainstreaming work previously published by small presses and regional journals (xxix). Dexter Fisher is noted in Lauter's *Reconstructing American Literature* for two previous anthologies, *Minority Language and Literature: Retrospective and Perspective* (1977) and as co-editor (with Robert B. Stepto) of *Afro-American Literature: The Reconstruction of Instruction* (1979), both also published by the Modern Language Association. The second book is *Teaching Women's Literature from a Regional Perspective*, edited by Leonore Hoffmann and Deborah Rosenfelt, which I'll refer to again in this chapter. Published by the MLA in 1982, *Regional* describes and shares materials from the 1976–1979 MLA project from which the book's title is drawn. Supported by the Fund for the Improvement of Postsecondary Education and directed by Leonore Hoffmann, the project recruited teachers and students in a nationwide "recovery" of women's literature. Forty-two faculty participants in thirty-six colleges over the three-year period offered semester and year-long courses in which students quickly acquired advanced research skills—including archival searches, transcriptions of unpublished materials, oral histories—which permitted them to design and carry through complex projects utilizing noncanonical materials out of which they made public presentations to their communities. The nationally visible project and the regionally visible courses (as Hoffmann names them, 11) inextricably tied research and pedagogy together in a self-consciously feminist methodology. Project and courses, unusually demanding in time and commitment, have not always continued beyond the time of the funded project. This book has a practical and utopian vision of feminist teaching and feminist intervention into literary production, centering the academy as a liberatory resource.

Dexter Fisher's *The Third Woman* participates in the processes reconstructing political and cultural identities that are seen in the comparison of *The Politics of Literature* and *Reconstructing American Literature*. What emerges from these processes is the conceptual and political fracturing of the very canon (and in a very short time) that Fisher's work puts together (its pedagogical variants have longer lives). These national identities she focuses on—American Indian, Black (American), Chicana (American), and Asian American—in their very description generate more and more marked categories, subverting the very horizon of a canon. At the same time, the seemingly unmarked category "white" is also pulled apart. (*Teaching Women's Literature from a Regional Perspective* is also very much involved in the deconstruction of the category "white" in the creation of marginal literatures.) Fisher is able to build upon white feminists' valorization of female identification to reframe earlier consolidations of "women's tradition"—as seen in feminist work emblematizing Emily Dickinson. "Poet" as political identity and "poetry" as political action are discreetly mobilized as well. These strategies work to assimilate each racial/ethnic location to these already valorized points of political meaning in the white women's movement (with sometimes racist consequences, as Mohanty's work articulates). As the apparatus for the production of feminist culture operated in the mid-seventies to produce many lesbianisms to which all feminists—lesbian and not—had some access (think of Rich's later lesbian continuum consolidating these conversations), so you can see Fisher's textbook similarly producing forms of empathetic identification through which this canon of races becomes multiply accessible as well. (This pedagogical tactic is still very powerful in women's studies, although always highly problematic. Notice, for example, how in Fisher's book it continues to place white women at the center of its audience. Subsequent anthologies, such as Lauter's, have tried to subvert this effect.[27]) In chapter 2 I've talked about the consolidation and deconstruction of the political object "women"; an examination of race and ethnicity is one of the powerful forces in feminism accomplishing this deconstruction. But to understand in detail how this happens one needs to look closely at how Dexter Fisher constructs racial and ethnic identities.

Fisher likens the "third woman" to the Third World, describing both as "emerging" in the sense that they are "discovered" and visible to Euro-America now (1980), though in fact they have existed prior to such "discovery."[28] The pun Fisher exploits here leads her to construct this single metaphoric "third woman," who is magically single and multiple, visible and invisible, created and eternal, infinitely revealing herself to "us," and in doing so, giving "us" new life, tradition, language and imagination, while remaining always "American." The gifts of this third woman thus are appropriated from the margins, an imaginary place of continual renewal, while "she" herself is left there, other, in commentary neither author nor reader, while at the same time, in the volume, contained within her canons of identity, her authorship and readership are celebrated. This magical third woman contradicts the pedagogical politics Dexter Fisher also displays. Far from intending such an appropriation of this third woman, Fisher wishes to give legitimation and value to the literary forms of an extremely various range of particular women writers. Legitimation here is practical and institutional: inclusion in syllabi and textbooks of colleges and universities in the United States, facilitated by this textbook's location—published by the Modern Language Association, the professional society of academic literary studies in the United States. What appear as the "gifts" of the third woman are in fact the values not yet bestowed on her by a dominant culture, values Fisher intends to wrest for her from the academy. As a textbook *The Third Woman* is both book and magical offering. It exists through the strategy of a brokering translator— white woman staff member of this professional association, hired to encourage the study and teaching of minority literature. Presented for adoption by teachers in need of arguments for their administrations (or themselves) for the inclusion of these materials in their classes, it is also presented to students who are structurally imagined by the book *not* to belong to the races and ethnicities offered. The "us"

the book is structured for is not "the third woman" herself. Explained, contextualized, offered as metaphor, the book is structured for those ignorant of these facts,
fictions, poems, not for minority women themselves wanting more and different
works by others sharing their heritages, although they might very well encounter
and use the book for these purposes. Such minority women as might encounter and
read the book are invisibly included within the generic student. These generic students are "Americans" sharing in "our" heritage. These consequences of the construction of the text are institutional at the same time that Dexter Fisher herself
becomes accountable for them. They are pedagogical tactics for inclusion and legitimation. They target a large textbook market, not the specialized markets of regional/
ethnic literatures from which the particular pieces are taken.

The sequence of minority Americans documented by the textbook is historically successive. First are the American Indians, or Native Americans ("America's
first natives," as Fisher footnotes the term, 5); then Blacks, kidnapped as slaves; then
Chicanas, an identity unique to the United States; then Asian Americans, whose literary history in the United States is represented as new in 1980 and in formation.
Each section on a different group has a teleological structure. It begins with an
introduction, where historical and cultural circumstances are specified. In "Contexts," this history and culture "nurturing" literature (xxx) are exemplified by legends, folklore, and autobiographical histories and described in interviews and essays. What follows are "Traditions, Narratives, and Fiction," which "imaginatively
amplify" (xxx) these contexts; myths and folktales intervene into the genres of short
story and novel (published and unpublished ones are excerpted in this section); and
forms which are neither one nor the other (an autobiographical narrative framing
a series of creatively retold "folktales," for example) powerfully confuse what
counts as fiction. However, the telos of this plethora of literary forms is the poem,
which "illustrates . . . linguistic versatility" (xxx). Poetry is a category that is not de-
stabilized by cultural specificity, and it appears universal here. This privileging of
poetry I will return to shortly. The unique literacy of each group of minority writers
is constructed by Fisher in a story told about what counts as the oral and the written.
The boundaries, intersections, interconnections, and the consequences of relations
between the oral and the written shift in each story.

American Indian women's writing is about "story" itself—conventionally displayed as the essence of the oral tradition. "Storytelling" names the performative
"preliterate" practice of literary art. In the following "story" (my ideological term)
about a unique American Indian "literacy" (my extended term), Fisher constructs
an object "story" *intersecting* the oral and the written:

> Storytelling . . . is integral to the oral tradition because it is a way of storing
> knowledge, and as long as a tribe exists as a community, the word as spoken is
> sufficient. But what happens to storytelling and the oral tradition when the com-
> munity begins to break down under the pressure of external conflicts, the advent
> of reservation life, and the introduction of English-based education? In short,
> what happens when a way of life that has existed for centuries suddenly undergoes

cataclysmic and brutal changes, such as occurred for many American Indians during the nineteenth century? Writing became a means to perpetuate tradition in
the face of cultural disintegration, and it also created new audiences and gave Native Americans a chance to tell their side of the story. By the end of the nineteenth
century, a written language was beginning to emerge out of the oral tradition that
would reach fruition in the 1960s and 1970s in the works of contemporary American Indians. The word continued to be equated with ways of knowing and of passing knowledge on. (6–7)

Here "story" and "the word" provide a continuity, still essentially oral, into writing.
Writing here appears as a new "emerging" kind of orality, one which both conserves
cultural tradition and permits political intervention. This configuration of writing
upsets the oral/written division as radically disjunctive, creating qualitatively different forms of consciousness and different types of cultures. In such a typological understanding, orality is conservative and homeostatic; oral knowledge is not
analytical, but typical, while writing is revolutionary, allowing for objectivity and
critical thought.[29] But Fisher manages to exploit these typological theories too:

> To study American Indian literature is to study the power of language to shape
> one's perception of human experience. The word has power because it is the vehi-
> cle of the imagination and the means of clarifying relationships between individu-
> als and their landscapes, communities, visions. (5)

The power of the word to determine reality, or the perception of reality, is simultaneously poignantly ironic and imaginatively compelling in Fisher's history. In
Fisher's history of American Indian women writers, a history structured by a particular relationship between the oral and the written, the word as spoken is only
sufficient in a homeostatic community. But in writing, the orality preserved by story
itself is, at the least, the means of survival and, at best, creative of a new politics.
Fisher creates another outline for the romanticizing shadows the Sapir-Whorf hy-
pothesis casts, exploiting its imaginative power, its magic defamiliarizing Euro-
American experience, but manages to imply as well that words by American Indian
women writers will yet determine a new reality.

The oral tradition essentialized but ideologically interrogated as "story" gives
way to a discussion of "literacy" (meaning the ability to read and write) and "the
literary tradition" in Fisher's historical perspective on Black American women writers. "Freedom" and "literacy" are synonymous in this way of talking about the
boundaries between the oral and the written:

> Achieving literacy before and during slavery was an extreme political act for a
> black person because slaves were prohibited from learning to read and write. The
> "quest for freedom" was synonymous with the "quest for literacy," and each act
> of writing became a political and historical event. (139)

The importance of writing here, writing which *is itself* freedom, contrasts sharply
with the power of the oral word continued through writing in the story of American
Indian women writers. The denial of writing finds its compensation in an elaborate

system of "verbal traditions that became, during slavery, creative outlets for individual expression" (139). Both entertainment and safety valves and arising from denied education and literacy, Fisher offers as examples of these verbal traditions "oral storytelling, sermons, proverbs, boasts, elaborate courtship rituals, toasts, work songs, and spirituals" (139). Fisher borrows from and elaborates upon the ideologies of literacy which give it the power of presence and define its opposite companions—nonliteracy, pre-literacy, aliteracy, illiteracy—as its absence. Stressing the cathartic value of art emphasizes the terrible oppression of the denial of writing. Emphasizing the persistence of these verbal traditions in modern black writing names the unique contribution and value of Black literature. The slave is "the consummate verbal artist" (139), and modern Black literature is characterized as "verbal complexity and the imaginative transformation of oral forms into literary art" (140).

Fisher describes the project of Black women writers to discover and create a literary tradition. In each of her literary histories, Fisher begins to name a canon of racial/ethnic writers, but the list she offers here in speaking of Black women writers is the most elaborated. For Fisher, such a canon powerfully locates "literary models" (140). Such "models" and "tradition" name feminist alternatives to "literary black nationalism" as espoused by Black men, as struggled for in the Harlem Renaissance, and as inherited in the sixties. Fisher suggests that Black women writers, disenfranchised from male literary circles, also consciously dissented from such nationalism, creating instead "a distinctively black female literary tradition" (142). This use of the idea of "tradition" echoes in its overlapping meanings the redefinitions and shifts in the notion of "culture." The verbal art informing written practice among Black writers as recounted by Fisher survives the transformation to writing. "Culture" and "tradition," as in folk culture and tradition, contain "survivals" of the archaic past: the formulas and rituals that remain though their original meanings, myths, functions are passed away. At the same time, "culture" also means the art forms of "civilization" (correcting its ideological opposite, an artless condition of "savagery"—here the debased condition of slavery) "cultivating" the self: permitting access to the structures of bourgeois personhood and subjectivity.[30] A Black female literary tradition is constructed from the objects of this culture: short story, autobiography, novel, poem are the genres offered by Fisher. There is little blurring of genres such as we saw in the writings of American Indian women. The one generically ambiguous literary piece is excerpted from Zora Neale Hurston's book of folklore, *Mules and Men*.

Names for contested "selves" center the story of the oral and the written in Fisher's account of Chicana writers:

> At the core of the Chicano literary imagination is a profound sense of heritage. Born of the forced union between the Indian mother and the European father, Chicanos are descendants of the Aztecs and offspring of the Spanish conquistadors, inheritors of the dichotomy between conditions of power and powerlessness. Inhabiting the landscape between two cultures, they are Mexican Americans, generally able to converse easily in Spanish and English, yet unable to identify totally

with either Mexico or the United States. They seek through their literature to articulate the paradox of their past, to understand what Lorna Dee Cervantes has expressed as "a name / that fights me." (307)

The range of possible names from which Fisher suggests these women writers chose "Chicana"—"Mexican American," "Hispanic," "Latina," "Mexican," "La Raza," and "Mestiza"—reflect dimensions of personal identification and of community and national loyalties. The strong pull of these identifications, communities, and loyalties is what Fisher is particularizing. The story of La Malinche (alluded to as "the forced union between the Indian mother and the European father") grounds the term "Mestiza"—mixed (mentioned by Fisher in a footnote, not in the body of the text). "Mexican American" is the term belonging to Fisher's strategically parallel list of ethnicities: American Indian, Afro-American, Asian American. Each embodies and renames its own powerful irony: the American Indian, the first natives; Afro-American, generations from Africa, culturally fractured by slavery; Asian American, an identity only made singular in America. Among these, simultaneously the Mexican American is bicultural, bilingual, but also ironically without language and culture, but yet again also the maker of a new Chicano culture creatively mixing languages. "American" denotes, on the one hand, the nationalist pluralism of the melting pot and on the other, the naming of hemispheric imperialism. Fisher juggles these many superimposed meanings, aiming them at different readerships of her textbook.

The creative mix of languages reflecting the power-charged histories of imperialism is made central to a unique Chicana literacy by Fisher.

> In spite of this marginal position between two cultures—or perhaps because of it—Chicanos have forged a distinct culture of their own and created a unique literature that fuses characteristics from their Indian, Spanish, and Anglo-American heritage. Their literature abounds with linguistic innovations; new sounds and rhythms are created by the juxtaposition of English with Spanish and even with Nahuatl. Myth informs symbolism, and folklore and legends influence genre and theme. (308)

The sounds and rhythms of language and the forms of myth, folklore, and legends constrain and enable the writings of Chicanas—the oral constrains and enables the written, which together create something new, neither only oral or written, but instead a linguistic innovation.

Fisher consolidates her canon of racial literacies by finishing up with the Asian American woman writer. Published in 1980, this book's sense of canonical closure with these particular identities belies the eventual effect such pedagogies will have in feminist conversations. The use of the term "minority" figures here. The unmarked categories of white, middle-class American culture start to dissolve in the solvent of feminist identity politics. The image of the American Midwesterner seemingly without ethnicity or culture is evicted by a proliferation of marked identities. Following this kind of canonical construction in the late seventies, exemplified by Fisher's book, feminist anthologies began to focus on and construct in historical detail the multiplicities within seemingly single identities and began to include feminist and other political material often about the politics of identity itself. Jewish lesbians and Italian American feminists are examples of two mixed identity literatures suddenly opening up in the early and mid-eighties.[31] Fisher's textbook pointedly disavows feminist or political principles of selection in favor of pedagogical and aesthetic criteria, but these later anthologies, constructed for a feminist rather than a school market, strategically target a feminist readership and stress their feminist politics.

At first, Fisher's history of Asian American women writers seems to tell no obvious story about relations between the oral and the written. Instead, Fisher focuses on rehistoricizations of identity. For example, divergent historical constructions of heterosexuality actually as a political achievement for Chinese and Japanese immigrants to the United States structures the discussion of women's oppression; so too does the differential treatment of Chinese and Japanese during the "relocations" of World War II. Few Chinese women came to the United States between 1882 and 1943 because of the Chinese Exclusion Act. Left in China, women were forced to be separated from their husbands. Japanese women, in contrast, as picture brides were brought to the United States, where they faced poverty and discrimination. Culturally and historically specific conditions separate the experiences of Chinese and Japanese women here. Similarly, during World War II, Chinese and Japanese Americans were pitted against each other by a racist policy of relocation which assumed that all Japanese were enemies of the United States. Meanwhile, Chinese Americans were even recruited to spy on Japanese Americans.

The differences by nationality here only begin to suggest how tenuous a unified "Asian" identity, a commonality of political purposes, could be for Asian American women writers.

> "Asian American" is a term that embraces a plurality of cultures—Chinese, Japanese, Filipino, Hawaiian, Korean, Malaysian, and so on—and as diverse as these backgrounds are, so are the voices in Asian American literature. (437)

How problematic that unity is and how much it is in creation now is expressed here. And here a tenuous, small story about the oral and the written does emerge: oral voices in their plurality make up what is becoming written literature. Pluralities and unities of identity and their coming into being through Asian American cultural productions, as suggested here in this tiny oral/written story, are more explicitly spoken about in the 1981 feminist film *Mitsuye and Nellie*.[32]

The subjects of the film are Mitsuye Yamada and Nellie Wong, Japanese and Chinese feminist poets. Their poems in voice-over through this documentary-style film recount the histories of the Yamada and Wong families: in discussion among family members, in conventional documentary narration, in film clips and photo montage, and in visits to sites of family events. The depiction of feminist activities and cultural events among Asian American women—especially artists, poets, playwrights—contextualizes the present historical positioning of these two families. It is in this depiction that the problematic but powerful construction of the unity of Asian American women is displayed. It is suggested that these women would not have a ground for unity *as women* (because outweighed by the complexities of historical nationalisms) except in the context of feminism in the United States; at the same time it is possible to see that any common grounds for political and cultural action are in the act of being created. "The poem" as privileged production (though not at all the only kind of cultural product in evidence and appreciated in the film) is also the subject of the film—as moving voice-over during the viewing of a relocation camp, of family photos, of visits to particular locations in the narrative of family history and as the locus of meaning for the work of Mitsuye and Nellie.

Notice again the feminist strategies that structure how and why the poem is the privileged object in this film and in the structure of Dexter Fisher's anthology. As I've indicated in my analysis, one way to look at the canon of ethnic literacies Dexter Fisher has assembled is to approach each as a story about the relations between the oral and the written. Fisher contends that poetry displays the "linguistic versatility" of each minority group. Although the generic boundaries of narrative prose writings are slippery and shifting in Fisher's canon, the generic boundary of poetry appears unproblematic, stable, even natural. The poem (like the "story" which essentially defines, but also ideologically subverts the oral tradition in Fisher's discussion of American Indian women writers) marks continuity across cultures as well as across the oral/written distinction. As "song" the poem moves in the direction of the oral. In discussions of oral poetry, the "song" and the "poem" are usually interchangeable.[33] In the context of Fisher's work, the poem is the object that connects the oral and the written in a stable and seemingly natural relation. Although unique linguistic skills are evidenced in the different poems of the different minority groups (for example, the use of both Spanish and English in the poetry of Chicanas), the object "the poem" is itself unproblematized. But although the poem operates in Fisher's textbook as a natural connection between the oral and the written, the poems presented there are rather narrowly conceived. That is, in a Euro-American modernist art tradition, they are typographically defined and belong to a particular art world.

Dramatic examples of the appropriation by high modernism of "oral poetry" come in the sixties; one fascinating example is the "assemblage" *Technicians of the Sacred: A Range of Poetries from Africa, America, Asia, Europe and Oceania*, edited with commentaries by Jerome Rothenberg.[34] In Rothenberg's preface (1967), he parallels (visually on the page) what he calls "Primitive and Modern: Intersections and Analogies." On the left (primitive) side he discursively describes characteristics of oral poetry, for example:

(1) the poem carried by the voice: a
"pre"-literate situation of poetry
composed to be spoken, chanted, or,

more accurately, sung; compare this
to the "post-literate" situation, in
McLuhan's good phrase, or where-we-are-today . . . (xxix)

while to the right (modern) side he briefly and schematically lists associations with
modern poetry (paralleling the above example):

> written poem as score
> public readings
> performance poetry
>
> poets' theaters
> jazz poetry
> rock poetry etc.

The mid-sixties of Rothenberg's first edition of *Technicians of the Sacred* is indebted
to the early sixties of Marshall McLuhan's *Gutenberg Galaxy: The Making of Typographic Man*.[35] Investments in orality are culturally oppositional in both Rothenberg and McLuhan. Rothenberg follows his lists of primitive/modern parallels with
the statement:

> In all this the ties feel very close—not that "we" and "they" are identical, but that
> the systems of thought and the poetry they've achieved are, like what we're after,
> distinct from something in the official "west," and we can now see and value them
> because of it. (xxx)

while a similar statement of McLuhan's reads:

> we also live in an electric or post-literate time when the jazz musician uses all the
> techniques of oral poetry. Empathetic identification with all the oral modes is not
> difficult in our century.
>   In the electronic age which succeeds the typographic and mechanical era of the
> past five hundred years, we encounter new shapes and structures of human inter-
> dependence and of expression which are "oral" in form even when the components
> of the situation may be non-verbal. (2)

These oppositional investments in orality and oral poetry are political attempts to
create something new by reinventing its origins, by simultaneously locating it in the
coming-into-being future and the past. Walter Ong's 1982 summary of several decades of his work, *Orality and Literacy: The Technologizing of the Word*, sandwiches
"literacy" between "primary orality" and "secondary orality." Ong nostalgically eu-
logizes the loss of the "oral" (that is, primary orality associated with traditional cultures), while McLuhan celebrates the epiphany of new oralities (that is, secondary
orality associated with "electronic" or "post-literate" culture; these new oralities
are brought into being by the domination of sight, first in print technology—literacy—and now in visual/aural electronic media—secondary orality).

   Such are the avant garde aesthetics and political investments from one academic location in the United States and Canada during the sixties in "the poem."

From another academic location in the mid-seventies, British anthropologist Ruth Finnegan (a critic of Ong) emphasizes a wide range of differing, even opposing, issues, politics, and especially disciplinary interests in oral literature and the emotional power of the layerings of meaning onto what is constructed as a single phenomenon:

> Many emotions are also involved. For some, like the traditional folklorists and earlier anthropologists, the topic is closely connected with "tradition," with nationalist movements, or with the faith in progress which expresses itself in the theory of social evolution. For others it forms part of a left-wing faith and a belief in "popular" culture, along with a revolt against "bourgeois art forms" or "the establishment." In others it goes with a romantic ideal of the noble savage and of the pure natural impulses which, it is felt, we have lost in the urban mechanical way of life today. Many of the positions taken up implicitly link with scholarly controversies about the development of society, the nature of art and communication, or various models of man. (7)

"The poem" then, like the word "culture," carries unwillingly a range of meanings and investments from which it is never wholly divorced, no matter through what political strategies the object itself is mobilized. At the same time, this wealth of investment, history, values, and subtle tones of meaning are great political resources. Feminists are very much in the middle of the contests for meaning and the deployments of value that both objects—"the poem" and "culture"—generate.

Mitsuye and Nellie resources the entire range of primary and secondary orality and the written in its use of the poem. As visual medium—film—combining sight and sound, juxtaposing images and poetic voice-over, *Mitsuye and Nellie* constructs Asian American women's issues of identity and cultural production in the midst of the technologies of secondary orality. Here, as in Rothenberg's modernist appropriation, the poem spans communications technologies, while also distinguishing among them.

I want now to introduce more fully this field I draw upon in my previous description and discussion, this field I call feminism and writing technologies. I started to construct my understanding of this field as I studied bibliography, or textual studies, which became for me a powerful window through which I had a chance to glimpse relationships that in contemporary literary interpretation seemed so infrequently detailed, taken for granted without commentary, or sometimes just not collected together in the same discourse. Especially I found this a window through which to consider the mobility of "what counts as the material." Still, only when I studied international art activism and the literature of decolonization could I begin to see sharply the currents of the powerful political uses of literary production that I understood in the cultural frames and accountabilities of feminist criticism today. Then I could begin to imagine how the political histories of the technologies of print culture opened up by textual studies could be matched by parallel analyses of contemporary transnational cultural technologies, analyses of a feminist apparatus of literary production under the rubric of feminism and writing technologies. So you might guess that it was as a feminist culture critic that I turned to learn from textual scholarship skills, approaches, histories, preoccupations, in order to examine literary production. The apparatus of literary production, simultaneously *object* for analysis and *tool* of analysis, intersects in art, business, and technology, an intersection currently determining "literature," both literary works and the academic disciplines of literature. From this perspective it becomes clear that interpretation is itself an element within the apparatus of literary production, rather than a transparent activity "reading," and itself requires analysis and positioning. A study of the apparatus of literary production potentially exposes our cultural expressions in a global economy of language, technology, and multinational capital.

Two views of this literary discipline bibliography suggest how its very historical location in the academy contributes to an understanding of the apparatus of literary production: we can notice that its locations in the academy begin to flesh out the organization of a literary division of labor, and we can learn from the studies, histories, editions, commentaries produced in bibliographic practice about texts in a world of technology and commerce, about historical specificity and commodity formation. In the academy, the currently marginal historical status of bibliography and textual criticism mark out what counts as the center of literary studies in a kind of institutional geography: bibliography and textual studies are located in specific places on campus and more and less visible in different genres and periods. Both challenge a modernist preoccupation with interpretation as the center of literary practice and challenge the department or the classroom—as opposed to, say, the library and the archive—as the center of critical production. This literary division of labor roughly separates out workers in the construction of texts and workers in the interpretation of texts. This separation is sharper as texts are more contemporary and more fluid as they are historically and linguistically distanced. Under new criticism, the acceptance or rejection of authorial intention as a central constraint also sharpened this distinction, while recent textual theory ruminating on multiple authority and textual process has softened it. Still, it is close reading that usually focuses introductory courses in literary studies, while textual criticism and bibliography are considered technical subspecialties, rarely engaged in before graduate study and often little known to literary scholars working in English in recent periods.

Literary practitioners may actually occupy different epistemological relationships to literary objects, constrained by their positions at points in an object's actual construction—from radical skeptic during the critique and reconception of, say, an edition, to stanch realist as their edition is physically embodied.[36] It's no wonder that scholars who privilege interpretation will have different points of view about the center of literary studies and may see not just different elements in the apparatus of literary production, but perhaps also fewer elements. Our locations within this division of labor may require us to maintain attitudes toward it and positions in relation to the apparatus of literary production as actual forms of knowing. And as we also know, poems, texts, and books are not only occasions for reading, but also artifacts with institutional statuses.[37]

Now, I just said that textual criticism opens a window on technology, commerce, historical specificity, and commodity formation. The subjects and topics essential to such work and investigations in the sociology of literature suggest differing models of an apparatus of literary production, with differing and shifting elements within it. In 1958, Robert Escarpit, in approaching internationally what he called "the literary fact," suggested as categories items such as: (a) political regime, (b) cultural institutions, (c) social classes, (d) social categories and levels, (e) jobs, (f) uses of leisure time, (g) degrees of illiteracy, (h) economic and legal statuses of writers, booksellers, and the public, (i) linguistic problems, (j) the history of books, and so on.[38] Richard Peterson, a U.S. sociologist of literature, outlined in 1985 what he called "six constraints on the production of literary works"; they are: (1) technology, (2) law, (3) industry structure, (4) organizational structure, (5) occupational careers, and (6) the market.[39] Obviously, feminists would be struck by how unself-consciously gender- and race-blind or gender- and race-sensitive Escarpit's and Peterson's suggestive nodes of analysis could be, depending on whose interests are described and taken into account in an apparatus of literary production. Sex and race, the history of decolonization, could be simply added as more "elements" or they might more powerfully be seen as constructing constraints affecting or determining elements. How to imagine this second alternative requires putting together in new packages knowledge we already have and engaging in new research. Communications theorist Mark Schulman's 1988 work on "gender and typographic culture" outlines a research program producing a history of "the effect of the technology of printing on women."[40] Schulman challenges the centrality of originary moments of artistic creation, and the book as the singular object of literature, by strategically opening analysis of "the four phases of print cultural movement" with "women as consumers of print"—thus forefronting large social formations rather than individual authors or acts of creation. He then moves on to suggest research issues in relation to "women as distributors of print," "women as producers of print," and "women as creators of print." His phrase "starting with reading and ending with writing" establishes an argument that describes women's practices in relation to social constraints and possibilities, as well as histories of women's alternative print culture.

For the purpose of describing a specific program of "historicist textual criticism" in a 1983 talk and a 1987 essay, Jerome McGann details a series of subjects and topics "essential" to textual criticism, while requiring for each element of his outline "a socio-historical analysis."[41] The outline organizes around three "moments" of production: (A) the originary textual moment, (B) secondary moments of textual production and reproduction, and (C) the immediate moment of textual criticism. Each moment is systematically examined in terms of: (1) an author or critic; (2) "other persons and groups involved in the [initial] process of production";

(3) "phases or stages in the [initial] productive process"—"personal, textual, or social"; (4) "materials, means, and modes of the [initial] productive process"—"physical, psychological, ideological." McGann's scheme might hint at the possibilities of critical sensitivity to the issues of race/class/sex and the politics of colonialism, for example, since it calls for: the analysis of ideology in "materials, means, and modes" of production; study of the author and critic as interested reconstructions "in the minds of various people and the ideologies of different classes, institutions, and groups"; and a kind of self-consciousness and accountability on the part of the critic, which even include historicizing the present.

Appropriating McGann's powerful schematization for the purposes of imagining the apparatus of literary production is especially helpful in considering ranges of activities covered by the terms production and reproduction, dramatically elaborating textual criticism's investments in authority and transmission. These same investments still locate the author (even in the guise of the critic) as the nodal site of production, unlike the very deliberate restatements of more sociological approaches, Marxist and not. For example, in Peterson's work, law and the market structure reception, while the author is only one of many so-called "occupational careers" in an industry of production. Peterson's work locates itself in contemporary Euro-American capitalism, not aspiring to much historical or cross-cultural and multinational analysis. The academy as a site for any of the processes of creation, production, distribution, or consumption is invisible.

"Feminism and Writing Technologies" names my own strategy for examining a set of systems of literary production in feminist terms. It's a large rubric under which an array of disciplinarily distinct kinds of work can be drawn together. It both centers on and makes problematic what currently might be called "literatures" or literary products or disciplines, deliberately raising questions such as: What counts as literacy? Who is literate? Which communications forms have elaborated literacies? What are the interpenetrated practices of reading/writing and other communications technologies in the United States? How are the United States and other Euro-centers parts of a world economy delineating particular literacies, including non-written ones?[42] I locate as the heart of the terrain of feminism and writing technologies the stories we tell about the shifting, problematic, and always multiple boundaries between those only seeming stabilities "the oral" and "the written."[43] The deeply problematic term "we" here runs the gamut of agents and levels of abstraction from local to global and implicates the multiple historical and political identities mobilized in cultural production and description. Mapping out stories about the oral and the written also includes understanding how these stories are produced and how they situate their makers and receivers in strategic relationships. This mapping begins a project to make visible our cultural expressions within that global economy of language, technology, and multinational capital I mentioned before.[44]

I like to describe four powerful but not exhaustive groupings of stories that suggest approaches to this large field of feminism and writing technologies, each encoding race, sex, and class. I use the word "stories" here to describe the complicated ideological agencies of cultural production. *Stories about origins* continually retell "the" difference between the oral and the written: one powerful Western version speaks the importance of the alphabet (only one of many forms of writing) as establishing a unique relationship between "spoken sound and inscribed sign." The histories of printing in the West set into motion technologies of copying, reproduction, and the making of simulacra—copies without originals. I look at the histories and social relations embodied in actual writing technologies: alphabet, moveable type, index, pencil, typewriter, photocopying machine, computer. Current technologies are situated in the international, integrated circuit of women, the multinational sexual division of labor, made up of (1) the sexual segregation of jobs and the sex stereotyping of women, (2) the earnings gap between women and men, and (3) the double or triple burden of so-called "women's work," which means that women do wage labor and/or subsistence work and on top of that do household work too. *The stories of crisis* require a feminist critique of the influential communications theories of Marshall McLuhan and the orality/literacy orthodoxies of Walter Ong, exposing especially their neo-colonial assumptions, their narratives of progress, their implication in development policy, their centering of a West with its heart in the Homeric hero. They are the stories of loss and opportunity: the Gutenberg galaxy made room for by the loss of the harmonious sociality of spoken memory; the invasion of new "oralities"—the television/radio/film technologies that some see as enervating literacy and others see as a post-literate orality that creates new pleasures of mind and body. Stories of crisis also include the leftover colonialisms of development and modernization theory, where literacy is the harbinger of logical thought, healthy and economical family life, cost-accounting, and threshold levels of national industry. *Stories about identity* examine the politics of decolonization and the investments of U.S. feminism in specific ethnic/racial/sexual literacies. They include a self-examination of the politics of English in a world in which English is increasingly the language of science, multinational capital and banking, a map of one set of colonial histories, and the bridge between tribal and regional languages in the construction of new nationalisms and national literatures. Within the U.S. feminist literacies speak the "Spanglish" of the Chicana, or envision often narrow utopias of "women's language," "women's culture," "women's writing." Song and poetry and storytelling are all the elements of this new set of narratives, not simply their forms, but their contents as well. The dramas of national literacy campaigns make very explicit the politics of the boundaries between the oral and the written (shifting as they are): as in Nicaragua's winning of the UNESCO literacy campaign award in 1982, while the United States' subsequent pulling out of UNESCO suggested our insistence on maintaining hegemony in global information production.

Finally, *stories about the production of stories* require feminists to engage in this story-making, not merely analyze it—there are no innocent positions from which one can only look on. It is in this set of stories that the apparatus of literary production is most directly addressed. In the fifties Escarpit's "literary fact" was measured by the amount of paper consumed in a country, rather than by the volumes of so-called "books" published. In the nineties, where in Silver Spring, Maryland, (my 1993 residence) one goes to the public library as much to take out audio tapes or videos as paperbacks, taking literally the materiality of "the literary fact" has to be strategized beyond paper itself. The systems of publication and other forms of production, the valuations of the academy and the market, the explicit and implicit "political" uses of literacies (in the plural) both within the United States and internationally—all must be taken into account in an examination of the apparatus of literary production.

Thinking about these stories about the production of stories returns us to the issues of academic divisions of labor. I said before that within the academy textual criticism and bibliography are often considered technical subspecialties rarely engaged in before graduate study. In the seventies and eighties many feminist textual critics engaged in the so-called recovery of women's texts. As with other problematic and suggestive explications of the construction of editions currently, feminist textual critics in this process opened up enormous questions. They explicitly challenged assumptions about literary value and often implicitly challenged assumptions about the nature and ontology of the text.[45] A decade and more ago, from 1976 to 1979, the MLA sponsored a project headed by Leonore Hoffmann out of which came that 1982 book *Teaching Women's Literature from a Regional Perspective* that I described earlier.[46] In this project, rather than solely focusing students' energies on close reading, instead the focus was on the acquisition of archival skills, with the purpose of recovering women's literature specifically in the regions in which students lived. "Regions" and "recovery" were defined very differently in the parallel classrooms all over the country in which the project took place: from examining long out-of-print texts in a large cultural/geographical area like "the South," to knocking door to door asking which women were writing poetry within an area of a few blocks in an urban city, and the gamut of possibilities in between. I would say that, rather than "recovering" women's literature, these students and teachers were "making" it, very much participants in the processes of literary production, creators of literary value. We have traditionally reserved this kind of "making" for specific, authorized groups of literary practitioners; the striking thing about the MLA project is that this power to make literature was given directly to students and didn't require long apprenticeships to possess advanced skills. Rather than being only positioned in relation to literary production, students were also positioning.

Feminist pedagogy aspires to empowering students, and this project suggests one form of empowerment that both challenges the divisions of literary labor in the academy and is theoretically very suggestive. When I've raised these issues of text production with students, I am often told "we haven't talked about how the text is made in literature or women's studies classes." These are more than just disciplinarily specific questions, rather they are feminist epistemological concerns. In this project, students had a sense of their own acts of production—not only as the writers they all are, or similarly as readers and critics, but also seeing themselves positioned and positioning in a much larger apparatus. Here the apparatus especially points to schools and the university, the publication industry, the laws of copyright and literary ownership, the library, and book collecting and connoisseurship. The MLA project also encouraged classes to make public presentations of the fruits of their research in academic contexts such as colloquia and in community contexts, including dramatic readings, audiovisual programs, and displays. Academic forms of consumption of literary materials were powerfully engaged, but only as one form within a variety of forms of consumption. It is this exemplary project that has informed my own conceptions of the "making" of "theory."

Now, as Schulman has pointed out, women have engaged in the making of an alternative print culture for at least the last century. He says that close to forty feminist presses existed in the United States in 1985, enlarging and politicizing women's powers of production and distribution and acting as the site for new feminist forms of art-theoretical writing. Some of my own work examines the politics of feminist publishing, taking as a compelling instance the art activist work of Audre Lorde.[47] Audre Lorde was a Black feminist lesbian poet, novelist, and essayist whose work has slowly gained prominence in the United States and Great Britain since the sixties. She was nominated for the National Book Award in the United States in 1973 for her volume of poetry *From a Land Where Other People Live* and has been and currently is published by both small arts presses and commercial mainstream presses. Lorde died recently, just after her 1982 book *Chosen Poems* had been reissued and revised as *Undersong*.[48] Lorde's work raises questions and theoretical suggestions about the apparatus for the production of feminist culture and offers one example of its operation, as well as detailing production, distribution, and reception of feminist theory. Her publication in small arts presses and mainstream presses and her manipulation of art-theoretical genres highlight the convergence of "audience" and "market" in their political, racial, gender distinctions, and in the codes of elite and popular culture.

Such mixed genres—combining poetry, polemic, fragments of autobiographical fiction, and description—especially mark the writing of specific ethnic/national/racial/sexual literacies still (in 1993) proliferating in feminist small press publication.[49] Studying the apparatus of literary production necessarily debunks the term "reading" as a gloss for the academic practices of "interpretation," instead requiring the acknowledgment of the cultures and varieties of literary, and I would also say, theoretical, consumption. For example, some of the work of these mixed genre writers is only sold in print after it has been initially encountered in performance. In that oddly dated but still stunning essay, *A Movement of Poets* (1982), Jan Clausen celebrates Lorde's shift from small press to commercial publication as a feminist event of the mid-seventies. Clausen describes "the increasing prominence of openly lesbian poets" within seventies feminism, an account that emphasizes the fusion of small press and mainstream press publication, creating "a lesbian-feminist poetry movement with non-lesbian adherents."[50] Notice the implications Clausen's observations have for how locations of publication are political, how they create specific audiences and identities, and how they constrain and construct possibilities for action.[51] In Lorde's work the distinctions between small press and commercial publication are political in these very ways.

Lorde's uses of the material and semiotic distinctions between small press and mainstream publication and of the varieties of forms of writing—she worked not only in poetry and prose, but also in genres such as the polemical essay, novel, speeches, interviews, and published letters—these various forms of writing create and reflect her multiple identities, mobilize various audiences, and passionately focus Lorde's deep commitments to global feminism and the international struggle against apartheid in South Africa. Instances of publication finely lacquer together the separate historical moments Lorde speaks from, constitute her autobiographical traces, are strategically appropriated to craft audiences and markets, and manage Lorde's own ideological distinctions between poetry and prose. Lorde was one of the founders of both Kitchen Table: Women of Color Press, which deals specifically with publishing the work of Third World women, and of SISA: Sisters in Support of Sisters in South Africa.[52] SISA educates an international public about everyday life for Black people in South Africa and fund-raises for projects in South Africa such as those establishing women's self-help groups, providing financial assistance to high school and university students, and assisting old-age pensioners and the disabled with rent and food. SISA is an example of the growing networks of international art activism, as is another group Art Against Apartheid, whose visual and literary artists do grass-roots organizing specifically in the United States.[53] Like Reagon, Lorde exemplifies the political opportunities that the apparatus for the production of feminist culture opened up, opportunities that brought together most powerfully the so-called white women's movement and Third World feminisms.

In this chapter I've done two things: first, I've made an argument that the apparatus for the production of feminist culture is the primary location for the elaboration of feminist identity politics in the United States in the seventies and eighties, an art-theoretical movement that has influenced all forms of feminist theory during this time period. To do this I've outlined several key "writing technologies" that produce, distribute, and consume feminist theory, and which extend today's conventional boundaries of this multiple object. These writing technologies "song," "story," and "poem" also make visible more conversational terrain in the travels of theory. Thus, I've considerably complicated the edges of the "academy" in U.S. forms of feminist theory by showing how the apparatus for the production of feminist culture profoundly reconfigures so-called academic feminisms. Second, I've introduced my own configuration of this field feminism and writing technologies and sketched out the conceptual map it produces, on which this chapter's argument is highlighted, understood as exemplary but also local.

Currently, we face historical realignments in the apparatus of cultural production, realignments reflecting the global economies of cultural interpenetration and the ruptures in the cultural hegemony of the United States, along with reconfigurations in what counts as "the West." The humanities in the United States, too, are necessarily reconfiguring in the shifting institutionalizations of the university, reflecting current economic imperatives and competing political demands for educational justice and for revivals of old orthodoxies, reconfiguring as well within the investments of the humanities in "literature." In these contexts, "academic freedom" is repoliticized, and the interconnections between feminism and the humanities become a sign of these historical trends, new resources for understanding them, and cautionary tales. Many feminisms are just now developing the intellectual, methodological, human tools that are required in the cultural frames and accountabilities of feminist theory today. These are some of the new directions women's studies will be constructed from, reflective of, and agents in as U.S. universities move into the next century.

4

Lesbianism as Feminism's Magical Sign Contests for Meaning and U.S. Women's Movements, 1968–1972 (1986)

ORIGIN STORIES ABOUT the women's movement are interested stories, all of them. They construct the present moment, and a political position in it, by invoking a point in time out of which that present moment unfolds—if not inevitably, then at least with a certain coherence. The period 1968–1972 is especially potent as an originary "moment" for feminism in the United States; both recent enough for the personal memories of many and yet made distant by the political, cultural, and personal mythologies of "the sixties."

I began thinking about lesbianism as a magical sign in the context of two recent debates within U.S. feminism: the critique of the anti-pornography movement and the emerging discourse on antiracist practice. The period 1968–1972 appears powerful in both conversations within feminism. On the one hand, the term "radical feminist" is used to ground current distinctions and disagreements in an early contest for a "politics of sexuality" and for competing images of "the lesbian";[1] on the other hand, into that period are read fundamental assumptions about the history of "the women's movement"—its constituencies and strategies, its stakes in "difference," and its commitments to antiracism.[2] It seems to me that both discourses challenge the current taxonomies of feminism as well as any unitary "history" of "the women's movement."

In this spirit I speak about "conversations" in feminist thinking rather than taxonomizing feminist theory, feminist history, or feminism. These conversations, which remain deeply embedded in various feminist practices, are sometimes local, very much historically (almost "momentarily") located, and are continually rewritten or reinscribed with new meanings by feminist practitioners. Besides these geographical and historical specifics (which are often unself-consciously generalized— a point to which I'll return), these conversations are marked by the specific ideological and rhetorical strategies of their speakers. These include strategies to describe ideology theoretically, to construct specific feminist ideologies, and to ground feminist action and practice in ideology. It's the "real" story that the origin story appears to capture. And to the extent that this "real" story looks new, the displacement that this "newness" offers is a moment of ideological ambiguity, the means by which another political position is constructed.

In this essay, I describe examples of this ambiguity or displacement. The examples I use are chiefly drawn from the writings of U.S. feminists between 1968 and 1972; they are instances of contests for meaning within U.S. feminism, moments where whole systems of signifiers are reduced to one. My argument is that lesbianism comes to function as this single, privileged signifier. But my own narration reinscribes the "origin" with another story, one also interested, which is both a commentary on, and an example of, a contest for meaning. This suggests two questions: What are the political effects of situating lesbianism as a magical sign? And how can we be politically accountable in the midst of our contests for meaning, accountable for the moments in which we reconstruct feminism?

FEMINISM IS THE THEORY, AND LESBIANISM IS THE PRACTICE

Ideology can change the ways we read back into our history. Evidences of these changes can be examined rhetorically: seemingly small verbal changes, changes in articles and conjunctions, may alter meaning profoundly. For example, most women in the U.S. women's movement have heard the phrase linked to Ti-Grace Atkinson, "Feminism is the theory, and Lesbianism is the practice." It's usually heard as a claim for an inherent (or similarly powerful) connection between feminism and lesbianism, a claim that feminism finds its proper practice in lesbianism, in fact that lesbianism is privileged as the expression of feminism.

In 1971, Anne Koedt published an essay titled "Lesbianism and Feminism" in *Notes from the Third Year*, using this phrase as an epigraph.[3] Her version uses no copulative "and," but rather a compounding semicolon. She guardedly does not say Atkinson said it, but rather says "*attributed* to Ti-Grace Atkinson." Koedt's essay exists in a historical context in which lesbians and feminists are not automatically assumed to be necessarily overlapping categories, and in which this phrase is being newly invoked in the women's movement in order to privilege lesbianism.

But Atkinson apparently did not use the phrase this way herself. Instead, it dates from a 1970 talk to the New York Chapter of Daughters of Bilitis (DOB), in which she asserted that lesbians and feminists were different groups, groups that perhaps could not work together at all. She said, "Feminism is a theory; but Lesbianism is a practice." Not "the" but "a"; not connected with "and" but distinguished by "but." The value is on "theory" here, as politically transformatory, not on "practice," which is enacted without revolutionary reflection.[4]

This exemplifies a displacement of meaning—what I call the necker cube effect. A necker cube is that "three-dimensional" drawing of a box one commonly makes, an optical illusion in which the front and back sides appear to each present themselves as forward first. In the origin story I'm giving here, the phrase is revealed to have been transformed historically in the women's movement to mean its actual opposite. Suddenly the phrase looks strange and our history means something different. Ti-Grace Atkinson looks like a different person. It's a willingness to check out the necker cube effect I'm asking for here. The necker cube effect marks examples of contested moments and tells us something about what we have at stake in our history, what different groups have at stake in our history, and how we erase and/or create our own historical memories.

To establish or construct the context for thinking about our own historical memories of this early period of the U.S. women's movement, I will examine two books as "ethnographic" objects of this period. They are Cellestine Ware's *Woman Power: The Movement for Women's Liberation* (1970) and Sidney Abbott and Barbara Love's *Sappho Was a Right-On Woman: A Liberated View of Lesbianism* (1972). I will also refer to several essays in *Radical Feminism* (1973), an anthology of writings between 1968 and 1972 from the feminist periodical *Notes*.[5]

OBJECTS: CELLESTINE WARE

Only two colors are used for the cover of Ware's book—black and orange, an extreme contrast. The cover, especially the front cover, is rather stark, graphically very simple, almost austere. It looks like a poster, and the back cover looks and sounds rather like a leaflet. The only image is the graphic of the women's symbol, and this is not really a picture, but an icon, that is, a symbol with a baggage of charged associations. A comment appears at the bottom of the front cover: "A brilliant interpretation of the struggle in America for complete social revolution through Women's Rights." Today the phrase "Women's Rights" seems a bit antiquated and at least has a reformist edge to it, but here it is paired with claims about "complete social revolution." The poster-like front cover presents itself uncompromisingly, even aggressively.

The back cover uses battle rhetoric; the first thing we see is the phrase "MARCHING WOMEN," and then "MEN ARE THE ENEMY." These phrases are sensational, but they are also not in substantial contradiction to the contents of the book. The book presents itself as dangerous. Other pieces of battle rhetoric are: "underground revolution" and "they intend to fight."

Each occurrence of the term "feminist" is preceded by the word "new." The sense of urgency, immediacy, difference is very strong. This "leaflet" takes itself very seriously, and its claims are enormous: "Complete equality: social, political, and economic" and "Revolution." Its claims are also very broad, as mobilization is presented in terms of masses of women, "major cities and small towns," "women young and old." But in fact it is unself-consciously class specific. This apparent cross section of women, we read, are found "on campuses and in living rooms"; they are "consoled with minis and maxis, nail polish and afternoon TV." The women's magazine style of the final pitch suggests this as well: "Learn how the women's liberation movement is going to affect you: your sex life, your marriage, your children, your whole life." The picture settles into the suburban housewife whose whole life is reduced to her husband, kids, and sex life.

In the place of epigraph or dedication in *Woman Power* is an initial page titled "Goals." It says:

> Radical feminism is working for the eradication of domination and elitism in all human relationships. This would make self-determination the ultimate good and require the downfall of society as we know it today.

Notice that the word "women" is not used. Or "men." Or "sex" or "gender." What we've got are "all human relationships." What we're for is "self-determination," and we get it by "the eradication of domination and elitism" and "the downfall of society." The word "radical" defines a position from which total revolution is possible; it means "complete," "total." It means the sweeping claims it makes. By focusing on the key term "domination," these goals take for granted the inclusion of struggle against domination in terms of race and class as well as gender. (See bell hooks, *Feminist Theory* 19 and 83, for comments on Ware.)

The table of contents functions as a map of the women's liberation movement. Having it as a map allows us to follow the author in her uncompromisingly impersonal narrative attitude. The map (1) privileges a problematic: "the relationship of Black Women to WLM"; (2) focuses action on abortion; and (3) claims a history: "19th-Century Feminism." Problematic, focus of action, and history immediately place us in a political stance in relation to the text.

This history of the women's movement, approximately covering the years 1968–1970, is written by a Black woman. It reminds us of the historical connections between feminism and the Black movement, as well as presenting us with a troubling irony about this movement that today seems so much more accurately labeled "the *white* women's movement."

Three issues in Ware's book are important in subsequent contests for meaning. They are (1) consciousness-raising groups, (2) the term "radical feminist" (which in a way is a discussion of ideological taxonomies, or systems of classification of different political groups), and (3) the purpose of Ware's book.

In Ware's description, consciousness-raising (CR) and consciousness-raising groups are not about *experience* but about *theory*, particularly for the groups Redstockings and New York Radical Feminists (NYRF). Therapy and T-grouping are exactly the wrong models; the right one (in Ware) is revolutionary self-criticism groups, even though CR significantly departs from them as well. Although Ware invokes the T-group (108 ff.) she uses it to mark the *differences* of the CR-group. The CR-group is *not* the vehicle of socialization (as the T-group is) but rather of DEsocialization. Its uses are (1) to build group intimacy, (2) to establish internal democracy, (3) to direct anger toward institutionalized oppression, and (4) to give women skills in understanding and taking advantage of the nature of political action.

Pam Allen, in her 1970 essay "Free Space," talks about four processes in CR: opening up, sharing, analyzing, and abstracting.[6] CR is not to exchange or relive experience, nor is it cathartic; rather, its purpose is to teach women to think abstractly in order to make theory, and the purpose of theory is to clarify and to clear a ground for action. For Ware, CR shouldn't be about the exchange of experience, but rather should construct experience as the resource for theory. Also, CR is not intuitive but counter-intuitive; its purpose is "thought-reformation" (40). CR gives women the skills to make theory belong to them; it is not something set in opposition to theory, or to action.

Ware also values the CR-group for its function within feminism as a cadre organization. *Woman Power* simultaneously calls for dissociation from the New Left and for revolutionary models. A women-blind Marxism and its privileging of the economic analysis of capitalism are rejected; the CR-group instead invokes revolutionary method, discipline, and action. China and Guatemala are models for revolutionary action. Actually, of course, this was true in the New Left at the time too, so the distinction is clearly an ideological or interested one. The CR-group then stands for this dissociation from the left, but also for the commitment to revolutionary action. In the same spirit, NYRF in their "Organizing Principles" use the term "cadre," a military term describing a core membership or initial framework, to describe the construction of their "brigades."

Today, the term "radical feminist" often is associated with a socialist/nonsocialist distinction. But talking about the CR-group suggests that this is not only too schematic to describe this early radical feminism of the 1960s and 1970s, but also reduces a whole system of terms or signifiers to one. These terms are NOT synonymous in Ware: socialist, Marxist, politico, New Left, anti-capitalist, revolutionary, radical, radicalism, radical women, women radicals. The word "radical" itself has a large range of meanings, including both its association with and dissociation from revolutionary theory, or even specifically socialist analysis; it is a dissociation from subordination and trivialization of the issue of women. Ware divides the women's movement into three categories. They are: (1) NOW, that is, reform feminism; (2) the WLM, the women's liberation movement, that is, mixed positions on feminism all *short of revolution*; and (3) radical feminism. Radical feminism includes ONLY the following groups: The Feminists, NYRF (New York Radical Feminists), and WITCH. She specifically questions whether Redstockings is a revolutionary group, but finally locates them as marking the boundary between radical feminism and the WLM. The "politico" faction of NYRW (New York Radical Women, from which both Redstockings and WITCH bud) becomes WITCH, so socialism is not a distinctive feature in the division between radical feminism and the WLM. So in fact for Ware, the word "radical" means "revolutionary." It is the position from which *total* revolution is possible. And the *sign* for this position, that is, the thing that stands for it, and marks its boundary or edge, is the advocacy of the elimination of marriage.

What's interesting about the phrase "radical feminism" (in contentions of recent years) is the way its use appropriates a "historical" reading of the women's movement (an appropriation I'm complicit with in this chapter). The taxonomy that accompanies it in Ware is not the same one taken for granted today. Examples of more current taxonomies in which "radical feminism" is a distinctive feature can be found in Lydia Sargent's *Women and Revolution*, 1981; Robin Linden's *Against Sadomasochism*, 1982; and Shulamith Firestone's *Dialectic of Sex*, 1970. The most recent and most fully drawn out taxonomic analysis of feminism and feminist theory is *Feminist Politics and Human Nature* by Alison Jaggar, 1983.[7] Firestone's taxonomy of the women's movement (32–40) is like a little machine set in motion to inexorably generate from itself the position "radical feminist." The taxonomies of Sargent and Jaggar do the same thing for the term "socialist feminist." (See chapter 2 for discussion of Jaggar and the taxonomic analysis of feminism.)

Ware doesn't generate "radical feminist" quite so obviously, perhaps because her interest lies not so much in distinguishing "radical feminism" as positioning herself with NYRF. Her book is very much "reports from the front lines." The immediacy of revolution is the power behind the "goals" of the book. Ware's book has two purposes. One is a kind of historical mission. She wants to record the "myriad significant happenings" of "one of the great revolutions in the history of Western civilization" (49). She's worried, however, that being too explicit will give the U.S. Justice Department material they shouldn't have—this is revolution; people will be arrested. This might appear ironic today, when much of the work of fighting sexism is often given to the government, even when it works against the government, but it underscores the sense of immediacy. Ware's concerns were justified; through the Freedom of Information Act we know now how extensive the interests of the Justice Department were in this period—and how invasive their manipulations of radical organizations. Zap actions like the Miss America protest resulted in the arrest and police surveillance of some women, and one lost her job (33).

Ware's other purpose is less explicit. Her book is not just history but also political platform. It is, after all, an origin story and interested. And the political platform is not feminism, or even radical feminism, but a far more specific contest for a history, a theoretical center, and a strategic practice for a particular ideological position within a small segment of the women's movement, that is, for the Stanton-Anthony Brigade and the NYRF. The fact is that this contest was lost. Comparing the number of printings of Ware's book (one) with the number of Firestone's (nine by 1979) you can also note that today no one distinguishes radical feminism from other positions within the women's movement by claiming that radical feminism is about revolution.[8]

Ware's specific platform here suggests powerfully how "our" history of "the women's movement" has always been marked by the interests and by the personal political histories of those telling it. This historicization has characterized a "women's movement" that is unitary and generalized beyond its narrow geographical boundaries. Early anthologies and histories privilege a particular social network: the same names of individuals and organizations coming up again and again. Ware's book both participates in this unitary history and challenges it. It challenges it by making explicit her strategic stakes in the construction of an extremely specific feminist ideology.

We won't learn from Ware's book what political struggles were taking place in geographical locations other than New York City, the Boston area, Chicago, and (very briefly) the San Francisco Bay area. These are highly privileged locations in the "history of the women's movement," and a unitary history exaggerates (as well as evidences) their importance. The social networks that tie these locations together construct a "women's movement" that is altogether too narrow to encompass the political actions of women on our own behalf during (and before) this time period. (Recently I heard a prominent feminist, in reply to a question about historical changes in feminist concerns for children, state that these were the result of "women becoming older." Of course what she meant was that it was the result of a specific cohort of women becoming older: her friends and her political network, who do indeed constitute "feminism" in important structural ways. The "women" of "women becoming older" is an example of the specificity of a seemingly generic term, the kind of hidden specificity that is challenged by the current discourse on antiracist practice. During this time period what we have are "women's movements" not "the women's movement.")

Access to mainstream publication at this time, and particularly in New York, creates one visibility for this set of social networks and obscures its historical and geographical specificity. Publication fixes and generalizes "the women's movement." Microfilm materials (another form of publication) from the Women's History Research Center are suggestive of other geographical locations of "the women's movement" in the late sixties and early seventies. The reconceptualization of "women's movements" would allow us to document and make visible the plurality of "our" history.

OBJECTS: ABBOTT AND LOVE

Ware never invokes the personal mode in writing *Woman Power*, and doesn't explicitly identify herself as Black.[9] In contrast, Abbott and Love's *Sappho Was a Right-On Woman* appears highly personal. The picture on the front cover is presumably of "Sappho," here a hippie, not a dyke. The term "liberated" in the subtitle is used unself-consciously, rather than with the edge of irony that goes with the phrase "there are no liberated women." Here clearly there are. Kate Millett's name is invoked on both front and back covers as a member of an established discourse within which the book can be judged. Already there are the beginnings of a literature on women and feminism (Ware's book in contrast seems isolated). Still, the bookstore classification on the back cover reads "Sociology/General," rather than "Women's Studies" as it might today. Also on this back cover are substantive comments from prominent feminists Kate Millett, Caroline Bird, and Isabel Miller: Millett, obviously the most significant and well-known, even notorious for her bisexuality and the furor caused by *Time* magazine (see Abbott and Love, 118–25, and Ti-Grace Atkinson, *Amazon Odyssey*, 131–34); Bird, a reform feminist who pointedly mentions the reaction of her husband; and Miller, whose lesbian novel *Patience and Sarah* had originally been self-published but was later picked up by the commercial paperback book trade.[10] The front inside cover gives other media comments, not names so much as publications, and a gamut of them at that: *Women's Wear Daily, Detroit Free Press, Playboy, Gay*. The word "feminist" is not invoked once here. Millett, in contrast, specifically speaks of feminism on the back cover, even mentioning the history the book gives of the "new" women's movement.

Unlike Ware's book, Abbott and Love's dedication is not politically programmatic, but rather retrospective (as is the first half of the book). Individual women are invoked, their names given, and their deaths described as the severe consequences of their lesbianism. Here we see a rhetoric of "suffering" rather than "oppression," and an invocation of the personal rather than a specifically political statement.

The table of contents divides itself into the past and the future. In the past are located "Guilt," "Sanctuary," and "The Necessity for the Bizarre." In the future are "Innocence," "Curing," and "Beauty." "Guilt" and "Innocence" conflate the languages of psychology and purity. The religious edge to purity is realized in the word "Sanctuary," as the mental health edge to psychology is in the phrase "Curing Society." Unlike Ware's seemingly comprehensive mapping of a new political phenomenon, Abbott and Love here offer a mapping of the individual lesbian psyche. "Guilt," "the Bizarre," and "Beauty" locate the problematic, and "Necessity" points to its constrictive structure. This problematic and its attendant history are expressed in an existential moment between the past and the future, while action is called "Curing Society."

The introduction establishes the authors as belonging to Gay Liberation; the first sentence says that the issue is not about "hiding," but instead about becoming "most ordinary people." These are not claims about revolution, or even particularly about political action. The second paragraph reveals the vacuum in which the book is written, the scarcity of information about lesbianism: two books in the 1960s, both written by men. What Abbott and Love want here are "psychological or social-psychological" studies on "the Lesbian"; they want the "facts" of lesbian existence, and the social sciences, especially psychology, are to provide the authority for these facts. The sense of scarcity here certainly contrasts with the rich proliferation of feminist literature on lesbianism produced since—of which this book marks a beginning—a literature that includes literary material, polemic, and social science work.[11]

Abbott and Love say too on this opening page that lesbians are coming "into the open" "in Women's Liberation or Gay Liberation." The "or" reveals these to be different places to function. The phrase "gay sister" is used self-consciously but synonymously with "Lesbian" (14). It claims a "pride" following "fear, guilt, and self-hatred." This is not about coming out in the women's movement, that is, choosing lesbianism, but rather revealing or discovering something that already exists and has existed in the context of "fear, guilt, and self-hatred," all terms of psychological isolation.

Looking further down this second page of the introduction, society is defined as "nameless and faceless strangers." This is not a political definition, but again a psychological one. Psychological costs are invoked in many forms, "alcoholism, suicide, or drug abuse," "self-degradation," or recurrent loss: "lost jobs, lost homes . . . lost children." It is called a "war" with "permanently psychologically disabled" casualties.

Abbott and Love talk about the book as divided into two parts in terms of "the Lesbian in the first part" and "the Lesbian in the second half"; this division underlines the sense of psychological isolation and is explained to reflect "the Lesbian's existential struggle between the past and the future, between shame and pride." This is congruent with Abbott and Love's statement: "At the time of this writing, the Lesbian's own liberation movement is highly introspective, more concerned with internal than with external changes."

Psychology is the language and context of lesbianism here. It is invoked to provide the "facts" of lesbian existence, but that hope resonates with the shadow of the costs of psychiatric institutions for lesbians as well. It is both a source of oppression and a hope of redemption; the desire expressed is to be "most ordinary people."

Abbott and Love also express an explicit fear that the history of this specifically lesbian oppression will be lost, and the first half of the book is particularly directed to "our younger sisters" who are reminded not to forget "historical process." Liberation is called a "psychological process" that feminists, Black activists, and student activists have also experienced. Feminists here are a group separate from lesbians.

However, this psychological overshadowing of the political is altered on the final page of the introduction, which first invokes consciousness-raising groups and then feminism, specifically NOW. It is asserted that "the common political goals" of feminists and lesbians (still distinct categories) "make sexual preference seem an unimportant difference." And lesbianism is finally claimed as "a political stance" in itself.

RACE AND SEX

A striking difference between *Woman Power* and *Sappho* is that Abbott and Love's book signals the beginning of the elaboration of lesbianism in the women's movement both as a sign and as a practice, while Ware's doesn't signal such an elaboration on antiracism despite her clear statements about the importance of the relationship of Black women to WLM and even her specific discussion of how to make this relationship more formal.

Ware talks specifically about needs for the women's movement to address class differences, concerns about political alliances with men, and collective identity around race. She says that class differences among Black women affect their relationship to specific political practices (75–96). She offers a program for the women's movement that would centralize a set of concerns which would also then be about the concerns of Black women. These include (1) a focus on issues of domestic labor, especially the improvement of employment conditions—including social security, medical insurance, disability, old age benefits. This would be accomplished by (2) setting as a feminist priority a visionary restructuring of domestic labor to be professionalized and offered on a contract basis and to offer both a full living wage and professional respectability. Professional mobility would be enhanced by optional training in other fields as well. It would also be accomplished by (3) more immediately placing a priority on adult literacy and vocational training and (4) orienting the issues of parenthood specifically around problems of welfare rights, women-headed households, unwed mothers and other forms of single-parenthood, and strong emphasis on full-time, community-based child care (96–99). Finally, she suggests (5) the development of a feminist vocabulary to speak to important differences among women in an effort to build a mass movement (117–18).

From the perspective on racism we are trying to construct today, the metonymic reduction of "race" to "Black," that is, how "Black" becomes the symbol, as a part to some whole, for all consideration of racism, seems a glaring problem in Ware's analysis. At the time, the white focus on the Black movement overshadowed this understanding. Ware's essay "Black Feminism" in *Radical Feminism* (81–84), a very-much-shortened version of chapter 2 of *Woman Power*, also suggests ways in which "women's oppression" in feminist rhetoric was being set into the same metonymic relationship to all oppression. That is, the oppression of women was allowed to stand for all oppression such that other forms of oppression became comparatively invisible. Firestone's chapter on racism is an almost caricatured example of this, highly elaborated through the metaphor of the "Family of Man."[12] Ware, in contrast, underscores the importance of considering sex, since there is already a rhetoric at this point considering race, or at least Black oppression, but only the beginnings of a rhetoric on sex. Ware also compares race and sex to persuade Black women to align with white women *as women*. She is trying to construct a category "Woman" to which many women will have access. But this pitting of race and sex against each other doesn't end up working to make that alliance. Her discussion of the importance of collective identity for Black women explains the dilemma in which this places the Black woman (75–96).

Abbott and Love's book and the quotation from Ti-Grace Atkinson I mentioned earlier uneasily juxtapose sexual preference and sex in a somewhat similar move. But the words used to describe this relation end up being not homosexual and woman (like Black and woman), but lesbianism and feminism. The origin story I told about the quotation from Ti-Grace Atkinson says something about how these words start off being exclusive of each other but end up, for better or worse, defining each other. Nothing similar happens with Black women and feminism in the early and mid-seventies.[13]

ANY WOMAN CAN BE A LESBIAN

One reason has to do with what becomes a highly elaborated rhetoric of choice around the idea and practice of lesbianism. One statement is offered by Alix Dobkin on her album *Lavender Jane Loves Women*: "Any woman can be a lesbian."[14] Today this is an important assumption in the women's movement and is confirmed (if occasionally uneasily) by the experience of many women. The idea that homosexuality is a choice was not always taken for granted, however, especially outside the feminist movement.[15]

To the extent in the 1960s and 1970s that lesbianism was *not* seen as a matter of choice, it appeared to feminists as a civil rights issue and not as a point of feminist revolution. It's this understanding that Ti-Grace Atkinson's speech to DOB reflected, an understanding in which feminism is a theory clarifying the grounds for revolution, while lesbianism is simply a sexual practice among a relatively small group of women whose rights should be respected.[16] Comparing this understanding with the claims made by Monique Wittig (in "One is Not Born a Woman," 1981) that heterosexuality is the source of the oppression of women and that the lesbian is the person who is outside of the collaborating categories of male and female, we can see that lesbianism means something very different in the women's movement today.[17]

But the rhetoric of choice didn't guarantee that lesbianism would be seen as a revolutionary practice. In a Redstockings editorial published in 1975 but probably written around 1973 or 1974—that is, concurrently with Atkinson's *Amazon Odyssey*—the rhetoric of choice was used to make lesbianism an issue different from feminism.[18] Redstockings (whose membership was by then very different from the founding membership in 1968) contended that because lesbianism was a choice it was not analogous to such issues as the oppression of women, people of color, or class oppression. These were all oppressions people had no voluntary control over by Redstockings' reasoning, therefore these oppressions were "primary." And because they were not questions of choice they were not subject to criticism, but lesbianism *was* a question of choice and therefore open to be critically examined in revolutionary terms.

The anthology *Radical Feminism* includes an interview in which Anne Koedt talks with a feminist who has recently initiated a relationship with another woman (85–93). Both were formerly in only heterosexual relationships. The interview includes discussion of how their lesbian relationship began, whether sex is "different with a woman," how their attitudes toward gay and lesbian groups have changed, and whether the women's movement influenced their decision to have a relationship. In effect, the interview describes how to construct oneself as a lesbian: it offers a blueprint in creating sexual tension, bringing the subject up, making a sexual move, thinking about lesbian sex, constructing differences between lesbian and heterosexual relationships, and assigning value to these as different experiences. Elaborating upon the rhetoric of choice, the interview implicitly argues that any woman can become a lesbian. The woman being interviewed says at one point that "once we got over the initial week or so of just getting used to this entirely new thing, it very quickly became natural—natural is really the word I'd use for it." This is such an "entirely new thing" that it takes only a week or so to get used to! This happens, she implies, because in some fundamental sense it's so "natural." Her comment is without irony and seemingly without consciousness of the language that revokes the conventional wisdom that lesbianism is "unnatural." Yet the natural/unnatural edge helps describe and create her experience. Lesbianism thus operates here as a visible sign of change in individual lives; elsewhere (as in Wittig) it stands for the possibility of radical change in all women's lives.

Lesbianism stands as a sign of something "entirely new" for both lesbians and non-lesbians. Knowing about lesbians, being in association with lesbians, having control of the arguments about lesbianism, these are all accesses to lesbianism that one doesn't have to practice lesbianism to have. Signs have a sort of magic attached to them, and magic operates by contiguity, or nearness; in other words, it works by rubbing off on you. There are many ways the women's movement offers lesbianism as a magical sign to feminists. The Ti-Grace Atkinson quotation is one powerful example. But there's also women's music and writing, which often offer lesbianism as a sign in a way that non-lesbians are certainly able to enjoy. A legacy of lesbianism as magical sign is Adrienne Rich's utopian idea of the lesbian continuum, a cross-cultural and trans-historical continuity of the "lesbian" to which all women have access and in which they may all be "spiritually" lesbians.[19] As Ware notes that the goal to eliminate marriage distinguishes one feminist group from another, so lesbianism and/or the knowledges of lesbianism can also be used as such a sign, distinguishing among feminist groups and delineating who has the right to the word "feminist." In this sense the context for the word "feminist" is historically intertwined with the contest for the word "lesbian."

RHETORIC AND ACCOUNTABILITY

How we construct rhetoric matters, what contests it is about matters, and what the stakes in it are also matters. Rhetoric is action, verbal action. It is not opposed to action, a substitution for action, an ornamentation on action, or a pale double of action. It is because it *is* action that it matters; it has political effects and so is necessarily called to political accountability. Calling rhetoric to accountability requires us to examine its construction and the stakes underlying this construction as well as requiring us to ask particular rhetorical elaborations and ourselves about the meanings we contest. In looking at the situation of lesbianism as feminism's magical sign, I've tried to make problematic terms such as "consciousness-raising" and "radical feminism," tried to make complex the construction of lesbianism as a political identity, and tried to challenge a unified history of "the women's movement."

"Radical feminism" as a signifier has come to solidify a taxonomic analysis of feminism. I want to challenge these taxonomies as inadequate to describe the terrain of feminist ideologies, either historically (diachronically) or currently (synchronically). In one conversation "radical feminism" and "socialist feminism" struggle, each attempting to require the other to give it birth (compare Firestone with Jaggar). In another conversation "radical feminism" distinguishes itself from "cultural feminism" by a particular historical reinscription that sees "cultural feminism" as the malignant gender-hypnotized child of an older, austere, gender-breaking parent (suggested by the formulations of Willis, Echols, and Rubin).

"Consciousness-raising" has been both the subject of criticism and revived as a practice. It has been criticized as the instrument by which the white women's movement encoded "white" and "middle class" into "women" of "the women's movement" through "experience" and as the means of the disengagement of "experience" (the personal) from political practice. It has been used to distinguish "feminism" from "Marxism" and "radical feminism" from "socialist feminism" (cf. MacKinnon, 1982) or as the sign distinguishing sexuality and experience from labor and politics, the anti-pornography movement from "the politics of sexuality." Simultaneously it has been offered as a method for unlearning racism; for constructing a varied, fragile, and essential "unity" within "women of color"; and for reassessing "differences," both of race/class/ethnicity and of sexual heterodoxy.[20]

The construction of political identity in terms of lesbianism as a magical sign forms the pattern into which the feminist taxonomic identities of recent years attempt to assimilate themselves. I am sympathetic to lesbianism as magical sign, appreciative, but critical. Identifying with lesbianism falsely implies that one knows all about heterosexism and homophobia magically through identity or association. The "experience" of lesbianism is offered as salvation from the individual practice of heterosexism and homophobia and as the source of intuitive institutional and structural understanding of them. The power of lesbianism as a privileged signifier makes analysis of heterosexism and homophobia difficult, since it obscures the need for counter-intuitive challenges to ideology.

The current discourse on the politics of sexuality directs our attention to the homophobias we practice and project against each other. Rubin's "The Leather Menace" in *Coming to Power* (1981) is a powerful statement about this kind of homophobia. Being a lesbian is not insurance against it. The discourse on antiracist practice calls feminist political identities into question (as does bell hooks) and offers nonunified or contingent constructions of identity in their place (as do Ché Sandoval and Cherríe Moraga).

Contested meanings tell us how we are interested and how we are politically positioned and positioning. Our erasure and creation of historical memory constructs who we are, our political—and momentary or ephemeral—identity. The reinscription of our history which this construction of identity requires obscures identity's ephemeral, shifting, and contested nature. Often it appears to be "real," "discoverable," and unchanging.

In this chapter I've described lesbianism as a constantly shifting construction in the women's movement. There is not "lesbianism" but rather many "lesbianisms" and similarly many "lesbians." The one word situates a number of constructions, each bound in a specific moment, a political moment, a moment in time and place. But to call this specific moment "historical" only and to criticize the construction of "lesbianism" in the singular as simply "ahistorical" is to remain unaccountable for the construction of history, unaccountable for the constant reinscription of an origin. It reduces the complexity of signification and accountability. This isn't the "real" story, it's one story. Origin stories about the women's movement are interested stories, all of them.

5

Producing Sex, Theory, and Culture
Gay/Straight ReMappings in
Contemporary Feminism (1990)

This chapter will explore the shifting feminist politics of sexual preference from three directions: the first—the "Sex Debates"—historically situating some of the issues at stake and redrawing the map of what was once called "the gay/straight split," the second and third—theory in press and the apparatus for the production of feminist culture—constructing an argument for how these issues look currently and suggesting some ironic and hopeful interconnections across differences.

THE TERM "gay/straight split" marks out, specifies, and layers together several historical moments in gay liberation, feminism, lesbian feminism, and feminist lesbianisms. In one meaning, it refers to a time when homosexual women and men shared the term "gay," when "lesbian" and "gay woman" were used interchangeably, when gay women and men were alike recruited from the bar scene, the homophile movement, and new gay liberation. Inside feminism, the first gay/straight splits revolved around passionate worries over the stigmatizing of feminism by the presence of a lesbian minority and passionate affirmations of the importance of resisting dyke-baiting and examining homophobia as central feminist projects, engaging in the critique of the institution of heterosexuality.

In another meaning it refers to a time when U.S. lesbians were increasingly recruited inside "the women's movement" itself, with investments in specifying nonparallel experiences of homosexual women and men, constructing sometimes alliances and often times distinctions across the categories of "lesbians and gay men." Inside feminism, lesbianism was constructed as privileged signifier, as magical sign: a vanguardism retreating as lesbianism became more and more acceptable in feminism, an avant-garde activism and theory ranging from lesbian as outside the collaborating categories of male and female to the lesbian continuum defining woman. The gay/straight splits quieted as lesbian vanguardism quieted and as homophobia and heterosexism were successfully challenged, though hardly eradicated; still, resentments smoldered under this magical sign.

In yet a third meaning it refers to a time when gay has a new salience among some lesbians, who see gay men bashed on the streets, denounced by other lesbian feminists as perverts, increasingly caught up in state repression, and dying from and living with AIDS. Inside feminism, the term gay/straight split marks a kind of mistake: the assumption that differences among women are only bipolar. Instead, differences come to be seen as simultaneously creating and created, strategically positioned. Situationally other differences that cannot be imagined as opposites may be as salient or more salient: race, class, nationality, language, religion, ability. All suggest that sexualities are too plural, too politically granulated to be named in a gay/straight division, as women have too many genders, sexes to be seen simply across such a "gay/straight" divide; indeed, any such centering of a gay/straight divide is in itself deeply divisive—mystifying the power dynamics feminists play with each other, and our accountabilities to each other.[1]

My own moment of coming out: in 1970 when the homophile movement, feminism, gay liberation, children's liberation, and mental patients' liberation seemed very closely pulled together for gay youth, harassed by and also protected in the academy in Santa Cruz, California. My own first feminist mentor was a gay man running a women's bookstore in Berkeley and doing feminist theory, convinced and convincing that only feminist theory could provide the theoretical grounding for understanding gay oppression and for mobilizing against it.

Time and space are deliberately problematized in the production of multiple stories in this essay. Feminists too easily believe "we" already know "the history" or even histories of feminism, even in the United States. What are taken as history are some privileged and published histories of feminism, which have been all too quickly naturalized. What I've just produced here is a series of overlapping—in time and space—historical "moments," what I've sometimes called conversations in feminism. I've located myself a bit because I believe this to account for my own place in time and space, to describe some of my political origins. These three "meanings" of "gay/straight split" are roughly successive historically. One can locate examples documenting each statement I've made in a place and time, but as periods in feminism they actually overlap, since they also describe different realities for slightly different political unities shifting over time. Also they describe *kinds* of events that might have happened in some places in different times than at other places. This may not be *your* historical memory, but maybe that means you are overhearing, eavesdropping on a recentered history.

This chapter connects and separates two threads of argument in a kind of weaving together and apart: Each section begins with a dense set of summary statements, that sometimes summarize issues of that section, sometimes contextualize issues of that section, sometimes generalize from examples offered in that section. I've made some of my arguments out of seemingly "local" issues and conversations precisely because I can be accountable to my own political communities for my stories about events and meanings. I consider these stories exempla illustrating large structural issues of general importance to feminist theory, thus a form in which theorizing takes place.

At the same time, this chapter as a whole has a rather sweeping agenda. I've

tried to give a sense of dynamic play among differing historical moments and feminist conversations, sometimes engaging each other, sometimes not, changing in the
middle into something else, and turning out to be right and wrong in unexpected
forms. So, while sometimes the argument may seem too local and detailed, at other
times it may seem too global and sketchy. Within this space this is the best way I
know how to tell the stories I think are important.

SHIFTING THE GROUND OF
THE "GAY/STRAIGHT SPLIT": "SEX WARS"

> *First direction—the "Sex Debates," in which divergent investments in "the lesbian" and
> her meanings and political activism in feminism fractured, and alliances (between some
> lesbians, heterosexual women, and gay men) reformed along the lines of a critique of the
> anti-pornography movement, the reperiodization of "radical feminism," and the indict-
> ment of cultural feminism.*[2]

The scope of the so-called "Sex Debates"—or my favorite term (lifted from
Gayle Rubin and Ruby Rich) "Sex Wars"—currently is too narrowly drawn around
the April 1982 Barnard conference and its synecdochic expansion, the academy.[3]
The Barnard conference and its products identify only one range of activity and
activism. Some of the very feminists who appropriately pointed out how white-centered these "Sex Debates" are also are among those responsible for reconceptualiz-
ing sexual politics, indeed sexualities, the meanings of race/sex identities, and the
blurred boundaries between these, the site of proliferations of both.[4]

So right from the beginning, we need to expand what's going to count as these
"Sex Wars," seeing as not the whole but only a *part* of this field the critique of the
anti-porn movement, the reduction of cultural feminism (which unfortunately contributed to an invisibility of the work of some women of color, some lesbians), and
the valorization of lesbian s/m and proliferated perversions. I begin with Ruby
Rich's troubled descriptions and questions at the end of her insightful 1986 review
essay in *Feminist Studies*. I begin with it in order to examine and reconfigure that
formative intertwining of sex and theory drawn in her essay in a generic economy
constructed in the academy—sex and theory in production, distribution, and reception, that is, sex and theory in the apparatus for the production of feminist culture.

Rich herself calls for such a reconfiguration, insisting on the significance of the
contributions of women of color to feminist concerns in sexuality; she demonstrates
in her questions the very premises on which their exclusion depends, but her questions actually reproduce these problematic premises in her critique.[5] Rich names
the generic politics: women of color contributing *"outside* the nonfiction books that
constitute the official discourse, in texts that exist on the margins of the debate, as
currently constituted." Here, as she herself constitutes one version of the debate for
Feminist Studies, she helplessly but critically "discovers" an "official discourse," a set
of "certified theorists," and a reign of "polemicists" who are *not* these women of
color. She critically names but also continues to establish a generic hierarchy: aca-

demic polemics and histories vs. non-academic autobiographical testimonies, each differently valued "currency in this theoretical economy." She laments the "inevitable dominance" of "theorized issues" "within feminist debates." Why is such dominance "inevitable"? Certainly it is currently powerful, and I think she means here to emphasize and problematize it. Here too, the term "feminist" ranges from a specific group of women physically present at the Barnard conference and/or represented in publication in Carole S. Vance's collection of papers and in the books centered in Rich's review article, to a larger group of feminists (who yet do not exhaust the category "feminist") writing and discussing these materials. The local/global shift assumed here in the ranges of "feminist debates" matters in examining these "Sex Wars."

The problem is how to criticize a white-centered discussion of sexuality without making visible only white women's participation in the large, feminist, interweaving conversations about sex. What's called for is similar to the historical reappropriation that draws a tension between critical histories of "the white women's movement" on the one hand, and reconceptualizations of simultaneous women's movements on the other. It must be possible to critique the formation in the United States of a "white women's movement" without simultaneously constructing a bogus history that makes invisible the contributions to feminist social justice that actually center in the political work of women of color, in the United States and elsewhere. In other words, the critique of the "white women's movement" doesn't mean relinquishing "ownership" of feminism in the United States to white women. Chicana theorist Chela Sandoval puts it this way: "the U.S. women's movement of the seventies was officially renamed the 'white women's movement' by U.S. feminists of color, a renaming which insisted on the recognition of other, simultaneously existing women's movements." Notice how the agents doing the "official" naming in Sandoval's description differ from those in Rich's.[6]

A similar refiguration redraws the map of what counts as "sex," "theory," and these "sex wars." Compare these shifts also to bell hooks's distinction between "the feminist movement" as an object and "feminist movement" as an action. Note also the power of publication to center and make visible particular histories of feminism and particular mappings of the current "Sex Wars."[7] Any "gay/straight split" is numerously fragmented in these new mappings which the "Sex Wars" demand, confounded with other markings. White heterosexual socialist feminists find themselves aligning with white lesbian s/m people to critique the anti-porn movement and a consolidated radical/cultural feminism.[8] Black feminist lesbians find themselves aligning with white self-proclaimed radical feminists to critique the symbolic and erotic uses of the paraphernalia of domination/"domination."[9] A different group of white self-proclaimed radical feminists align with the anti-porn critique and draw distinctions between an early radical feminism and a later developing cultural feminism.[10] Lesbian s/m people point out that they have most in common in terms of legal criminalization and street bashing with gay men, especially s/m gay men, s/m heterosexuals, and other visible and/or ostracized sex perverts.[11]

The renewed salience of the term "gay" among some lesbians invites both a re-vision of an early radical feminism and a continuity across gender in alliances with gay men, as it makes visible lesbian homophobia against gay men and corrosive judgments about gay male sexuality. Heterosexual women's fascination with gay men meets/overlaps with the possibly sexually specific perversions of fag-hagging.[12] Butch and femme roles conflate/separate in erotic dances with s/m, with the roles of top/bottom. An erotic analysis of power among Black and white lesbians, shifting across time, across the historical meanings of butch and femme, contributes to an examination of what counts as "sex" in these "Sex Wars".[13] Women of color working as artists, writers, and theorists produce breathtaking new analyses of the "race of sex"/"sex of race"—gender and sexuality and sex acts and sex meanings and memo-ries—for example, Moraga's "My brother's sex was white. Mine, brown."[14]

Women in several countries continue and begin analyses of sex tourism in the context of an emerging interconnected, international sexual division of labor. The sex industry (domestic and international) becomes the site of more writing and identity making, producing personal stories, films, and continuing moves for de-criminalization.[15] Anti-porn activisms are sometimes distinguished from a critical, but academic, theoreticism.

Some shifts have been in the making a while, some are old allegiances newly refreshed, some are momentary and fleeting, some emerge from old wounds of the early gay/straight splits and are fueled by still-smoldering resentments. These long-standing resentments are against the formation of lesbianism as if at the center, the very heart of feminism—they fan homophobia, internalized and external, as groups struggle for both vanguard perversion and gatekeeping sexuality, for political cen-trality, for new political identities, for new strategies of activism. The work, the labor, active and written, of lesbians of color is central. Such work creates new critiques of homophobia in various separated and connected communities, new critiques of ra-cism among feminists, and, most powerfully, insists on the specificity and overlap-ping necessities of political positioning—not simply a simultaneity of oppressions, but the complex interdefining, interacting movements of power, for change and against it.

Gayle Rubin's Foucauldian historical proliferation of perversions under attack by the Reagan new right contrasts here with the old Norman O. Brown celebration of polymorphous perversity that colored the beginnings of gay liberation in the late sixties and early seventies. Sexual identities and sexual acts merge and pull apart. The moments of reidentification, of the consolidation of new identities, are deeply distressing when unmanaged.[16] Polymorphous perversity suggested that sex was an-other set of hallucinogenic drugs, each to be savored for their specific reconstitu-tions of reality, for their special insights and truths. Proliferated perversions suggest that people can orchestrate, stage, contract for sex acts regardless of sexual identity, or in complex dances with sexual identities, just offering even more senses of varia-tion, variety, and especially specificity. The struggle over the giveness or the choice, the possible subtleties within, the psychic subtleties of sexual identity are heightened. Personally, I've begun to wonder if the dualist distinction here isn't rather between those who are erotic specialists and those who are erotic generalists.

Some subtle and not so subtle reinterpretations of events are evident in my stories, all pointing toward my own investments in challenging the ways that most participants in these debates use the term "cultural feminism." I contend that at this moment, cultural feminism is best seen as the very apparatus for the production of feminist culture and thus the important political site in which race, sexuality, art activism, and new forms of gay culture are being interconnected. Understanding such connections requires us to not separate away from one another debates about sexuality and race from sex radical debates, for example, about s/m. I want to focus less on the contents of these debates—summaries now often ritualized—and more on the political terrain and how it's sculpted, textured, crafted by all of us involved in these conversations, specific and momentary, but strategically important. I also agree with Gayle Rubin, that we don't need a "middle ground" in analysis of our "Sex Wars"—a reconciliation of the contents of debate, the conservative answer to conflict and struggle—but I think we need to do some mapping, some rehistoricizing, some understanding of our multiple mediations, a term I use in Lata Mani's meaning as the analysis of the political receptions of feminist theory and its products.[17]

THEORY IN PRESS

Second—redefinitions of feminist "theory," especially as influenced by the powerful explanatory systems of poststructuralist practice in the academy or by Euro-centered philosophical traditions. In 1979, Barbara Smith and Lorraine Bethel could recommend conditions: the black women's issue *(later expanded and reprinted as* Home Girls: A Black Feminist Anthology*) as a text for feminist theory courses, (implicitly) including as theoretical genres poetry, prose poems, fiction and autobiography, journals, essays, song lyrics, and reviews. In 1989, "theory" is more narrowly defined from a number of disciplinary and political perspectives. The academic and commercial success of feminist publication vs. movement and small press publication has effectively recreated both a straight/gay split and a white/women of color split sometimes now coded as "theory" vs. "experience."*

So, it's deeply important to understand that what was once called the "gay/straight split" has been irrecoverably altered, now positioned on many axes of meaning and political investment. This doesn't mean that gay people have no interests in common: we do. But our coalitions and identities are in flux and appropriately so.

The second site of the reconstitution of such meanings is the academy: for feminism in the United States that vexed and valued sometimes "home"—in that desiring and subjecting sense brought out by Bernice Reagon. It is only home for some, and even for them, only sometimes; yet it is one center for the proselytizing of feminism, within the academy and beyond.[18] A new gay/straight:women of color/white split emerges in the academy in the late eighties. The commercial success of feminist work, the new interests of university presses in trade books, and of commercial houses in feminist academic work combine in a visibility of feminist "theory" unstably and tensely inside and outside of literary theory, shading into cultural theory. Disciplines are mined for and mired in commercially successful appeals to the niches of reading and writing markets of the academy. Feminists laughingly and ruefully say to each other that they have sold their souls to some trade house with a feminist line, generating reviews and reports, anthologies and collections, and texts for classes (but not textbooks).[19]

Lesbian theory, fiction, scholarship, and activist writing, once occupying a center (if not the center) of feminist "thought," has now been displaced in the academy. One might chart who is publishing and who is reading lesbian writing, that proliferating work in mixed genres, creating new forms of intertextuality and abstraction. Such work may call for a vigorous reinvention of reading protocols on the part of academic theorists. Especially now, in that context, note what counts as theory and for whom. How is that assessment affected by the genres in which theory is written? Consider which bookstores carry which kinds of writing, and what clientele they attract. These questions of distribution are part of the apparatus in which theory is produced for feminist consumption.

As mixed genres emerging from and theorizing mixed complex identities are produced in the feminist press, genres of academic feminist writing are increasingly compartmentalized in production, distribution, and consumption in the academic and commercial presses. Political meanings are assigned to all these activities, redrawing political communities. "Theory" here has shifted from an activity possibly (though not without exception) embodied in many written genres to a genre of writing itself. The precedence of the rationalist essay becomes murky in these generic valuations. The hierarchies of value produced, as suggested by Ruby Rich in her discussion of the "Sex Debates," complexly crosses the race and sex exclusions of the academy.[20] These are indications about how theory travels and in what forms, the local/global structures theory repositions, and which structures get to count as object-language and which meta-language. Theory finds different uses in different locations.[21]

Some of the categorizing feminist work has been subjected to is indeed the fallout of the "Sex Wars" (and of commercial constraints). The equation of cultural feminism with a naturalizing, unself-consciously universalizing, theoretically naive anti-porn activism—or in the case of Catharine MacKinnon, a theoretically sophisticated but essentializing anti-porn activism—has certainly deflated the value of a much broader segment of work for a range of academic feminist theorists. The big three—essentializing, universalizing, naturalizing, the "sins" of feminist theory— are currently powerful gatekeepers among a particular grouping of feminists.[22] Non-academic lesbian writing has been assumed to be and sometimes insensitively read as simply replicating these sins.[23] Reconstructions of the history of feminist theory have facilitated these sometimes correct and sometimes incorrect readings of lesbian materials. The work of women of color, lesbians and heterosexuals, has also been marked by these practices.[24]

These histories and gatekeeping practices—although only having currency inside the feminist academy, and even there only among a relatively small grouping of feminist intellectuals—are currently disproportionately powerful in visible university and trade publications. They reify a division of labor that is sometimes characterized as the "theory" of white women, built on the "experience" of women of color, or, in a move that keeps these ranges inappropriately separated, the "theory" of heterosexual academics, built on the "experience" of lesbians. Gatekeeping works both ways across these divides: see, for example, the increasing code terms for "accessible language and style" in feminist journals and among editors and publishers; once meant to encourage interdisciplinary submissions, now they are also often meant to transform, discourage, or admonish "theorists," especially deconstructionists.

An error feminists make over and over is to mistake the *part* of a particular theoretical reading, especially a published reading, for the *whole* of the many forms theorizing takes: active thinking, speaking, conversation, action grounded in theory, action producing theory, action suggesting theory, drafts, letters, unpublished manuscripts, stories in writing and not, poems said and written, art events such as shows, readings, enactments, zap actions such as ACT UP does; or for that matter, incomplete theorizing, sporadic suggestiveness, generalizations correct and incorrect, inadequate theory, images and actions inciting theoretical interventions, and so on.[25] It's not that all human actions are equivalent to theorizing, but rather that a particular product of many forms of theorizing should not be mistaken for the processes of production themselves. Theorizing can find its embodiments in a variety of forms, written or not, published or not, academic or not, individual or not. Like the other forms of cultural production I look at—the poem, the art work, art activism—the exchangeable product with a single, valorized author/actor is the visible and venerated metonym oversimplifying the intersecting systems of production and reception.[26] Issues of the production and reception of theoretical work are meaningful, and feminists are now struggling over these meanings. As I said in the introduction to this book, these issues of the production and reception of theory become visible as sharply disciplinized, colored by race and racial privilege in the academy, strangely fixed by sexual identity, defined by a division of labor and a generic hierarchy, and consumed within politicized systems of publication and distribution.[27]

Barbara Christian's "The Race for Theory" attempts an intervention into some of the statuses accorded a particular reified product called "theory" in the academy. The title of her article plays on the commodification of theory in a factory-sped-up university system where publication defines a particular "fast track"; similarly it also plays on the theorizing activities of black people, seeing theorizing-as-a-verb as a necessity for survival by oppressed people.[28] The passion of Christian's work and the passion it provokes in reaction reflects on the struggles over "theory" in U.S. feminism today. It is one of the areas in which the so-called "gay/straight split" might be said to appear in reconstituted forms.[29] Christian and others contesting the spoils system in the academy, especially in relation to literary and cultural studies, may be surprised to discover that those seen as the standard bearers of high theory themselves feel embattled and devalued. The "stars" rewarded by the academy for the practice of "high theory" may benefit from this spoils system, but most practitioners of these specific schools of theoretical practice, especially in literature (sometimes the only ones perceived as, or perceiving themselves as, the "theorists"), find themselves solitary workers in departments of hostile "non-theorist" critics.[30]

Chicana theorist Chela Sandoval has spent many years working out a theory of what she calls "oppositional consciousness," a theory of the production of theory and specifically of a descriptive but also utopian form of it, "differential consciousness," which she sees as pointing and contributing to alternative theoretical paradigms, ones already and potentially departing from "hegemonic feminist theory."[31] Sandoval is a theorist influential in specific circles, who, in the manner of some other feminist workers—Gayle Rubin and Alice Echols come immediately to mind—has been a graduate student working on a long-awaited doctoral thesis. Sandoval has been published only sporadically and eccentrically, yet her circulating unpublished manuscripts are much-cited and often-appropriated, even while the range of her influence is rarely understood. Belonging to several national networks of women of color, she has described, helped develop, and herself been influenced by the feminist theoretical work of lesbians of color. Sandoval has deeply influenced what might be a nascent "school of feminist theory" housed in the History of Consciousness program at the University of California at Santa Cruz. (This names one of my own formative intellectual communities, one among many such places of feminist academic theorizing.) A story of the uses of Sandoval's work offers a kind of parable about the apparatus that reifies theory in the academy and the abilities of this apparatus to hide the race-consolidated structures of power in which knowledge is produced. `

Sandoval has described some processes in which the theory produced by U.S. Third World women has been appropriated by white academic feminism. She, like many other women of color, has seen this firsthand: her own work on "oppositional consciousness" is attributed to her teacher Donna Haraway in Sandra Harding's insightful and sometimes surprising book *The Science Question in Feminism*. Haraway is an imaginative as well as an astonishingly broad-ranging synthesizer of and a powerful contributor to the theorizing occurring at the History of Consciousness programs. She scrupulously attempts acknowledgment in her publications of her own indebtedness to this active work, thus making some of these systems of production within the program visible, as in the notes to her "Manifesto for Cyborgs." "Cyborgs" is presumably the work from which Harding extracts the idea of "oppositional consciousness," but without reproducing Haraway's acknowledgment of Sandoval. More recently Teresa de Lauretis, a prolific thinker producing exacting and absorbing theory and description, has moved to, been influenced by, and has influenced this "HistCon" theorizing. The footnotes to her essay on "Sexual Indifference and Lesbian Representation" follow a different strategy for acknowledgment and authorization than Haraway's, and her recent "Eccentric Subjects" is also clearly indebted to Sandoval's work.[32] Haraway and de Lauretis are more visible in terms of publishing and career trajectories than Sandoval (and other HistCon feminist theorists), and so may acquire cultural capital in the work they actively mentor but are also imaginatively indebted to. The processes that institutionalize Sandoval's work as Haraway's through publication and citation exemplify processes in which reified "theory" in the academy depends upon communities *theorizing*.

These processes—despite the intentions of individual authors—are not simply not innocent of racism and heterosexism. In fact, they are constituted in structures that depend upon wide and ongoing theorizing work done by whole communities, but most prized when decontextualized, exchangeable, race- and sex-consolidated in their published forms, forms mystifying their own processes of production. Thus, this term "theory" has to be bracketed in feminist thinking now, used ironically and proudly, shamefacedly and shrewdly, gloriously and preposterously, if it is really to convey anything like what feminists are doing in the academy and elsewhere.

THE APPARATUS FOR THE PRODUCTION OF FEMINIST CULTURE

Third—Proliferations of lesbian sexualities/ethnicities (both in the plural). The powerful critique of cultural feminism emerging from the "sex debates" was especially helpful in drawing attention to the homophobia among lesbians practiced against gay men and against other sexual minorities among lesbians. However, the reduction of cultural feminism to the anti-pornography movement was premature and narrow. In the 1980's, cultural feminism (that is, the apparatus for the production of feminist "culture") also becomes the site for political art activism and for art-theoretical elaborations of multiple identities and the antiracist critique of "the white women's movement." Mixed literary/ theoretical genres connect women's lived experience with the shiftings of what Chela Sandoval calls "differential consciousness." Lesbianism is remade in this continuing "cultural" blossoming of art activism, intertwined now with race, ethnicity, religion, national origin, decolonization, language, region, ability, and so on. Multiple identities refigure and make more complex any simple "gay/straight split" now, since coalitions among many differences may be profound while historically momentary.

The zealous narrowing of cultural feminism to the movement arm of anti-pornography activisms led to challenges redirecting feminist energies and calling us to accountability. The challenges to lesbianism as magical sign were profound and largely successful. The challenges to a coalition with the new right around pornography and violence against women have been cautionary; they have split apart groups within "cultural feminism" and decentered anti-porn practice. The challenges to the equation of fantasy with violence against women have made such an equation harder and harder to sustain. The challenges to unexamined assumptions about s/m and other proliferating sexualities have opened up new paths of inquiry about heterosexualities and homosexualities supplanting simple dichotomies when it comes to thinking about sex. The challenges to an international feminism founded in ahistorical, acultural "crimes against women" have required U.S. feminists to examine some of their cultural hubris, and feminism itself, as a kind of cultural imperialism.[33]

The zealous narrowing of cultural feminism to the movement arm of anti-pornography activisms was also premature and problematic. It solidified a particular form of U.S. socialist feminism expensively writing a taxonomic history of the women's movements, pedagogically powerful but historically mystifying, as I discuss in chapters 1, 2, and 3. Beyond that it overgeneralized—or perhaps better, *intervened* in—the ubiquity of the anti-porn imperative in lesbian politics and in current U.S. feminism, though undoubtedly *not* overgeneralizing its power in national politics. Its critique of lesbianism as magical sign revealed homophobia among some heterosexual feminists who mistakenly equated cultural feminism with lesbian feminism (a shift the critique of femin*in*ism made all too easy). It downplayed the tremendous pleasures provided for all feminists in the often lesbian-centered but not exclusively lesbian alternative institutions in its cautioning against entrepreneurial capitalism. Many alternative cultural institutions and cultural activisms in feminism became tarred with the brush of this narrowed, pejorative vision of "cultural feminism."[34]

Bernice Reagon's "Coalition Politics" offered a critique of cultural feminism from the angle of identity politics. Cultural feminism and identity politics may be shifting and overlapping terms, may be historically successive as centers of feminist practice. Despite some early fears that its political strategies might deflect attention *away* from an analysis of racism, identity politics has often turned out to be the site of antiracist work in current U.S. feminism.[35] Much powerful antiracist work has been in what might be called the "cultural" camp of feminism, or among those who sometimes call themselves "cultural workers" (a term with a powerful history in nationalist movements around the world). Early on, lesbian-centered alternative institutions were figured in women's music, women's bookstores and coffeehouses, women's buildings: sites of the production, distribution and consumption of feminist "culture."

Cultural analysis, critique, even theory in agitprop and other art activist forms similarly and strikingly marks AIDS political interventions, sex radical productions of gay culture.[36] Within a range of forms of art activism, one might see a coming together of cultural feminism, anti-imperialist work, AIDS activism combined with sex radicalism, and antiracist cultural products and strategies. Some of the politics and possibilities overlapping with this cultural analysis/activism have altered the terrain of what counts as the "gay and lesbian community" and "cultural feminism." AIDS activism combined with sex radicalism produces "sex-positive" political demands for respect for gay male sex practices and "liberated heterosexuality," while at the same time challenging reformist gay politics.[37] Successful coalitions in urban communities, such as San Francisco, make for pockets of support, even public documentation of the history of gay activism.[38]

Lesbian interests in AIDS activism produce new community with gay men; lesbian interests in safe sex offer opportunities for redefinitions of lesbian sex practices and meanings, forms of public lesbian sex.[39] A backlash, or troubled sense of priorities, incites some lesbians to challenge involvement in AIDS work or policy priorities for AIDS, while other lesbians and heterosexual women, women of color, prostitutes, drug users make new coalitions to describe AIDS as a "women's disease."[40] Calls are made by sex radicals for a return to, but at the same time a revision of, the consciousness-raising group as a site for the production of theory about sex, while anti-essentialist, anti-autobiographical individual and collective writing and film projects re-structure/re-vision bodies and body parts.[41]

AIDS activism domestically and internationally draws upon Foucauldian histories and anthropologies of sexuality, literalizing such theory in interventions into forms of global gay organization and local homosexualities.[42] The cultural and historical appropriations that create homosexual continuities across time and space are in tension with the imperatives of transnational influences and realities creating some kinds of gay organization globally. The flows of capital that appear to be linked to the possibilities of gay urban formations, intervening into family forms of organization, intersect with flows of sexual repressions and license. Lesbianisms in specific cultural locations are subject to multinational receptions.[43]

Meanwhile, feminist presses become the site for the production of proliferating lesbian sexualities/ethnicities, new genders, new sex, restatements and mixtures of sexuality and identity, colonialisms and decolonizations, essentialisms and anti-essentialisms, sex and language, sex and diverse bodies.[44] Not simply are the contents of recent materials about such mixing (Sandoval notes "U.S. third world feminists are 'new mestizas' " describing "this in-between space, this third category"), but the written genres themselves mix life stories—autobiographical and anti-biographical—letters, journals, poems, short stories; many are theoretical interventions, origins, and supplements in "white hegemonic feminist theory." It is no accident that academic high theorists discover/convert to feminism, or that academic feminists turn to the powerful, destabilizing, theoretical tools of poststructuralist thought at the same time in the United States that identity politics and cultural feminism elaborate issues of "difference." Our theorizing communities across feminisms have produced intersecting conversations, mutually influencing. Sandoval connects these ranges of production, sometimes differentiated in a division of labor: "such contemporary theoretical spaces as poststructuralism, dominant feminism, ethnic studies, and the critique of colonial discourse meet and intersect in the analytic space represented by U.S. third world feminism." Sandoval points out that "this other kind of feminist theoretical activity" caused "a rupture," "a crisis in the terms of dominant feminist theory and activity." "A theory of difference—imported from Europe—could subsume, if not solve it." "This recognition but concomitant deflection or sublimation of U.S. third world feminism can be tracked throughout the text of hegemonic feminist theory."[45]

HOPEFUL IRONIES

An emphasis on multiple identities and nonunified subjects brings together political investments across several "divides" here. Ironically, academic feminism is deeply indebted theoretically to this proliferation of lesbian identities, even though this influence is not always understood or acknowledged. I think drawing from this interconnection is hopeful, pointing to the possibilities of conscious and appreciated *mutual influences. Current academic work "theorizing lesbianism" shifts the "theory" vs. "experience" divide in the "straight/lesbian split," as does current work on race, but challenges to what counts as theory are still needed.*

6

Global Gay Formations
and Local Homosexualities
AIDS Activism and Feminist Theory (1992)

The juncture between all of these interests is comprised of the differential form of oppositional consciousness which postmodern cultural conditions are making available to all of its citizenry in *a historically unique democratization of oppression* which crosses class, race, and gender identifications. Its practice contains the possibility for the emergence of a new historical moment—a new citizen—and a new arena for unity between peoples.

Chela Sandoval, "U.S. Third World Feminism: The Theory and Method of Oppositional Consciousness in the Postmodern World"[1]

AIDS activists know that silence equals death, but we also know that this cannot be *said*, it must be *performed* in an anarchistic politics that sometimes coincides with and supports the political action of our allies working within the unitary power system, but sometimes contradicts it, or seems simply mad in the traditional public realm. The insight that "silence equals death" has spawned an *international agitprop activism that circulates* around the meanings elided in the legitimated discourses of science, media, public politics.

Cindy Patton, *Inventing AIDS*[2]

The shift seems to be away from psychic identity as an ever slipping fiction of coherence through language and representation to an emphasis, particularly on the part of chicana, black, and other theorists and critics, on ideological processes of subject positioning. The operations associated with "identity" are now seen as more fully implicated in social formations. . . . Feminism is focusing increasingly on the *identity-effects* produced by those contradictory social realities and "identity" has emerged—as the semantically surfeited term it is—to occupy large areas within feminist work: multiple identities, strategic identities, identity politics.

Elizabeth Weed, "Introduction: Terms of Reference"[3]

WITH CHELA SANDOVAL, I wonder too at the meanings and possibilities of what she calls "postmodern cultural conditions," although I tend to think instead in terms of "transnational culture/s." I prefer to focus on the debates about subjectivity and the limits of agency within the contexts of what we see happening in Cindy Patton's "international agitprop activism," which is contemporary AIDS activism. You might call this arguing "from the activism *up*"; I say this believing that theory is always already action, even if its scope and sphere worry us, seem too limited, or claim too much; activism is always mired in theory, whether it deploys theory self-consciously or not. What actions are meaningful, produce change, mobilize and/or restrain various "powers," create new political groupings—I take it that these issues are what matter when discussing the politics of agency, and for that matter, the meanings of theory in feminism.

I display two major interests in this chapter. First of all, I'm concerned with what I call global gay formations and local homosexualities, a single example of many interconnected and complex current historical shifts. I'm interested in these global gay formations and local homosexualities, on the one hand, as a theoretical apparatus in production and, on the other hand, as naming the historical circumstances this apparatus describes and even shapes. Second, I connect this apparatus with another interest, one in the construction of political identities. I'm concerned with both the political identities that cluster around the term "Gay" and the political identities mobilized by feminist theorists as they construct apparatus that locate them theoretically and politically. A guide through this chapter is an emphasis on these historical conditions, called both postmodern and transnational. I especially use the work of Chela Sandoval to make some of these links but implicitly refer back to the epigraphs by Cindy Patton and Elizabeth Weed as well. Feminists as theoretical agents are both accountable to and shaped by these shifts radically altering transnational locations of power. An attention to AIDS activism and its international art activism requires feminist theorists to swim in this rich sea of reconfiguring alliances, descriptions of reality, and political interests. Ergo this chapter.

I'm making a case here about the complex interactions *between* so-called global gay formations *and* local homosexualities; I try especially to unpack the meanings of "global gay formations" in the illustrations I give at some length. The relation between "global" and "local" is not the relation "universal" to "particular" (although, to be fair, it plays with this relation to some extent). My point here is to highlight the historical specificity of these abstract relations, to suggest indeed that they may determine the horizon of our abilities to conceptualize gay theory at this time. This is the point of returning to meanings of the term "postmodern." My *method* tries very hard to enact the shifts of political meanings and alliances as it describes them (indeed, I doubt they can be adequately described any other way). Although one might call the political purposes here very generally "historical" since I criticize unitary histories, I try not to reproduce them. Instead, I want to emphasize movement and change—how political objects look like one thing at one time and turn out to be something else quite different later on. It's at this level of insight that I think I have something specific to say about the feminist debates on agency and how they enact theoretical agencies: how they make certain kinds of political change inside feminist theory.

So rather than mobilizing the term "poststructuralist" in considering these debates—a term that names a set of powerful theoretical tools honed by some very divergent theorists in more and less politically engaged variants, in Euro-centers and peripheries, in self-consciously Third World appropriations, and in U.S. theoretical geographies—like Sandoval I prefer to consider a set of historical conditions. Indebted to that theoretical stew Elizabeth Weed says shifts a focus from psychic identity to subject positioning, indeed, to what she calls "identity-effects produced by those contradictory social realities," the historical conditions I'm most interested in right now I call "global gay formations and local homosexualities." One visual emblem of these conditions I take from the objects produced in AIDS art-theoretical activism: the ACT UP appropriation of Barbara Kruger's appropriation art, a hand grasping the statement "I am out therefore I am." I'll return to this visual emblem after some preliminary remarks.

As I pointed out in the previous chapter, AIDS activism domestically and internationally draws from Foucauldian histories and anthropologies of sexuality—particularly drawing on the periodizations and inventions of sexualities—literalizing, refiguring, imploding such theory in interventions into forms of global gay formations and local homosexualities.[4] Such activism has three direct consequences for feminist theory. First is a new appreciation for "cultural feminism," which I claim is the proper name for our apparatus for the production of feminist culture: a sometimes essentialist and sometimes anti-essentialist synthesis of identity politics and sex radical productions of feminist and gay culture.[5]

Second, in AIDS activism we see an altered terrain in the United States for what counts as the "gay and lesbian community"; for example, there are new coalitions among feminists—lesbian and other. Who and what these "others" are is under contention as "heterosexual" destabilizes as a category. Note again that we see lesbian interests in AIDS activism producing new community with gay men, lesbian interests in safe sex redefining lesbian sex *practices* and meanings. At the same time, a backlash, or troubled sense of priorities, incites some lesbians to challenge involvement in AIDS work or policy priorities for AIDS, while other lesbians, heterosexual women, women of color, female prostitutes, and drug users—these overlapping groupings of women—make new coalitions to describe AIDS as a "women's disease." Lesbian sex radicals call for a return to, but at the same time a revision of, the consciousness-raising group as a site for the production of theory about sex, while anti-essentialist, anti-autobiographical individual and collective feminist writing and film projects restructure and revision bodies and body parts. These coalitions and alliances I situate inside "international art-theoretical activism," that is, cultural analysis, critique, even theory in agitprop and other art activist forms, which are sex radical productions of gay culture.[6]

The third consequence for feminist theory comes from the new visibilities created by such activism, visibilities that suggest directions for gay/lesbian/feminist/gender studies in global gay formations and local homosexualities. As I pointed out in the last chapter, the cultural and historical appropriations that create homosexual continuities across time and space are in material tension with the impera-

tives of transnational influences and realities creating some kinds of gay organization globally. The flows of capital that appear to be linked to the possibilities of gay
urban formations, intervening into family forms of organization, intersect with
flows of sexual repressions and license. International feminists begin to understand
that lesbianisms in specific cultural locations are subject to multinational receptions. Such contemporary material circumstances offer us new insight into the
global formations of historical continuities and the local understandings of historical specificity.

Let me be a little clearer about my evocation of Sandoval's use of "postmodern
cultural conditions." Sandoval's use of the term "postmodern" diverges from Fredric Jameson's precisely as Sandoval emphasizes utopian possibilities of the present
moment over dystopian analysis of the lost project of modernism. Jameson's coinage
retains a Frankfurt school pessimism about the homogenization of "world culture."[7] Sandoval's stunning shift is instead to describe as "differential consciousness" the results of "a historically unique democratization of oppression." This
utopianism ironically builds itself upon and counters distopian analysis. I'm less
comfortable than Sandoval is with such assertive utopianism and tend rather to emphasize a range of complex contradictions, as if they could be shorn of either celebration or denunciation. But I know they can't be. I'm not as single-hearted as Sandoval, although I find courage and power in her reframings. I'd like to claim, for
example, that my use of "global gay formations and local homosexualities" is only
descriptive. I'd like to, but I can't believe that it is possible to simply describe conditions without being politically implicated in the powers identified, framed, and reconstructed in such naming. I do claim that agency is a heady mixture of historical,
group, and individual movement, that intention plays a smaller role than the fiction
of heroic actors would suggest, that political people can often only respond to social
conditions that are too complex to be fully understood, rationally trying to make
the most of circumstances of which they are not in control. It is the assertive belief
(I might call it hope) that one can do all this that Sandoval's utopianism energizes.

It is to illustrate these concerns that I take another visual emblem—one that
shows the complexities of power in its transnational forms, its problems and pleasures—a work of international art activism by the Japanese artist Masami Teraoka:
his painting from the AIDS series *Black Ships and Geisha*.[8] I wouldn't press to describe Teraoka's painting specifically as resistance art, unlike ACT UP's art-theoretical objects. Rather, I want to stress how, as a kind of postmodern art, it ambivalently and carefully paints uniquely postmodern interests that are *not yet* decidably
politically progressive or recuperative, that despite and because of such uncertainty
require our recognition and intervention. Its humor depends upon and empowers
uncertainty. Its ambicultural, multilinguistic locations are not reciprocal, but
aligned along paths of commodification, the production of cultural identities in the
United States, and along points of political, artistic, and commercial reception.
Teraoka's work very effectively places its own cultural production inside the transnational systems that I mean to resonate with global gay formations, where I at-

tempt to make more complex (less utopian?) the celebratory resonances of the word "gay," but without denying their appropriate traces. Global gay formations among other multinational systems are depicted, parodied, and politicized in Teraoka's work. Teraoka's technique simulates ukiyoe woodblocks but in watercolors, linking his images with U.S. pop art and commerce. Throughout the AIDS series, Teraoka uses Kabuki imagery. This particular painting is set up as a theatrical scene, and written across the top, as if the entire scene were a Kabuki illustration, is a description of four aspects of the action.[9] The inclusion of two women samisen players decorating the narrative suggest its genre: a Kabuki chant. The chant names the cast and then describes the four acts. In the first act, Surgeon General Koop arrives in the black ship for a special symposium between the United States and Japan. In the second scene described in the chant, trade friction is depicted in a condom trading agreement negotiated between Japan and the United States while the stock market crash is also discussed. In the third, dinosaurs sink the To-Shi-Ba boat engaging in secret trading; the text describes the sound the boat makes sinking. In the final act, an international conference on condoms is being held, in which women train to use a super-giant version.

Presiding over the scene is the head courtesan, a Kabuki female impersonator identified by the orange cloth over her head. She holds a long scroll on which is written: "New educational material for sex—your spirit must be prepared for the use of condoms." The condom packages—their brand name is "Safe"—have written on them "giant size, bargain price." Multinational commerce is the site in Teraoka's work of new engagements of people and everyday life, cultural imperialisms wryly shown to be eagerly embraced, of links between old and new sexualized pleasures, and new sources of exploitation and power. Teraoka presents sexuality as various and not centrifugally centered in dichotomous homosexuality/heterosexuality. I first discovered a catalog of Teraoka's work in a gay men's bookstore in Toronto, a bookstore specializing in international gay travel. The catalog, as an object, is itself embedded in global gay formations, moving along the lines of tourism and multinational capital.

Now I return to the emblem from ACT UP, reflecting again on Elizabeth Weed's point that " 'identity' has emerged . . . to occupy large areas within feminist work: multiple identities, strategic identities, identity politics."[10] Some of the objects produced in ACT UP's strategic activism comment on the limits of art activism and the implications of the New York art world in the national, willful ignorance of AIDS. They facilitate direct action, draw from gay and lesbian resources, and model citizen health research and citizen intervention into health institutions and regulatory mechanisms. Such activism literalizes radical theoretical insights into the social construction of disease; for example, it insists on explicitly politicizing such construction and engaging in political struggle to participate in such construction, thus affecting and changing the systems that produce disease as social objects and produce drugs to manage disease. In the coalitions produced by AIDS activism, sexual identities are becoming politically subordinated to the permutating meanings and reconfigurations of specific sex practices, just as sex practices must be prioritized over earlier euphemized "risk groups" (defined by race, sex, and class) in education on HIV transmission.[11]

Consider, for example, something like the benefit performance for the Santa Cruz, California, AIDS project "Feeling the Heat: An Evening of Erotic Entertainment, for Women Only." This sex radical, safe-sex performance participates in redefinitions of lesbian sex practices and meanings, perhaps even producing forms of what one might call "public lesbian sex."[12] Not only do such events support and elaborate lesbian sex (and safe-sex) practices, but such reframings along the lines in which gay men's sex practices are usually stigmatized (as "public," in which lesbians are somehow seen as innocent) reflect some new meanings of "sex radical." Such deliberately constructed similarities drawn between lesbians and gay men reflect some lesbians' refusal to collude with the stigmatizing of gay men's sexual practices. The emphasis on women's pleasure *and* safety publicly displayed is mirrored in the homemade lesbian safe-sex posters plastered around my neighborhood in Washington, D.C. Immediately defaced, they once graphically depicted women's genitals being touched through dental dams, with the slogan "Dam It Janet!" My neighborhood gay bookstore sells dental dams along with condoms, but interestingly enough, dental dams are not sold at the feminist bookstore a few blocks away. Feminists and lesbians are still in contention over sex radical politics. All of these examples reflect political realignments affected by AIDS activism and by new emphasis on sexual practice. Earlier versions of such political realignments emphasizing shared interests between gay men and lesbians and challenging sexual stigma occurred in the feminist debates on lesbian s/m.

In such activist engagement and political realliances, overlapping AIDS activisms challenge the simple binaries and the misleading charges of essentialism that academics use to process, categorize, and taxonomize political identities, struggles, and literatures and to manage political alliances in U.S. feminism. The political alliances emerging from AIDS art-theoretical activism exceed management within this framework. And, indeed, we need such theoretical-activisms to overflow in these messy ways in order to avoid what Eve Sedgwick analyzes as the genocidal "Western project or fantasy of eradicating [individual gay] identity."[13] I am especially interested in the analogues between the social construction of political identities and—as revealed by AIDS activism—the social construction of disease, or more broadly, of scientific objects of knowledge. As we know and have been talking about for a long time, identities are produced; I would emphasize here the *nodes* of their dynamic political production—processes, positions, moments, chronologies, epistemologies—an apparatus for description which I'm developing here. "I am out therefore I am"; the political struggles within which identities are produced; their production over time; the kind of playing with, parodying, literalizing that takes place in AIDS art-theoretical activism—each of these elements in the nodes of dynamic political production makes more visible that "essentialism" is often but one epistemological moment in the production of identities, not itself the essence of identity formation.[14] Such "moments" of essentialism consolidate political unities, sometimes only "momentarily," sometimes maintaining them "stably" at great cost.

Education about HIV infection and AIDS internationally underscores the real influence globally of historically white, Euro-American consolidations of sexual identity, that mutual social construction through which "heterosexuality" has defined itself against "homosexuality" in the last century, mostly in the United States and Europe, and there in several dominant discourses. (As the Oxford English Dictionary points out, the terms "heterosexual" and "homosexual" were invented in nineteenth-century sexology discourses—"heterosexual" is the more recent term. Notice how the word "invented" requires us counter-intuitively to separate names and practices that are not coterminous for all communities of people, even in the United States.) AIDS activists point out how educational efforts such as those of the World Health Organization have often seriously misrepresented the sexual practices and behaviors currently understood to transmit HIV because they are fascinated with reconstructing a heterosexuality innocent of, and mutually dichotomous with, homosexuality. In doing so, they ignore or appropriate local sexual practices.

Earlier, I suggested the insufficiency of the term "heterosexual" also in feminist alliances, that "heterosexual" is no longer a sufficiently stable or enveloping category to include those not named by the term "lesbian." Heterosexuality is politically granulating as feminist struggles over bisexuality—that sometimes third reification, sometimes overflow category, sometimes liminal impurity—are conflated with loss of control over the naming of sexual identity. The coming-out story as a technology to reconstruct sexual identity doesn't work when feminist life histories—not only from Euro-American centers but spoken and written transnationally—increasingly can't be captured in names only "heterosexual" or "lesbian" or "bisexual." The debates around essentialism as they have functioned in gay studies work as strategies to name collectivities. Other new social formations loosely allied under the rubric of "Queer Nation" include the "transpersons" mentioned by the National Coalition of Black Lesbians and Gays; the "queers" of Queer Nation, Queer theory, Queer writing; the "bisexuals" of LABIA (Lesbians and Bisexuals in Action); and "transgender"-ed people mentioned in the magazine *Anything That Moves* of the Bay Area Bisexual Network.[15]

So what does it mean to privilege the historical conditions named by this phrase "global gay formations and local homosexualities"? In what contexts is it meaningful? What does this examination add to feminist debates about agency? I want next to give two extended examples to illustrate my use of these terms and to show these vibrant examples as a rich sea of political interests shifting and refiguring.

One genre of AIDS discourse describes the realities of what work against AIDS means in specific cultures. "Silences: 'Hispanics,' AIDS, and Sexual Practices" by Ana Maria Alonso and Maria Teresa Koreck from the U.S. feminist journal *Differences* belongs to this written genre.[16] Alonso and Koreck place their analysis historically in terms of the multinational production and consumption of "Hispanics." I would also place it within the historical location of "transnational cultural studies," a term I borrow from the journal *Public Culture*. *Public Culture*'s editors, Arjun Appadurai and Carol Breckenridge, contend that "the state is increasingly dominated by elites who are transnational cultural producers and consumers." However, they also stress the "multiplicity of world-systems" that "now emerge from many centers and reach out to many peripheries."

> Furthermore, the dialogue between elites and masses, or from another point of view, between cultural producers and consumers, grows ever more complex. National elites raid each other's cultural repertoires for useful representations of themselves, while the masses, who are their audiences, themselves as tourists, television-watchers, immigrants, and *gastarbeiter*, constitute a partially deterritorialized and occasionally counter-cosmopolitan audience whose tastes and knowledge are ever-changing. Thus the foundations of the sort of critical theory that emerged from the Frankfurt school need fundamental rethinking before they can be brought to bear on the emergent global forms of public culture.[17]

Alonso and Koreck describe the "attractive packaging" of the "Hispanic" by U.S. media, corporations, and the state. The category "Hispanic" mystifies the significant differences among various Latino populations. They question the dominant assumption that disproportionate numbers of "Hispanics" and "blacks" are HIV positive because of greater intravenous drug use rather than because of sexual practices. This analysis refutes stereotypes about both drug use and sexual practices among the many groups reductively named in these two terms. For example, Alonso and Koreck cite studies that differentiate modes of HIV transmission among persons in the United States of Puerto Rican origin from those of Mexican and Cuban origin.

Alonso and Koreck's analysis deconstructs the terms "heterosexual," "homosexual," and "bisexual" as mainstream Anglos use them. Drawing from ethnographic research on sexuality in Mexico and focusing on receptive anal intercourse as "high risk" for HIV transmission, they locate two categories of male behavior: (1) men who engage exclusively in insertive anal intercourse with men and anal and vaginal intercourse with women and (2) men who engage, primarily or exclusively, in receptive anal intercourse with other men. The first group are not socially stigmatized, indeed their honor, power, and virility is enhanced by their sexual behavior. Reporting on a study by Mexican researchers in Guadalajara, Alonso and Koreck contrast both these local sexual behaviors with those by men who engage both in insertive *and* receptive anal intercourse with other men.

> Significantly, males playing both roles are called "internationals," a term which indexes the "foreignness" of practices which are much more like those of American gays than the ones discussed here. Carrier suggests that "internationals" tend to be middle class and that their divergence from the type of *macho-joto* relationship discussed here [a relationship between men of each category of behavior discussed above] is a result of influences from the U.S. and the impact of the gay liberation movement in Mexico. In the areas where we carried out our preliminary

study, where the population is largely composed of agriculturalists and rural workers, there were no "internationals." (114)

Here the designation "international" indexes one edge to what I'm calling
global gay formations, which are a complex mixture of transnational influences in
their layered representations: (1) as "foreign" within an indigenous set of sexual
practices, (2) as etic (outside, not local) analytic categories deconstructed but also
used by ethnographers both Mexican and U.S. North American, (3) as material im-
positions operating as explanatory indexes both for U.S. cultural comparison and
for U.S. cultural defamiliarization, and finally (4) as shadows of international political alliances, powerful and not innocent of domination. So, I offer this example of
one set of meanings bringing together "global gay formations and local homosexualities."

Alonso and Koreck have difficulties in this essay in shifting the ground in
which anal sex and homosexuality come to define each other; at times, they seem
eager to uncover a "real" homosexuality in disguise. Their work is directly connected to education about modes of HIV transmission, and they stress anal intercourse as risky sex requiring recognition and protective practices. Strangely, they
unproblematically accept the absence of lesbianism reported by informants, an un-
questioned absence rather than a similarly nuanced investigation considering practices not coextensive with identities. The AIDS education imperative may have appeared less urgent and motivated here. The difficulty lies in the overwhelming
power of the ideologies of sexual identity which seemingly specify sexual practices.

I want to switch gears here for a moment, before I go on to talk briefly about
the second ethnography I mentioned, in order to reflect on my use of several terms.
I said before that global gay formations are a complex mixture of transnational influences in their layered representations. I think of layerings of instance, of political
meanings constrained in particularity, inseparable and mutually constructing, while
distinct; differing patterns of abstraction, *dynamically* shifting ground and foreground, interacting and correcting and deconstructing each other. Precisely this
complexity of interaction marks these material systems as "postmodern" or "transnational." The terms global and local have begun functioning for me as layers of
abstraction with differing patterns. Saying this, I mean explicitly *not* to posit a bi-
nary between the abstract and the concrete, but instead to posit that relation as mobile. I want to look at abstractions layered next to each other in the *relation* of abstract to concrete or as map to territory.

Of course, this alters the common-sense meaning of the word "abstraction,"
since such layerings become both maps and territories. In a materialist discourse, it
requires one to ask the question: What counts as the material? The mobility of what
counts as the material I also claim is an aspect of what is meant by the term "postmodern."[18] When I now talk about "global gay formations and local homosexualities," I'm talking about layerings of maps and territories that also interact, correct,
and deconstruct each other, that describe distinct and important *systems* of *material*

circumstances.[19] Using the term "global gay formations" suggests how analytic models are sometimes material systems, as the term also refers to the models of sexual identity that gay liberation has dispersed through the world and made powerful in new political locations. The term "local homosexualities" also ironically displaying its own speciously generic use of the sexological term (homosexual), while pointing to local form(s), still keeps in view the sexological term's currency and power. The fluidity of sexual desire itself is what is currently stigmatized as *bisexual*—for example, in public policy discourses labeling "human vectors" of AIDS, or in politically recuperative feminist concerns about the stability of the category lesbian.

Now, given this use of layerings, global and local, I want to turn to a second ethnography. Earlier, I said that international feminists begin to understand that lesbianisms in specific cultural locations are subject to multinational receptions. For example, U.S. anthropologist and Japanologist Jennifer Robertson's theoretical apparatus depends on tensions between global gay formations and local homosexualities in her study of the Takarazuka Revue, an all-female Japanese theater founded in 1914. Her essay "Gender-Bending in Paradise: Doing 'Female' and 'Male' in Japan" is an ethnography of an international art practice.[20] "Paradise" is the name of the theater in which the gender specialists of the all-female Takarazuka Revue perform. Its theatrical locations resonate with Teraoka's investments in the Kabuki theater. Robertson's essay may be seen as part of a newly proliferating genre of lesbian writing that stabilizes and destabilizes constructions of "the lesbian," *but where and for whom*?

Paradoxically, according to Robertson, a genre of literature most associated with a lesbian author inspired the Takarazuka theater, yet the theater's purpose was to valorize *hetero*sexuality. Nonetheless, its teen-age and working women fans appropriated the theater as their model for a lesbian subculture, "namely, 'butch/femme' " says Robertson. The actors of the Takarazuka and their fans use the kinship terms "older brother" and "younger sister" for female couples or lesbian sex. Robertson distinguishes these terms from several other "expressions used in reference to female couples"—for example, a generic term meaning "same-sex love" and several slang terms, like "Class S," which conjures up the picture of crushed-out schoolgirls, a typical moment in the Japanese female life cycle. Another term, "take-out lunch box," alludes to the gender saturated meanings associated with rice.

The term that corresponds to "lesbian," Robertson says, "was not used to name a politicized female identity . . . until the 1970s." The Takarazuka expressions do not highlight the same-sex of the couple, as do the other Japanese terms, but rather "the differential gender roles." The configurations of the Takarazuka terms overlay two differentiated systems: *kinship*—both the "older brother"/"younger sister" distinction and ambiguously *gender transitivity/intransitivity*—"the asymmetrical but interdependent relationship" between the "male and female gender specialists" in the theater, specializations which complement but don't duplicate the all-men gender specialists of the Kabuki theater, which offer ideal representations of maleness and femaleness.[21] Robertson says "the division of sexual labor here recalls American butch/femme bar culture in the 1950s," and she suggests that while the same-sex terms represent socially innocuous couplings occupying a moment in a woman's life cycle, the oppositional Takarazuka couples confounded heterosexuality. In pre–World War II Japan, as nativism was increasingly valorized, outraged critics of the subculture saw "butch" sexuality in particular as Euro-American and un-Japanese. The oppositional possibilities of the Takarazuka Revue have shifted across historical moments. Note that this "international art practice" is not *necessarily* a politically resistant one, at least not over all the historical moments within which it has refigured.

I would locate Robertson's use of butch/femme distinctions as the "global gay formation" utilized here, not in a universalization of U.S. bar culture of the fifties, but as a key theoretical concept etically (not local, here not Japanese) used to distinguish among the varieties of local homosexualities in their more and less resistant forms and to encode Robertson's theoretical apparatus, which assumes a unified analysis of gender and kinship. It functions in the political shadows I've already described as "global gay formations." At the same time, global gay formations also structure some *consumptions* of these representations of Japanese lesbianisms.

In the last few years, materials have become available in the United States that point out and sometimes play out U.S. consumption of the global maps that include local and cosmopolitan lesbianisms: for example, between 1988 and 1990 I pair two evocative collections, edited by Ines Reider and Patricia Ruppelt, *AIDS: The Women*—connecting materials from the United States, Brazil, Denmark, Germany, Austria, the Philippines, Zimbabwe, Nicaragua, Haiti, the Netherlands—and edited by Reider alone, the "urban stories by women" *Cosmopolis*—drawing upon a similar though different range of locations and implicitly constructing local and cosmopolitan "lesbianisms." Ines Reider is one of the founders of *Connexions*, a magazine that translates into English materials in a variety of languages from international feminist movements and publications. Compare Reider's sex radical materials to 1990's *Finding the Lesbians: Personal Accounts from around the World*, ed. Julia Penelope and Sarah Valentine, from a quite different political location.[22] Who are these books for? What are the relations that permit them to exist in the United States, in English, for the consumption of U.S. lesbians, feminists, and overlapping cohorts? How are they similar to and different from the series of anthologies that proliferated new lesbianisms in the 1980s? How do they reflect or create alliances among feminist movements? How do they stabilize and destabilize constructions of "the lesbian" and *where* and *for whom*? U.S. feminists must work to locate the United States and U.S. feminism in transnational systems of power and to examine U.S. feminism in its constitutive appropriations of globally intertwining activisms and inside the history of decolonization.[23] These politicized systems map feminist conversations through which theory moves.

Thinking in terms of layerings requires locating oneself in the material systems dynamically modeled. In my work, I describe the reconfigurations of power and the new formations of identities in order to value which differences make a difference, which changes make change. Feminist debates about agency regularly polarize over how well feminist theoretical apparatus can adequately come to grips both with elaborating the varieties of power and domination and with charting the different abilities of individuals and groups to make effective change in opposition to domination or in deployment of such powers. For example, when Linda Gordon and Joan Scott stage themselves in debate in *Signs* as for and against poststructuralist theory, as against humanism or against determinism, *both* are struggling to claim and articulate the most dynamic and complex model of women's agency they can produce.[24] Connections translating *across* feminist uses of poststructuralism and social and political theory I consider especially significant in both Gordon's and Scott's theoretical practice, in contrast to the ritualized oppositions they produce in their staged debate—oppositions that obscure their actual practice and the theoretical reception of their work. Chela Sandoval's elaboration of "oppositional consciousness" similarly translates *across* feminist uses of poststructuralism and social and political theory, appropriating and dramatically transforming the work of Jameson and Foucault, predating but participating in current feminist uses of "positionality." "Positionality" is a term with poststructuralist resonances, which functions effectively to connect interlinking poststructuralisms—U.S., Euro-centered and Third World, profoundly produced and affected by feminism in its colonial, decolonized, and internally colonized manifestations—to a U.S. identity politics increasingly influenced by U.S. women of color as they understand and produce relations between, with, and about women in the "Third World." This is an identity politics also mapping across lesbianisms, mapping coalitions across classes, sexualities, religions, nationalities, and ethnicities.

In examining global gay formations and local homosexualities, I draw upon Sandoval's and science studies theorist Bruno Latour's work, with an eye to the ways they hint more complexly at the dynamic quality of the production of political and historical subject-positions, suggesting that such production occurs unstably over time and through several epistemological moments, each with new forms of agency/constraint, stability/instability, historical determination/universal use, and so on.[25] For example, Sandoval describes the making of the category "women of color" within political struggles in a specific and historically powerful location: the 1981 NWSA conference in Storrs, Connecticut.[26]

Thinking in layers means placing feminist theorists within the historical meanings of postmodernism, thinking of feminist theorists as theoretical agents and thinking of the political struggles within which identities are produced, within which theoretical agents play roles as "subject-effects." In other words, noting that, for example, not only are the meanings of lesbian and gay community consolidated "stably" in the costly epistemological moments of essentialization, but so are the theoretical identities of "poststructuralist feminist theorist" and "socialist feminist historian" (Scott's and Gordon's polarized locations in their staged debate). When

I say that theoretical agents play roles as "subject-effects," I deliberately conflate two partially overlapping, partially exclusive systems of analytic tools—which could be represented in the theoretical identities of "poststructuralist feminist theorist" and "socialist feminist historian"—creating simultaneous compartmentalizations and messy overflows. An emblematic example in the debates on agency is the meaning of the word "subject." To disentangle a bit of this wonderfully felted-together term, consider the following distinctions. On the one hand stands the dichotomy "subject/object"—an analytic tool with a long feminist history, a history to which Linda Gordon appeals in her critique of Joan Scott and of poststructuralism, claiming in the *Signs* debate that to describe agency as a "discursive effect" drains the word of any meaning. On the other hand stands the very duplicity of the terms "súbject/subjéct" (noun/verb)—an analytic tool that precisely balances on the undecidability of agency: Can agency be assumed prior to knowing what actions are meaningful, produce change, create new political groupings, mobilize and/or restrain various "powers"? To what extent does trying to locate "agency" make it impossible to see how power is shifting and moving? Is it the right unit of analysis?

I gave a version of this work on global gay formations and local homosexualities at an international feminist theory conference in Glasgow, Scotland, in the summer of 1991. I was struck there by the deep desire of international lesbians to produce an intellectually and materially autonomous lesbian studies innocent of, not dependent upon, not a supplement to or in any way indebted to anything from "gay studies." In my work, charting the courses of power in the formations we produce and work within seems necessary to any intellectual work on lesbianism. To know lesbianism "subjéct" (in some ways) to "global gay formations" doesn't destroy the active meanings of the political struggles of the differing groupings of lesbians found in either the International Lesbian and Gay Association (once called the International Gay Association and politically called to account, required to change its name and its politics by these lesbians) or the International Lesbian Information Service (a lesbian-only offshoot of the ILGA, separating from gay men in their own protest), however *not yet* decidably progressive or recuperative these struggles might be seen to be.[27]

Is agency a reflective, retrospective category, shot through with complicity, misunderstanding, contingency? Sandoval insists that we know agency exists: we (oppressed peoples, here a very *new* category of historical location) have already used it to make change—use it, know it daily, intimately. What does it mean that Sandoval challenges an emphasis on *women's* agency, instead describing a "democratization of oppression"? What units of analysis are shifting here, and for what historically significant reasons? Notice that Sandoval's "democratization of oppression" suggests world historical changes that substantively alter current feminist classifications of privilege and oppression. This "we," drawn together by new political interests, is made up of some of those who once (a past she claims is rapidly receding) were among the "privileged." This ironic, even bitter, but strangely hopeful "democratization of oppression" simultaneously names new extensions of oppressions on a world scale but also names "a new arena for unity among peoples" as power realigns on a scale yet to be understood or assessed.

Notice how the terms in which Sandoval names this ironic "democratization" reframe those now-canonical objections to postmodern politics: its putative relativism a misunderstanding by its critics of the very meanings of *tactical, mobile;* its apparent lack of political commitment, of radical politics precisely names critical misperception of the meanings of "differential consciousness"; its so-called inability to discuss power a misreading of those new skills actually reading the webs of power; a perception and concern that just as women are becoming subjects, men are destabilizing subjectivity, is seen as a misleading effect of white women's privileged male/female (unraced, unclassed) dichotomy out of which that "democratization of oppression" as a historically spreading transnational experience is invisible.[28]

I claim that within shifting feminist theoretical agencies (those named in new theoretical apparatus and those enacted by feminist theorists as historical conditions shift and theorists shape and are shaped by these conditions) the Gordon-Scott debate can best be understood emblematically. In this debate a putative dichotomy resynthesizes (in theoretical practice) as current reformulations in feminist theory destabilizing the political identity "socialist feminist" reconfigure in a formulation profoundly influenced by new coalitions among academic feminisms. This reshaped theoretical agency (reshaped for good and ill, not yet decidable) might be named "materialist feminist"—in which the meanings of "materialism" are transformed, in feminism, as they now must be transnationally (as a look at today's headlines in 1991 makes only too clear). Will we (theoretical agents recasting materialist feminism) work out the uses of "what counts as the material?"— an understanding provisional, historically shifting? Will we refigure our claims of what is prior, of what is given priority, importance, of what is immediate, immediately important in some "strategic materialism"? I hope that the book in which this chapter figures will be an example of such new provoking agencies.

Notes

FIRST, A STORY

1. The quoted phrase is from ftn. 9 of Donna J. Haraway's "In the Beginning Was the Word: The Genesis of Biological Theory," from *Simians, Cyborgs, and Women: The Reinvention of Nature* (New York: Routledge, 1991), 235; although I first encountered it in *Signs* 6 (1981).

2. See also Latour and Woolgar, *Laboratory Life: The Social Construction of Scientific Facts* (Beverly Hills: Sage, 1979); look esp. at 90, ftn. 20.

3. *Laboratory Life*, 176–77 for the description of the stabilization of a fact as an object; and 236 for the definitions of "agonistic" and "materialization."

4. Katherine Ruth King, "Canons without Innocence: Academic Practices and Feminist Practices Making the Poem in the Work of Emily Dickinson and Audre Lorde," diss., U of California, Santa Cruz, 1987.

1. WHAT COUNTS AS THEORY?

1. In discussion *Inscriptions* 3/4 (1988): 100.

2. "Displacing Hegemonic Discourses: Reflections on Feminist Theory in the 1980's," *Inscriptions* 3/4 (1988): 130–32.

3. "Teaching Feminist Theory," in *Theory in the Classroom*, ed. Cary Nelson (Urbana: U of Illinois P, 1986) 57–58.

4. "Displacing Hegemonic Discourses, 127–44; see also "Eccentric Subjects: Feminist Theory and Historical Consciousness," *Feminist Studies* 16 (Spring 1990). Allen, *free space: a perspective on the small group in women's liberation* (Washington: Times Change P, 1970); Ware, *Woman Power: The Movement for Women's Liberation* (New York: Tower, 1970).

5. Echols (Minneapolis: U of Minnesota P); Collins (New York: Routledge); Mohanty (Bloomington: Indiana UP); Gallop (New York: Routledge); Mitchell (New York: Pantheon); Cade (New York: Signet); Ware (New York: Tower); hooks (Boston: South End P); Parker (New York: Routledge); Gordon, *Inscriptions* 3/4; Clifford, *Inscriptions* 5; Eisenstein (Boston: Beacon).

6. *Feminist Studies* 16 (Spring 1990).

7. For example, in Sandoval's encyclopedia entry "U.S. Third World Feminism" in *The Oxford Companion to Women's Writing in the United States* (forthcoming). For my argument, see chapter 4.

8. Karen V. Hansen and Ilene J. Philipson, eds., *Women, Class, and the Feminist Imagination: A Socialist-Feminist Reader* (Philadelphia: Temple UP, 1990).

9. See, for example, June Sochen, *Choice* 27 (July 1990): 1883; Cynthia Harrison, *American Historical Review* 96 (April 1991): 638–39; Linda Kelly Alkana, *History: Reviews of New Books* 19 (Spring 1991): 105–106; Jo Freeman, *Contemporary Sociology* 20 (March 1991): 186–87; Rikki Abzug, "An Impassioned Radical History Lesson," *New Politics* 3 (Summer 1991): 187–89; Ellen Carol DuBois, " 'Dare to Struggle, Dare to Win,' " *Radical Histoy Review* 49 (1991): 129–34; Julie

Abraham, "The Way We Were," *The Nation* (August 27/September 3, 1990): 209–12; Rosalyn Fraad Baxandall, "Feminizing the Sixties," *Socialist Review* 21 (January 1991): 189–94.

10. Alice Echols, "Cultural Feminism: Feminist Capitalism and the Anti-pornography Movement," *Social Text* 3 (1983): 34–53; "The New Feminism of Yin and Yang," *Powers of Desire: The Politics of Sexuality*, ed. Ann Snitow, Cristine Stansell, and Sharon Thompson (New York: Monthly Review/New Feminist Library, 1983) 439–59; "The Taming of the Id: Feminist Sexual Politics, 1968–83," *Pleasure and Danger: Exploring Female Sexuality*, ed. Carole S. Vance (Boston: Routledge 1984) 50–72.

11. Hansen and Philipson, *Women, Class and the Feminist Imagination*.

12. Firestone (New York: Morrow, 1970) and hooks (Boston: South End, 1984).

13. Ed. Betty Roszak and Theodore Roszak (New York: Harper Colophon) iv.

14. The Roszaks give this citation: "From *Poor Black Women* (Boston: New England Free P, 1968). Reprinted by permission of the author."

15. *The Black Woman: An Anthology*, ed. Toni Cade (New York: New American Library/Signet/Times Mirror, 1970) 189–97.

16. Patricia Haden, Donna Middleton, and Patricia Robinson, "A Historical and Critical Essay for Black Women" in *Voices of Women's Liberation*, compiled and edited by Leslie B. Tanner (New York: New American Library/Mentor/Times Mirror, 1970) 316–24.

17. In Tanner, 215–16.

18. *Liberation Now! Writings from the Women's Liberation Movement* (New York: Dell, 1971) 185–97. The epigraph states (iv): "We have intentionally omitted our names from the cover of this anthology. It is our personal/political conviction that to single out only our own names for special notice would distort the fact that the book was made possible by the efforts of every woman whose work appears herein. (signed) THE EDITORS." They did include their names at the end of the table of contents: "Compiled by Deborah Babcox and Madeline Belkin" (xi), and the copyright is held in their names (ii). The introduction suggests the editors self-identify as "radical women in the women's liberation movement" (for whom they speak) (4).

19. *The New Women* (Greenwich: Fawcett Premier, 1970) 63–76.

20. *Sisterhood Is Powerful: An Anthology of Writings from the Women's Liberation Movement* (New York: Vintage, 1970) 340–53.

21. "Statement on Birth Control," Black Women's Liberation Group, Mount Vernon, New York (360–61); Eleanor Holmes Norton, "For Sadie and Maude" (353–59); Florynce Kennedy, "Institutionalized Oppression vs. the Female" (438–46).

22. Ed. Vivian Gornick and Barbara K. Moran (New York: New American Library/Signet/Times Mirror, 1971).

23. This is highly ironic considering Echols's description of the trivialization of women's liberation *Ramparts* indulged in earlier; see 108–109.

24. Echols notes that Ellen Willis was criticized within Redstockings for being too visible—this could be a strategy to respond to this internal critique; see 149.

25. Hacker's work drew from Gunnar Myrdal's appendix 5, "A Parallel to the Negro Problem," in *An American Dilemma* (New York: Harper, 1944) 1073–1078, as cited by the Roszaks in *Masculine/Feminine*, 131.

26. Appendix A, 369–77; Echols narrates 104–107.

27. Baxandall, "Feminizing the Sixties," *Socialist Review* 21 (January 1991).

28. In Tanner, *Voices from Women's Liberation*, 303–307.

29. Sandoval (New York: Oxford, forthcoming).

30. My survey of anthologies dates Beale's essay 1968; perhaps 1970 (the publication date of *Sisterhood Is Powerful*) names Sandoval's own initial participation in what she calls here Third World feminisms.

31. See Echols's ftn. 2, 314 for comments on terminology.

32. Joreen [Jo Freeman], "What in the Hell is Women's Liberation Anyway?" *The Voice of*

the *Women's Liberation Movement* (March 1968); Anne Koedt, "Women and the Radical Movement," *Notes from the First Year: Women's Liberation* (New York: New York Radical Women, June 1968); Evelyn Goldfield, "Towards the Next Step," *The Voice of the Women's Liberation Movement* (August 1968); Beverly Jones and Judith Brown, "Toward a Female Liberation Movement" ("published by Marlene Dixon in the Fall of 1968"). See Echols's citations, 316.

33. bell hooks and Cornel West (Boston: South End, 1991).

34. For examples, see "Haciendo caras, una entrada," in *Making Face, Making Soul: Haciendo Caras*, ed. Gloria Anzaldúa (San Francisco: Aunt Lute, 1990) xv–xxviii; Norma Alarcón, "The Theoretical Subject(s) of *This Bridge Called My Back* and Anglo-American Feminism," also in *Making Face, Making Soul*; Maria Lugones, "Playfulness, 'World'-Traveling, and Loving Perception," *Hypatia* 2 (1987); Henry Louis Gates, Jr., *The Signifying Monkey: A Theory of Afro-American Literary Criticism* (New York: Oxford, 1988).

35. Gloria Joseph with Jill Lewis, *Common Differences: Conflicts in Black and White Perspectives* (Garden City: Anchor, 1981).

36. Special issue of *Inscriptions* 3/4 (1988) on "Feminism and the Critique of Colonial Discourse," ed. by Deborah Gordon; special issue of *Inscriptions* 5 (1989) on "Traveling Theories, Traveling Theorists," ed. James Clifford and Vivek Dhareshwar.

37. *Nationalisms and Sexualities*, ed. Andrew Parker, Mary Russo, Doris Sommer, and Patricia Yaeger (New York: Routledge, 1992).

38. Chow (Minneapolis: U of Minnesota P, 1990).

39. Eisenstein (Boston: Beacon, 1991).

40. See "Under Western Eyes," 52.

41. "Writing and Sexual Difference," special issue of *Critical Inquiry* 8 (Winter 1981); rpt. ed. Elizabeth Abel (Chicago: U of Chicago P, 1982); *The New Feminist Criticism: Essays on Women, Literature, and Theory*, ed. Elaine Showalter (New York: Pantheon, 1985); "Simone de Beauvoir and the Women's Struggle," special issue of *L'Arc* 61 (1975); "French Feminism in an International Frame," special issue *Yale French Studies* 62 (1981); *The (M)Other Tongue: Essays in Psychoanalytic Feminist Interpretation*, ed. Shirley Nelson Garner, Claire Kahane, and Madelon Sprengnether (Ithaca: Cornell UP, 1985); *The Poetics of Gender*, ed. Nancy K. Miller (New York: Columbia, 1986); *Images of Women in Fiction: Feminist Perspectives*, ed. Susan Koppelman Cornillon (Bowling Green: Bowling Green U Popular P, 1973); *Feminist Literary Criticism: Explorations in Theory*, ed. Josephine Donovan (Lexington: UP Kentucky, 1975); *Feminist Criticism: Essays on Theory, Poetry, and Prose*, ed. Cheryl L. Brown and Karen Olson (Metuchen: Scarecrow, 1978); Marjorie Pryse and Hortense J. Spillers, *Conjuring* (Bloomington: Indiana UP, 1985); *Making a Difference: Feminist Literary Criticism*, ed. Gayle Greene and Coppélia Kahn (New York: Methuen, 1985); "Feminist Issues in Literary Scholarship," special issue of *Tulsa Studies in Women's Literature* 3 (1984), rpt. ed. Shari Benstock (Bloomington: Indiana UP, 1987).

42. Zimmerman, 205; Gallop's emphasis added.

43. Hester Eisenstein, *Gender Shock: Practicing Feminism on Two Continents* (Boston: Beacon, 1991) and Joyce Gelb, *Feminism and Politics: A Comparative Perspective* (Berkeley: U of California P, 1989).

2. WRITING CONVERSATIONS IN FEMINIST THEORY

1. hooks, *Feminist Theory* (Boston: South End, 1984) ix.

2. Sandoval, "U.S. Third World Feminism: The Theory and Method of Oppositional Consciousness in the Postmodern World," *Genders* 10 (Spring 1991): 1–24.

3. "The Psychology of the Generic Masculine" in *Women and Language in Literature and Society*, ed. Sally McConnell-Ginet, Ruth Borker, and Nelly Furman (New York: Praeger, 1980) 69–78. This material is based on Martyna's "Using and Understanding the Generic Masculine: A Social-Psychological Approach to Language and the Sexes," diss., Stanford, 1978, and explored fur-

ther in "Beyond the He/Man Approach: The Case for Language Change," *Signs* 5 (Spring, 1980): 482–93; revised version "Beyond the He/Man Approach: The Case for Nonsexist Language," rpt. in *Language, Gender, and Society*, ed. Barrie Thorne, Cheris Kramarae, and Nancy Henley (Rowley: Newbury, 1983) 25–37.

4. My own original use of marked and unmarked categories derives from John Lyons, *Semantics*, vol. 1 (Cambridge U P, 1977). For some useful discussion of linguistic markedness and feminist issues, see Francine Wattman Frank and Paula A. Treichler, *Language, Gender, and Professional Writing: Theoretical Approaches and Guidelines for Nonsexist Usage* (New York: Modern Language Association, 1989); for masculine marking as general feature, 85; for the asymmetries of markedness, 206; for a parody of sex-marking substituting race, 225; for a discussion of false universals, 227.

5. Wo-man, marked; ø-man, unmarked.

6. Martyna gives a metaphoric example; "One scientist describes a hypothetical researcher who produces a long list of publications, but little contribution to the enduring body of knowledge: 'His true position is that of a potent-but-sterile intellectual rake, who leaves in his merry path a long train of ravished maidens, but no viable scientific offspring.' " Martyna comments, "Such contexts leave little room for a generic interpretation. But even in a context explicitly designed to encourage a generic inference, the use of he allows a sex-exclusive inference to be drawn, and females to be excluded from the category of generic human beings." ("Psychology," 74. Martyna's example is from Paul Meehl, "Theory Testing in Physics: A Methodological Paradox," *Philosophy of Science* 34 [1967]: 103–115.)

7. Both examples were offered—undocumented—by Casey Miller and Kate Swift in their *The Handbook of Nonsexist Writing* (New York: Barnes, 1980) 12. Miller and Swift's explanation of "Man as a False Generic" is a particularly entertaining historical and practical discussion, persuasive, sharp, and generous.

8. This definition is found phrased identically in each of the three versions of Nancy C. M. Hartsock's argument on a feminist historical materialism: "Can There Be a Specifically Feminist Materialism?" (unpublished manuscript, n.d. but probably 1979) 2–3; "The Feminist Standpoint: Developing the Ground for a Specifically Feminist Historical Materialism," in *Discovering Reality: Feminist Perspectives on Epistemology, Metaphysics, Methodology, and the Philosophy of Science*, ed. Sandra Harding and Merrill B. Hintikka (Dordrecht: Reidel, 1983) 285; and *Money, Sex, and Power: Toward a Feminist Historical Materialism* (New York: Longman, 1983) 117. Hartsock has very generously given me permission to quote from her manuscripts.

9. Actually, Hartsock's discussion of the connections between these two viewpoints is much more detailed than my deliberately and appropriatively schematized description here. For one thing, she makes much more specific the ideological relation of the bourgeois vision with the proletarian, calling it "an inversion" of the other, both "partial and perverse." Hartsock gives a cogent summary of her own argument here on 232 of *Money, Sex, and Power*.

10. I'm relying heavily here on Sandoval's "Women Respond to Racism: A Report on the National Women's Studies Association Conference, Storrs, Connecticut," published by the Center for Third World Organizing, 4228 Telegraph Avenue, Oakland, CA 94609 [n.d. but 1982] in their Occasional Paper Series: The Struggle Within; and also on my attendance at talks given by Sandoval at the University of California, Santa Cruz, 1981–1983. Commenting and theorizing on events at the N.W.S.A.'s annual meeting in 1981, Sandoval makes an argument for a political stance that she calls "oppositional consciousness." An alternate version of this essay (which doesn't include some of the material I draw on here from the earlier version) is published by Sandoval "as Secretary to the National Third World Women's Alliance" and titled "Feminism and Racism: A Report on the 1981 National Women's Studies Association Conference" in *Making Face, Making Soul, Haciendo Caras: Creative and Critical Perspectives by Women of Color*, ed. Gloria Anzaldúa (San Francisco: Aunt Lute, 1990) 55–71.

11. Sandoval talks about this four-part model in "Racism," 21–23. See also Sandoval's

"Comment on Krieger's 'Lesbian Identity and Community: Recent Social Science Literature,' " *Signs* 9 (Summer, 1984): 725–29, rpt. in *The Lesbian Issue: Essays from* Signs, ed. Estelle B. Freedman, Barbara C. Gelpi, Susan L. Johnson, Kathleen M. Weston (Chicago: U of Chicago P, 1985) 241–45.

12. In this responsibility it contrasts strikingly with the privilege of the unmarked generic masculine. There the marked category is "eaten up" by the unmarked category. Imagine a group "men" responsible to coalitions among just its elements "men" and "women," let alone the implied elements of other categorizations of humans. It remains to be seen if "the women's movement" in the United States can learn this kind of coalition-building.

13. Jaggar and Rothenberg Struhl, eds. (New York: McGraw-Hill, 1978).

14. Roszak and Roszak, eds. (New York: Harper, 1969); Kourany, Sterba, and Tong, eds. (Englewood Cliffs: Prentice Hall, 1992).

15. This is not uniformly true of current women's studies textbooks. See, for example, Johnetta B. Cole, ed., *All American Women: Lines That Divide, Ties That Bind* (New York: Free P, 1986); Paula Rothenberg, *Racism and Sexism: An Integrated Study* (New York: St. Martin's P, 1988); Jo Whitehorse Cochran, Donna Langston, Carolyn Woodward, eds., *Changing Our Power: An Introduction to Women Studies*, 2nd. ed. (Kendall/Hunt, 1988, 1991); or older textbooks, such as Hunter College Women's Studies Collective, *Women's Realities, Women's Choices* (New York: Oxford, 1983).

16. Alison M. Jaggar, *Feminist Politics and Human Nature* (Totowa: Rowman & Allanheld, 1983); Rosemarie Tong, *Feminist Thought: A Comprehensive Introduction* (Boulder: Westview, 1989).

17. Nancy C. M. Hartsock (New York: Longman, 1983) and Alison M. Jaggar (Totowa: Rowman & Allanheld, 1983).

18. Patricia Hill Collins, *Black Feminist Thought: Knowledge, Consciousness, and the Politics of Empowerment* (New York: Routledge, 1990); Fredric Jameson, "History and Class Consciousness as an 'Unfinished Project,' " *Rethinking Marxism* 1 (1988); "Situated Knowledges: The Science Question in Feminism and the Privilege of Partial Perspective," in *Simians, Cyborgs, and Women: The Reinvention of Nature* (New York: Routledge, 1991).

19. Ftn. 35, 250; cf. 241 in the text of *Money, Sex, and Power*.

20. *Feminist Politics and Human Nature* (Totawa: Rowman, 1983; Sussex: Harvester). I will be largely referring to Jaggar's final chapter "Feminist Politics and Epistemology: Justifying Feminist Theory," 353–94, and especially to the section "Identifying the Standpoint of Women," 385ff. For Jaggar's debt to Hartsock in her criticism of abstract individualism, see 41; ref. 50, n. 35.

21. See Hartsock's discussion of the five epistemological claims made in the notion of a standpoint: the limits of material life; the inverse, partial, and perverse character of ruling-class vision; everyone's forced participation in this ruling-class vision; the achievement of liberatory vision through political struggle, analysis, and education; the historical and liberatory role of a standpoint (118 of *Money, Sex, and Power*).

22. For her argument, 386; also see her comments on written work by women of color, 10–11, and on radical feminist literary work, 381.

23. See note 8, above. That it is earlier is evident by comparing the versions: both the circulating manuscript, which predates it, and the Harding and Hintikka essay consistently use the phrasing "male" and "female" (as in "the male worker" or "the female contribution to subsistence"), where the book consistently reads "men" or "women" (as in "women's contribution to subsistence") in paragraphs that are otherwise identical.

24. Michelle Z. Rosaldo's influential essay "The Use and Abuse of Anthropology: Reflections on Feminism and Cross-Cultural Understanding" was published in *Signs* 5 (Spring, 1980): 389–417, and may very well have affected Hartsock's claims here, directly or indirectly in the comments of the readers of the manuscript. In the essay, Rosaldo calls feminist theory to account, including her own earlier work, as she questions how anthropology and cross-cultural claims are

used to construct origins and universals about women and their subordination. She suggests that "gender" is a radically specific social construction, history- and culture-bound, not at all universal in its implications or contents.

25. I believe this powerful use of the term "difference" can be attributed (at least in part) to the speech "The Master's Tools Will Never Dismantle the Master's House" given by Audre Lorde at the Second Sex Conference, New York, September 29, 1979, and subsequently published in *This Bridge Called My Back: Writings by Radical Women of Color*, ed. Cherríe Moraga and Gloria Anzaldúa, foreword by Toni Cade Bambara (Watertown: Persephone, 1981; rpt. New York: Kitchen Table: Women of Color P, 1984) 98–101. The essay is also rpt. in Audre Lorde, *Sister Outsider: Essays and Speeches* (Trumansburg: Crossing, 1984), 110–111. Compare also: *Common Differences: Conflicts in Black and White Feminist Perspectives*, Gloria I. Joseph and Jill Lewis, eds. (Garden City: Anchor/Doubleday, 1981). Acknowledgments mention Audre Lorde and Toni Cade Bambara.

26. In a discussion of the work of Sandra Harding, Jaggar names, for example, physically challenged women, lesbian women, women of color, colonized or immigrant women, working-class women, white/Anglo women, Hispanas, Black women, and "other historically silenced women," and facetiously puts them together into "physically challenged Jewish lesbians of color" in order to dispute the ranking of oppressions (386).

27. She cites Adrienne Rich, *On Lies, Secrets, and Silence* (New York: Norton, 1979); Elly Bulkin from *Sinister Wisdom* 6 (Spring, 1980); and bell hooks, *Ain't I a Woman?* (Boston: South End, 1981). Conspicuously missing are, say, *Common Differences* (1981), *This Bridge Called My Back* (1981), or earlier *conditions five: the black women's issue* (1979).

28. For an example of the same taxonomy operating to produce the position "radical feminism," see Hester Eisenstein, *Contemporary Feminist Thought* (London: Allen and Unwin, 1984).

29. "Socialist feminists believe, therefore, that a primary condition for the adequacy of a feminist theory, indeed for the adequacy of any theory, is that it should represent the world from the standpoint of women" (370). Keeping within the specialized meaning of the word "standpoint" this reduces the category "socialist feminist" radically. Without the specialized meaning, it could very well describe any feminist.

30. Because of this strong link with feminist object relations, the group of "standpoint theorists" seems to be missing someone: the name Nancy Chodorow appears conspicuously absent since it is her development of psychoanalytic theory that has grounded and inspired the work of most of these theorists. Chodorow is mentioned by Jaggar earlier, first in her description of socialist feminism and human nature (126, 140) and then in her discussion of the politics of socialist feminism (320). Jaggar cites criticisms of Chodorow by "socialist feminists" unnamed (163, n. 9 or 347, n. 37) except for Ann Ferguson (347, n. 37); impersonalized, while both full, citations to Chodorow's book are familiarly abbreviated: *Mothering* (163, 347), rather than *The Reproduction of Mothering: Psychoanalysis and the Sociology of Gender* (Berkeley: U of California P, 1978). My assumption is that Chodorow is not included because she does not explicitly make epistemological claims in Jaggar's terms.

31. Hartsock's work is indeed problematic in relation to Jaggar's taxonomy; however, it is also true here that Jaggar has misleadingly constructed the quotation from Hartsock that leads her to this particular observation. She has just quoted Hartsock attempting to describe how deeply material women's experience is in contrast with abstract masculinity, but appropriates her description out of context, giving a utopian cast—a vision of the future that the standpoint of women opens to—rather than the description of present possibility that may through achievement become the feminist standpoint. Jaggar's different notion of achievement here leads her to misread Hartsock in this instance.

32. Echols points out: "This book [*Feminist Politics and Human Nature*] has a great deal to recommend it, but it suffers from the failure to situate the women being studied within the move-

ment. As a consequence, Jaggar occasionally misidentifies certain individuals and groups as when she refers to the politico group WITCH as a radical feminist group" (ftn. 74, 306).

33. Ftn. 46, 392.

34. Jane Gallop, Marianne Hirsch, and Nancy K. Miller, "Criticizing Feminist Criticism," in *Conflicts in Feminism*, eds. Marianne Hirsch and Evelyn Fox Keller (New York: Routledge, 1990) 349–69.

35. Marjorie Pryse and Hortense J. Spillers, eds., *Conjuring: Black Women, Fiction, and Literary Tradition* (Bloomington: Indiana UP, 1985). Gallop's discussion of *Conjuring* in *Around 1981* contains a couple of strange elisions. One thread (of several) Gallop develops concerns interracial relations among white women and women of color. Gallop wonders that such interracial relations are somehow conspicuously absent at particular moments from this text. "The lesbian connections that Pryse, Walker, and Lorde celebrate are between black women. . . . The introduction's exploration of 'the bond between women' never once mentions interracial female bonds" (160). Of course, Gallop is wrong about Lorde, who does celebrate sexually interracial bonds, in her writing (Gallop mentions *Zami*) and in her life. And, oddly, Gallop never mentions that the editorial pair, Pryse and Spillers, represent an interracial collaboration. One wonders whether Gallop here unconsciously makes the point that white women do not always know an interracial relationship when they see one.

36. Jaggar, *Feminist Politics and Human Nature* (Totowa, New Jersey: Rowman and Allanheld; Sussex: Harvester; 1983) 10–11.

37. *Bridge, Home Girls*, and *Cuentos: Stories by Latinas*, ed. Alma Gomez, Cherríe Moraga, and Mariane Romo-Carmona (1983). See Stella Dong, "Kitchen Table: Publishing for Third World Women," *Small Press* 2 (January/February, 1985): 26–31.

38. Donna Haraway, "Situated Knowledges: The Science Question in Feminism and the Privilege of Partial Perspective," in *Simians, Cyborgs, and Women: The Reinvention of Nature* (New York: Routledge, 1991).

39. Chandra Talpade Mohanty, Ann Russo, and Lourdes Torres, eds., *Third World Women and the Politics of Feminism* (Bloomington: Indiana UP, 1991).

40. This is Hartsock's synthesis of critiques by Nancy Fraser and Linda Nicholson, Jane Flax, Iris Young, Susan Hekman, Kathy Ferguson, Teresa de Lauretis and possibly unnamed others. Hartsock's words here do not encapsulate my own understanding of these critiques, but entering into them is not my purpose here. I quote from Hartsock's talk with her permission.

41. Toril Moi, *Sexual/Textual Politics: Feminist Literary Theory* (New York: Routledge, 1985).

3. THE POLITICS OF THE ORAL AND THE WRITTEN

1. Bernice Johnson Reagon, "Coalition Politics: Turning the Century," in *Home Girls: A Black Feminist Anthology*, ed. Barbara Smith (New York: Kitchen Table: Women of Color P, 1983).

2. Che Sandoval, "Feminism and Racism," in *Making Face, Making Soul*, ed. Gloria Anzaldúa (San Francisco: Aunt Lute, 1990) 66.

3. Women who sang with Sweet Honey sometime in the period prior to "Coalition Politics," 1976–1983, were Bernice Johnson Reagon, Evelyn Maria Harris, Patricia Johnson, Louise Robinson, Carol Lynne Maillard, Ysaye Maria Barnwell, Yasmeen Bheti Williams, Aisha Kahlil. Some exemplary recordings of this period are: *Sweet Honey in the Rock* (Flying Fish Records, 22, 1976), *Believe I'll Move On . . . See What the End's Gonna Be* (Redwood Records, 3500, 1978), *Good News* (Flying Fish Records, 245, 1981), *We All . . . Everyone of Us* (Flying Fish, 317, 1983). See also *Give Your Hands to Struggle: The Evolution of a Freedom Fighter, Songs by Bernice Reagon* (Paredon, 1028, 1975). See also Bernice Johnson Reagon and Sweet Honey in the Rock, *We Who Believe in Freedom* (New York: Anchor Doubleday, 1993).

4. This jacket material is written by Ivy Young.

5. "No Hidin' Place" (1977, Thumbelina Music BMI); *Lesbian Concentrate* (Olivia Records, 915, 1977).

6. Many feminist artists and theorists have acutely and movingly contributed to this analysis/metaphor/destabilization of "home," or elaborated upon Reagon's use here. Among them I'll mention three highly influential academic essays that explicitly worked theoretically from/within the apparatus for the production of feminist culture: Minnie Bruce Pratt's art-theoretical essay "Identity: Skin Blood Heart," in *Yours in Struggle: Three Feminist Perspectives on Anti-Semitism and Racism*, ed. Elly Bulkin, Minnie Bruce Pratt, and Barbara Smith (Brooklyn: Long Haul P, 1984), and two essays that built upon it: Biddy Martin and Chandra Mohanty, "Feminist Politics: What's Home Got to Do with It?" in *Feminist Studies/Critical Studies*, ed. Teresa de Lauretis (Bloomington: Indiana UP, 1986) 191–212; and Caren Kaplan, "Deterritorializations: The Rewriting of Home and Exile in Western Feminist Discourse," *Cultural Critique* 9 (Spring 1987): 187–98.

7. Bernice Johnson Reagon, "The Power of Communal Song," in *Cultures in Contention*, ed. Douglas Kahn and Diane Neumaier (Seattle: Real Comet, 1985) 172–79; Holly Near, "Smile beneath Your Tears: Women's Song and Resistance in Uruguay," also in *Cultures in Contention*, 76–81.

8. Members of the Freedom Singers were Charles Neblett, Bernice Johnson, Cordell Reagon, and Rutha M. Harris (see photo in *Cultures in Contention*, 174).

9. Gail Jordan, Mattie Casey, Mary Ethel Jones, Jacqueline Howard, and Bernice Johnson Reagon (see photo in *Cultures in Contention*, 175).

10. ©1973 Hereford Music, new words added 1983; on Holly Near, *Watch Out!* (Redwood Records, 406, 1984).

11. Bernikow, introduction, *The World Split Open: Four Centuries of Women Poets in England and America, 1552–1950* (New York: Vintage/Random House, 1974) 41–42.

12. June Jordan, preface, *Passion: New Poems, 1977–1980* (Boston: Beacon P, 1980) xxv.

13. Jan Clausen, *A Movement of Poets: Thoughts on Poetry and Feminism* (Brooklyn: Long Haul P, 1982) 37.

14. Betsy Erkkila, "Dickinson and Rich: Toward a Theory of Female Poetic Influence," *American Literature* 56 (December 1984): 546.

15. *Snapshots, Necessities*, and *Patience* (New York: Norton).

16. From "Vesuvius" in *On Lies, Secrets, and Silence: Selected Prose 1966–1978* (New York: Norton, 1979) 160.

17. (New York: Norton).

18. In her call for a lesbian-feminist reading she is quoting Toni McNaron, 157. See Rebecca Patterson, *The Riddle of Emily Dickinson* (Boston: Houghton, 1951) and her posthumous collection of work, edited and with an introduction by Margaret H. Freeman, *Emily Dickinson's Imagery* (Amherst: U of Massachusetts P, 1979). Faderman's essay "Emily Dickinson's Letters to Sue Gilbert," *The Massachusetts Review* 18 (Summer 1977): 197–225, formed the basis for her book *Surpassing the Love of Men: Romantic Friendship and Love between Women from the Renaissance to the Present* (New York: Morrow, 1981); from her introduction: "This book began as a study of Emily Dickinson's love poems and letters to Sue Gilbert, the woman who became her sister-in-law." Fundamental to the acceptance of the lesbian identification of Dickinson (and constitutive of a historically specific construction of women's sexuality—our feminist stakes in the idea "lesbian") is the widely influential work of Carroll Smith-Rosenberg (to whom Faderman also refers in her introduction), "The Female World of Love and Ritual: Relations between Women in Nineteenth-Century America," *Signs* 1 (Autumn 1975): 1–29.

19. In *The Fact of a Doorframe: Poems Selected and New, 1950–1984* (New York, Norton, 1984).

20. *The Marriage of Emily Dickinson: A Study of the Fascicles* (Lexington: UP of Kentucky). In his acknowledgments, Shurr prominently states, "It will be recognized immediately that behind this book stands the editorial work of Ralph W. Franklin. Since the death of Emily Dickinson no

one has been able to study her poems exactly as Dickinson left them, until the reconstruction of the original booklets was published by Franklin" (ix).

21. *The Norton Anthology of Literature by Women: The Tradition in English* (New York: Norton, 1985); biographical introduction to Dickinson and selected poems and letters: 839–73, selected bibliography: 2399–400. Gilbert and Gubar's response to the contest for Dickinson as lesbian/poet is conspicuous silence in selections of poems, letters, and bibliographic materials. Their own stakes in a heterosexual analysis of the "Master" letters require this (they are the first two letters selected, 867–70); prominently in the introduction, they say of them: "Yet her 'Master' letters, with their deliberate effacement of the addressee's identity, are just as clearly explorations of the general relationship between male power and female powerlessness, male authority and female dependency, as they are pleas for romantic reassurance from a particular man" (841). The heterosexual recuperation of Dickinson in the *Norton*, constructed by the suppression or ignorance of contesting discourses, is agonistically declaimed in Suzanne Juhasz's *Feminist Critics Read Emily Dickinson* (Bloomington: Indiana UP, 1983). As Paula Bennett astutely notices in her review of Juhasz's collection (*The Women's Review of Books* 1 [March 1984]: 10–11), in the editorial construction of the collection an article offering a lesbian reading of Dickinson's work is followed immediately by a direct rebuttal, the only article so addressed, and without the opportunity of response (Adalaide Morris, " 'The Love of Thee—a Prism Be': Men and Women in the Love Poetry of Emily Dickinson," 98–113, is answered by Margaret Homans, " 'Oh, Vision of Language!': Dickinson's Poems of Love and Death," 114–32). The best current book addressing and reframing these issues is Martha Nell Smith's *Rowing in Eden: Rereading Emily Dickinson* (Austin: U of Texas P, 1992).

22. (Boston, Houghton Mifflin, 1980).

23. For this use of "literacy" I am inspired by a similar definition used by Robert Pattison in his book *On Literacy: The Politics of the Word from Homer to the Age of Rock* (Oxford: Oxford UP, 1982). This book is an opinionated and witty synthesis of a variety of literatures: for example, on cross-cultural anthropological and sociological materials about literacy, on the differences between "oral" and "written" "consciousness," on the history of print in the "West," on literacy and modernization in "developing" nations, and on current debates in the United States about the decline of reading and writing skills among children and the effects of television. See especially Pattison's engaging bibliographic essay, 221–35. Lamentably, it is also extremely problematic for feminist use. Pattison's text might very well stand as exemplar of the specious generic masculine, which pervades the text to such an extent and with such substantive effects on meaning as to make parts of it almost unusable.

24. For much of my understanding of the class valences the term "literacy" carries and for a strategy for examining it (in reading, writing, print, and communication technologies) as historically and culturally/economically specific, I am indebted to Richard Ohmann, "Literacy, Technology, and Monopoly Capital," *College English* 47 (1985): 675–89.

25. Donna Haraway also uses the term "story" to talk about ideological narratives in the production of the history of science. See, for example, her comments on story in "Primatology is Politics by Other Means" (edited version), in *Feminist Approaches to Science*, ed. Ruth Bleier (New York: Pergamon, 1986) 79–81. Haraway emphasizes what might be called the story-field. Within this field numbers of stories contest: "What determines a 'good' story in the natural and social sciences is partly decided by available social visions of these possible worlds. Description is determined by vision; facts and theories are perceived within stories; the worlds for which human beings contest are made of meanings. Meanings are tremendously material forces—much like food and sex. And, like food and sex, meanings are social constructions that determine the quality of people's lives." My use of the word "story" emphasizes the identities that each story constructs.

26. Paul Lauter, "Race and Gender in the Shaping of the American Literary Canon: A Case Study from the Twenties," *Feminist Studies* 9 (1983): 435–62.

27. See Bettina Aptheker, *Tapestries of Life: Women's Work, Women's Consciousness, and the Meaning of Daily Experience* (Amherst: Massachusetts UP, 1989) for theoretical and strategic dis-

cussion of "pivoting the center" in examination of the apparatus for the production of feminist culture.

28. "Just as the nations of the third world are 'emerging' in the sense that the Euro-American world has 'discovered' them, so is 'the Third Woman' revealing herself to us, though she has always been present. Her hyphenated existence—as Asian American, Black American, Mexican American, or American Indian—imbues her angle of vision with perceptions that revitalize our concepts of tradition and folklore, language and imagination" (xxvii). Fisher's delight in and strain for linguistic play can be seen in the titles of her other MLA books mentioned earlier, *Minority Language and Literature: Retrospective and Perspective* and *Afro-American Literature: The Reconstruction of Instruction.*

29. See, for example, Walter Ong's *Orality and Literacy: The Technologizing of the Word* (New York: Methuen, 1982). For a brief overview of these cultural types and their corresponding communications media, see Donald M. Lowe, *History of Bourgeois Perception* (Chicago: U of Chicago P, 1982) 2–5.

30. See also Raymond Williams, *Keywords: A Vocabulary of Culture and Society* (New York: Oxford UP, 1976) 76–82.

31. A mini-bibliography shows how rich these two literatures were in the early and mid-eighties: see Evelyn Torton Beck, ed., *Nice Jewish Girls: A Lesbian Anthology* (New York: Crossing, 1984; Watertown: Persephone, 1982); Susannah Heschel, ed., *On Being a Jewish Feminist: A Reader* (New York: Schocken, 1983); Melanie Kaye/Kantrowitz and Irene Klepfisz, eds., *The Tribe of Dina: A Jewish Women's Anthology*, special issue of *Sinister Wisdom* 29/30 (1986); Susan Weidman Schneider, ed., *Jewish and Female: A Guide and Source Book for Today's Jewish Woman* (New York: Simon, 1984); Elly Bulkin, Barbara Smith, Minnie Bruce Pratt, eds., *Yours in Struggle: Three Feminist Perspectives on Anti-Semitism and Racism* (New York: Long Haul, 1984); on Italian American feminists: an anthropological examination in Micaela di Leonardo, *The Varieties of Ethnic Experience: Kinship, Class, and Gender among California Italian Americans* (Ithaca: Cornell UP, 1985); and expressive writings from Helen Barolini, ed., *The Dream Book: An Anthology of Writings by Italian American Women* (New York: Schocken, 1985).

32. Dir. Allie Light and Irving Saraf, Light-Saraf Films, 1981.

33. Compare, for example, Ruth Finnegan's discussion of the lyric form in oral poetry: "Though certain oral poems like epics and some panegyrics are chanted or declaimed only, sung delivery is the most common characteristic of oral poetry. Throughout this book (as in many discussions of oral literature) the term 'song' is often used interchangeably with 'poem' in the sense of a lyric, and the quickest way to suggest the scope of 'oral poetry' is to say that it largely coincides with that of the popular term 'folk song.' Lyric is thus an extremely important and wide category of oral poetry." *Oral Poetry: Its Nature, Significance, and Social Context* (Cambridge: Cambridge UP, 1977) 13.

34. (Berkeley: U of California P, 1968, 2nd ed. revised and expanded 1985). "Assemblage" is Rothenberg's own term.

35. (Toronto: U of Toronto P, 1962).

36. I've discussed this kind of making of objects in my story "What is an Object?" and in chapter 1, describing my debts to Bruno Latour and Steve Woolgar, *Laboratory Life* (Beverly Hills: Sage, 1979). I've discussed the history of the editions of Emily Dickinson in similar terms in "Canons without Innocence: Academic Practices and Feminist Practices Making the Poem in the Work of Emily Dickinson and Audre Lorde" (diss. U of California, Santa Cruz, 1987).

37. Jerome J. McGann, "The Text, the Poem, and the Problem of Historical Method," *New Literary History* 12 (1980–81): 269–88.

38. Robert Escarpit, *The Sociology of Literature*, 2nd ed. (London: Frank Cass, 1971; first French edition, 1958).

39. Richard A. Peterson, "'Six Constraints on the Production of Literary Works," *Poetics* (1985): 45–68.

40. Mark Schulman, "Gender and Typographic Culture: Beginning to Unravel The 500-Year Mystery," *Technology and Women's Voices: Keeping in Touch*, ed. Cheris Kramarae (New York: Routledge, 1988) 98-115.

41. Jerome J. McGann, "Interpretation, Meaning, and Textual Criticism: A Homily," *Text 3: Transactions of the Society for Textual Scholarship*, ed. D. C. Greetham and W. Speed Hill (New York: AMS, 1987) 55-62.

42. International Commission for the Study of Communication Problems, UNESCO, *Many Voices, One World (The MacBride Report)* (UNESCO, 1980, 1984); Group for the Critical Study of Colonial Discourse, *Inscriptions*, special issue on Feminism and the Critique of Colonial Discourse 3/4 (1988); Heidi I. Hartmann, ed., *Computer Chips and Paper Clips: Technology and Women's Employment*, vol. II (National Academy, 1987); Louis Kampf and Paul Lauter, *The Politics of Literature: Dissenting Essays on the Teaching of English* (New York: Random/Pantheon, 1970).

43. Walter J. Ong, Marshall McLuhan, Eric Havelock; such as: Ong, *Orality and Literacy: the Technologizing of the Word* (New York: Methuen, 1982); McLuhan, *The Gutenberg Galaxy: The Making of Typographic Man* (U of Toronto P, 1968); Havelock, *Origins of Western Literacy* (Toronto: Ontario Institute for Studies in Education, 1976). Robert Pattison, Ruth Finnegan, Brian Stock; such as: Pattison, *On Literacy* (Oxford UP, 1982); Finnegan, *Oral Poetry: Its Nature, Significance, and Social Context* (Cambridge UP, 1977); Stock, *Implications of Literacy* (Princeton, 1983).

44. Donald M. Lowe, *History of Bourgeois Perception* (U of Chicago P, 1982); Armand Mattelart, *Transnationals and the Third World: The Struggle for Culture* (South Hadley, Mass.: Bergin and Garvey, 1983); Armand Mattelart, *Multinational Corporations and the Control of Culture* (New Jersey: Humanities, 1979); Edward W. Ploman and L. Clark Hamilton, *Copyright: Intellectual Property in the Information Age* (Cambridge: MIT, 1982).

45. Some materials I've found especially suggestive in imagining our implication in these elements and layerings of the apparatus of literary production are Judith Newton and Deborah Rosenfelt, "Introduction: Toward a Materialist-Feminist Criticism," *Feminist Criticism and Social Change: Sex, Class, and Race in Literature and Culture*, ed. Judith Newton and Deborah Rosenfelt (New York: Methuen, 1985) xv-xxxix; Lila Abu-Lughod, *Veiled Sentiments: Honor and Poetry in a Bedouin Society* (Berkeley: U of California P, 1986); and Paul Lauter, "Race and Gender in the Shaping of the American Literary Canon: A Case Study from the Twenties," *Feminist Studies* 9 (1983): 435-62.

46. Leonore Hoffmann and Deborah Rosenfelt, eds., *Teaching Women's Literature from a Regional Perspective* (New York: MLA, 1982).

47. Katie King, "Audre Lorde's Lacquered Layerings: The Lesbian Bar as a Site of Literary Production," *Cultural Studies* 2 (1988): 321-42; and also "Canons Without Innocence," 130-219.

48. *Chosen Poems: Old and New* (New York: Norton, 1982); *Undersong: Chosen Poems Old and New*, revised ed. (New York: Norton, 1992).

49. See chapter 5.

50. Jan Clausen, *A Movement of Poets: Thoughts on Poetry and Feminism* (Brooklyn: Long Haul, 1982) 16.

51. Another model for considering these politicizing concerns is Janice Winship, *Inside Women's Magazines* (London: Pandora, 1987).

52. Stella Dong, "Kitchen Table: Publishing for Third World Women," *Small Press* 2 (1985): 26-31.

53. *Heresies 20: The Activism Issue* (1985); esp. Blanche Wiesen Cook, "Sisters in Support of Sisters in South Africa" (42-44); Susan Ortega, "Art Against Apartheid" (45-50). *Heresies 22: Art in Unestablished Channels* (1987). Douglas Kahn and Diane Neumaier, eds., *Cultures in Contention* (Seattle: Real Comet, 1985); esp. DeeDee Halleck, "Paper Tiger Television" (36-41); Judith Francisca Baca, "Our People Are the Internal Exiles" (62-75); Holly Near, "Smile beneath Your Tears" (76-81); Honor Ford-Smith, "Sistren: Jamaican Women's Theater" (84-91); Martha Gever, "Video Politics: Early Feminist Projects" (92-101); Suzanne Lacy and Leslie Labowitz, "Feminist Media

Strategies for Political Performance" (122–33); Bernice Johnson Reagon, "The Power of Communal Song" (172–79); Peter King, "The Art of Billboard Utilizing" (198–203); Hans Haacke, "Where the Consciousness Industry is Concentrated" (204–235).

4. LESBIANISM AS FEMINISM'S MAGICAL SIGN

This essay originated in the early eighties as a lecture for Donna Haraway's feminist theory class at the University of California, Santa Cruz, and owes most to her enthusiasm, critical example, suggestive work, and acute questioning of feminist dogmas. I want to thank the following people for also having read and commented on it early on: Carolyn Clark, Chris Grella, Debbie Gordon, Barbara Gottfried, Lisa Lowe, Cathy Reback, Zoë Sofia, Paula Treichler. It is reprinted here, substantively unrevised, from *Communication* 9 (1986): 65–91.

   1. The critique of the anti-pornography movement is complexly intertwined with the examination of "the politics of sexuality." This phrase characterizes a feminist reappraisal of sexual practices, the sex industry, sexology, and sex laws. Among the first voices to question feminist anti-pornography strategies was Ellen Willis in her 1979 article "Feminism, Moralism, and Pornography," *The Village Voice* (October 15, 1979). Also striking in its polemical strengths and historical reinscription is the work of Alice Echols (such as "Cultural Feminism: Feminist Capitalism and the Anti-pornography Movement," *Social Text* 3 [1983]: 34–53). The anthology *Powers of Desire: The Politics of Sexuality*, ed. Ann Snitow, Christine Stansell, and Sharon Thompson (New York: Monthly Review/New Feminist Library, 1983) showcases the discourse on "the politics of sexuality," as do the papers given at the Ninth Conference on "The Scholar and the Feminist: Toward a Politics of Sexuality," held on April 24, 1982, at Barnard College in New York and now collected in Carole S. Vance, ed., *Pleasure and Danger: Exploring Female Sexuality* (Boston: Routledge, 1984). Coverage of the conference also sparked charged debate (see *Off Our Backs*, June 12, 1982, for initial reporting, and subsequent issues (July, September, and November) for replies and objections by Gayle Rubin, Amber Hollibaugh, and others, including a petition in support of the conference). Also prominent in this reappraisal of sexuality is the discussion of lesbian sadomasochism and it is from the position of its advocacy that theorists Gayle Rubin and Pat Califia criticize the anti-porn movement; see also Nancy Wechsler (1981) and many essays in *Coming to Power*, ed. Samois (Palo Alto: Up Press, 1981). Paired with *Coming to Power* in refutation is *Against Sadomasochism: A Radical Feminist Analysis*, ed. Robin Ruth Linden, Darleen R. Pagano, Diana E. H. Russell, and Susan Leigh Star (East Palo Alto: Frog in the Well, 1982).

   2. In the United States, the word "difference" is associated with cultural particularism and with race and class criticism of "the white women's movement." The literature of the discourse on antiracist practice is becoming increasingly extensive. *This Bridge Called My Back: Writings by Radical Women of Color*, ed. Cherríe Moraga and Gloria Anzaldúa (Watertown: Persephone, 1981) marks an important formulation of the constituencies of the category "women of color," and one beginning of the U.S. discourse on "difference." See also *Common Differences: Conflicts in Black and White Feminist Perspectives*, ed. Gloria I. Joseph and Jill Lewis (Garden City: Anchor/Doubleday, 1981); *All the Women Are White, All the Blacks are Men, but Some of Us Are Brave: Black Women's Studies*, ed. Gloria T. Hull, Patricia Bell Scott, and Barbara Smith (Old Westbury: Feminist, 1982); Bettina Aptheker, *Women's Legacy: Essays on Race, Sex, and Class* (Amherst: U of Massachusetts P, 1982). The formation of Kitchen Table: Women of Color Press provides an important visibility for antiracist work and literary, critical, and theoretical work by women of color; see, for example, *Home Girls: A Black Feminist Anthology*, ed. Barbara Smith (New York: Kitchen Table: Women of Color P, 1983). bell hooks's discussion of feminist theory in *Feminist Theory: from margin to center* (Boston: South End, 1984) challenges the unitary construction of "the women's movement"; on the politics of antiracist work and constructions of political identity, see the writing on "oppositional consciousness" by Chela Sandoval as well as the work of Cherríe Moraga, for example; see also Moraga's *Loving in the War Years* (Boston: South End, 1983).

3. In *Radical Feminism*, ed. Anne Koedt, Ellen Levine, and Anita Rapone (New York: Quadrangle/New York Times Book Co., 1973). This is an anthology of materials from *Notes from the First Year* (1968), *Notes from the Second Year* (1970), and *Notes from the Third Year* (1971).

4. See Sidney Abbott and Barbara Love's *Sappho Was a Right-On Woman* (New York: Stein, 1973) 117. The Daughters of Bilitis (DOB) is a homophile organization founded in the early fifties and predating gay liberation. See Ti-Grace Atkinson's *Amazon Odyssey* (New York: Links, 1974) both to confirm these sentiments and to note the subtle distinctions Atkinson draws around "lesbianism" for various audiences. Though this collection doesn't contain the text of the speech reported by Abbott and Love, it does contain the text of the speech delivered at DOB's opening of the first lesbian center in the United States, January 4, 1971 ("Strategy and Tactics: A Presentation of Political Lesbianism," 135–89). Atkinson's criticisms of homophile lesbianism are much the center of her statement, as they are also in "Lesbianism and Feminism," 83–88. A more sympathetic aspect emerges in her "Lesbianism and Feminism: Justice for Women as 'Unnatural,' " 131–34, originally prepared in response to the *Time* disclosure of Kate Millet's bisexuality, and she says "at the request of the *New York Times*, Op-Ed page." Rejected by the *Times*, it was published March 30, 1972, in Jill Johnston's *Village Voice* column.

5. Ware (New York: Tower, 1970). I chose these particular books because they impressed me so much at the time they came out and yet have not remained powerful in the women's movement; both seem semi-forgotten and terribly dated. Ware's book can be compared interestingly to Shulamith Firestone, *The Dialectic of Sex: The Case for Feminist Revolution* (New York: Morrow, 1970), a book that came out of the same political moment yet is a very different book with a different project, purpose, history, and taxonomy. Firestone is still current, Ware practically forgotten. Abbott and Love's book can be linked to Adrienne Rich's *Of Woman Born* (New York: Norton, 1976) in that Rich's book totally eclipses Abbott and Love in subsequent feminist constructions of lesbian experience. *Radical Feminism* is a general resource especially related to the construction of lesbianism as a political identity.

6. Pamela Allen, *Free Space: A Perspective on the Small Group in Women's Liberation* (Washington: Times Change, 1970); abridged rpt. in Koedt, Levine, Rapone, eds., *Radical Feminism*, 271–79.

7. Sargent, ed., *Women and Revolution: A Discussion of the Unhappy Marriage of Marxism and Feminism* (Boston: South End, 1981). Jaggar (Sussex: Harvester; Totowa: Rowman & Allenheld, 1983).

8. By March 1979, Bantam's edition of *The Dialectic of Sex* had gone through nine printings. In contrast, Atkinson's *Amazon Odyssey* went through only one printing. Atkinson speaks of her problems with publication and the circumstances of the publication of *Amazon Odyssey* in her afterword, ccxxxiii–cclviv.

9. Ware's only personal reference—she identifies herself as a founder of New York Radical Feminists—is in the third person (56).

10. Bird is characterized by Abbott and Love as "the first well-known Feminist to validate the Lesbian life-style" (in contrast to Ti-Grace Atkinson and Susan Brownmiller), 115–16. "Reform" has strong associations with lesbianism in this time period. In 1969, Miller published her book *A Place for Us* (New York: Bleecker Street P). In 1972, it was picked up by McGraw Hill and in 1973 published in paper by Fawcett Crest.

11. Rita Mae Brown's work, notably *Rubyfruit Jungle* (Plainfield: Daughters, 1973), marks a significant historical moment in this publication history. Adrienne Rich's poetry and polemic construct a new "lesbianism" that elaborates upon what I call "lesbianism as magical sign." Audre Lorde's autobiographical novel *Zami* (Watertown: Persephone, 1982) retells the lesbian stories of the fifties and makes visible and problematic the circumstances of "inclusion" for Black lesbians inside an essentially white bar culture. Especially significant for lesbian literature are the works of whole presses such as Diana, Daughters, and Persephone—now gone—and Naiad Press in Tallahassee, Florida. Ground-breaking anthologies explicitly discussing links and concerns between les-

bianism and antiracism and ethnicity include *This Bridge Called My Back* and *Nice Jewish Girls*, ed. Evelyn Torton Beck (Watertown: Persephone, 1982). Examples of scholarship include Blanche Wiesen Cook (1979), Ellen Ross and Rayna Rapp (1981), Ruddy Darty and Sandee Potter (1984), and the lesbian issue of *Signs* 9 (Summer 1984). Many other examples might be offered.

12. See especially chapter 5, titled "Racism: The Sexism of the Family of Man," 105–125. A striking contrast between Ware and Firestone is their differing uses of Calvin Hernton's *Sex and Racism in America* (New York: Grove, 1965). Firestone opens her chapter on racism citing it, and clearly the focus for her in the word sex is about sexuality—it leads directly into her description of "the thing" between white men and Black women, and white women and Black men. Firestone's look at racism is entirely through the lens of (hetero)sexuality. In contrast, Ware's reference to Hernton is a reference to "sex" as gender. Her discussion leads into the pitting of Black women and men against each other in employment practices. This is an example of the uneasy stake she has in promoting the alliance between Black and white women as women, paralleling the move she makes in "Black Feminism."

13. Another interesting point about the juxtaposition of these books is the common focus of feminism side-by-side with the complete invisibility of the concerns of each to the other. Ware's book is without mention of lesbianism, and Abbott and Love's invokes Black activists only as models to be emulated, as another "outsider" group. Firestone is also without mention of lesbianism though she mentions homosexuality, usually in association with men, and often homophobically. Her assumptions about heterosexuality, for example, include its preference for the sake of "sheer physical fit" (240).

14. (Women's Wax Works, A001, [no date?]).

15. The assumption seems to be coming back into feminist contention within the conversation on the politics of sexuality.

16. For some of the flow of this contest over the relation between the word "lesbian" and the word "feminist" just in Atkinson's own writing, see *Amazon Odyssey* and my comments on it above, note 4.

17. Monique Wittig, "One is Not Born a Woman," *Feminist Issues* 1 (1981): 47–54.

18. Redstockings of the Women's Liberation Movement, "The Pseudo-left/Lesbian Alliance against Feminism," in *Feminist Revolution: An Abridged Edition with Additional Writings* (New York: Redstockings, 1975); abridged rpt. (New York: Random House, 1978) 190–98.

19. See Rich's "Compulsory Heterosexuality and Lesbian Existence," *Signs* 5 (1980): 631–60.

20. Catharine A. MacKinnon, "Feminism, Marxism, Method, and the State: An Agenda for Theory," *Signs* 7 (1982): 515–44; and essays from *Pleasure and Danger*.

5. PRODUCING SEX, THEORY, AND CULTURE

When I first considered this essay I talked with some colleagues about making it fully collaborative, but practical time constraints enforced more single authorial responsibility, and it ends up being written in my style and with my special concerns centered. Still, quite a few people were involved in the thinking and writing of this essay. Biddy Martin and Evelyn Fox Keller urged me to undertake it for the book *Conflicts in Feminism*, and Lata Mani, Ruth Frankenberg, and Harryette Mullen all spent many hours talking about it and reading pieces while we still mulled over the possibilities of making it a collective effort and after. Caren Kaplan and Donna Haraway were enCOURAGEing readers during the processes of writing and Chela Sandoval was inspirational in the midst of life's traumas. Marianne Hirsch, Carla Freccero, and Juliana Schiesari were suggestive readers and editors, and Eve Sedgwick and her Duke graduate students in "Literature and the 'Invention of Homosexuality'" gave me a chance to argue my conclusions and see new connections with graduate student experiences in making theory. Chandra Mohanty helped in final revisions. A Mellon Fellowship from Cornell University gave me more time to work and write. This essay is reprinted here, substantively unrevised, from *Conflicts in Feminism*, ed. Marianne Hirsch and Evelyn Fox Keller (New York: Routledge, 1990).

1. Some of these formulations I've already argued in the previous chapter. For some specific purges of lesbians and lesbian zap actions 1968-1972, see Sidney Abbott and Barbara Love, *Sappho Was a Right-On Woman: A Liberated View of Lesbianism* (New York: Stein & Day, 1973). For the political locations of gay recruitment, see John D'Emilio, *Sexual Politics, Sexual Communities: The Making of a Homosexual Minority in the United States, 1940-1970* (Chicago: U of Chicago P, 1983). Contemplating and analyzing lesbian repositionings and new coalitions are: Gayle Rubin, "The Leather Menace: Comments on Politics and S/M," in *Coming to Power: Writings and Graphics on Lesbian S/M*, ed. Samois (Palo Alto: Up P, 1982); Combahee River Collective, "A Black Feminist Statement" (April 1977), in *Capitalist Patriarchy and the Case for Socialist Revolution*, ed. Zillah Eisenstein (New York: Monthly Review P, 1978); Chela Sandoval, "Chapter Two: Toward a Theory of Oppositional Consciousness: U.S. Third World Feminism and the U.S. Women's Movement" (March 14, 1988 draft unpublished diss. History of Consciousness, University of California, Santa Cruz). Compare with Donna Landry, "Beat Me! Beat Me! Feminist Appropriations of Sade" (ms. 1984).

2. In previous work, I've suggested how "lesbianism as magical sign"—the formation fractured in these "Sex Wars"—was historically constructed; I've also suggested that the polarization of the sex radicals from identity politics is currently in flux. See both the previous chapter and Katie King, "Audre Lorde's Lacquered Layerings: The Lesbian Bar as a Site of Literary Production," *Cultural Studies* 2 (1988): 321-42.

3. The controversial Scholar and the Feminist IX Conference, "Toward a Politics of Sexuality," held on April 24 at Barnard College, New York City.

4. Rubin, "The Leather Menace"; B. Ruby Rich, "Review Essay: Feminism and Sexuality in the 1980s," *Feminist Studies* 12 (1986): 525-61; Cherríe Moraga, "Played between White Hands: A Response to the Barnard Sexuality Conference Coverage," *off our backs* (July 1982); Barbara Smith, *Home Girls: A Black Feminist Anthology* (New York: Kitchen Table: Women of Color Press, 1983); Hortense Spillers, "Interstices: A Small Drama of Words," in *Pleasure and Danger: Exploring Female Sexuality*, ed. Carole S. Vance (Boston: Routledge, 1984) 73-100; see comments about proliferations of gender in Sandoval, "Oppositional Consciousness"; Barbara Smith, "Toward a Black Feminist Criticism" *conditions: two* (1977): 25-44; and reading of Smith in Teresa de Lauretis, "Eccentric Subjects: Feminist Theory and Historical Consciousness," *Feminist Studies* 16 (Spring 1990).

5. Forming, as they do, the ground of much feminist theory in the academy, I too find it difficult to extricate thinking from them.

6. Sandoval, "Oppositional Consciousness."

7. B. R. Rich, "Review Essay"; Sandoval, "Oppositional Consciousness"; bell hooks [Gloria Watkins], *Feminist Theory: from margin to center* (Boston: South End, 1984); and previous chapters 3 and 4.

8. Ellen Willis, "Feminism, Moralism, and Pornography," *The Village Voice* (October 15, 1979); Vance, *Pleasure and Danger*.

9. Audre Lorde, *Zami: a new spelling of my name* (Watertown: Persephone, 1982); Alice Walker, "A Letter of the Times, or Should This Sado-Masochism Be Saved?" in *Against Sadomasochism: A Radical Feminist Analysis*, ed. Robin Ruth Linden, Darlene R. Pagano, Diana E. H. Russell, Susan Leigh Star (East Palo Alto Calif.: Frog in the Well, 1982) 205-209; Linden, *Against Sadomasochism*.

10. Alice Echols, "The Taming of the Id: Feminist Sexual Politics, 1968-1983," in Vance, *Pleasure and Danger*, 50-72; cf. Hester Eisenstein, *Contemporary Feminist Thought* (Boston: Hall, 1983).

11. Rubin, "The Leather Menace" and "Thinking Sex: Notes for a Radical Theory of the Politics of Sexuality," in Vance, *Pleasure and Danger*, 267–319; Pat Califia, "Feminism and Sado-masochism," *Heresies* 12 (1981).

12. Camilla Decarnin, "Interview with Five Fag-Hagging Women," *Heresies* 12 (1981): 10–14.

13. Joan Nestle, *A Restricted Country* (Ithaca: Firebrand, 1987); Lorde, *Zami*; King, "Audre Lorde's Lacquered Layerings."

14. B. Smith, *Home Girls;* Aurora Levins Morales and Rosario Morales, *Getting Home Alive* (Ithaca: Firebrand, 1986); Cherríe Moraga, *Loving in the War Years* (Boston: South End, 1983); Cherríe Moraga, "The Shadow of a Man"; Dorothy Allison, Tomas Almaguer, and Jackie Goldsby, "An Interview with Cherríe Moraga," *Outlook* 4 (1989): 46–57; Oliva M. Espin, "Cultural and Historical Influences on Sexuality in Hispanic/Latin Women: Implications for Psychotherapy," in Vance, *Pleasure and Danger*, 149–64; Gloria Hull, *Color, Sex, and Poetry: Three Women Writers of the Harlem Renaissance* (Bloomington: Indiana U P, 1987); Cherríe Moraga and Gloria Anzaldúa, *This Bridge Called My Back: Writings by Radical Women of Color* (Watertown: Persephone, 1981); see comments by Chela Sandoval, "Oppositional Consciousness." See also white women commenting on the race of sex: Mab Segrest, *My Mama's Dead Squirrel: Lesbian Essays on Southern Culture* (Ithaca: Firebrand, 1985); Minnie Bruce Pratt, "Identity: Skin, Blood, Heart," in *Yours in Struggle: Feminist Perspectives on Racism and Anti-Semitism*, ed. Elly Bulkin, Minnie Bruce Pratt, and Barbara Smith (New York: Long Haul, 1984); Nestle, *Restricted Country*; Ruth Frankenberg, "The Social Construction of Whiteness" (paper delivered at Feminisms and Cultural Imperialism: Politics of Difference conference, Cornell University, April 23, 1989).

15. The sex you do for money and the sex you do for yourself may be the same or different, may situate one in terms of personal/political identities or may not. Swasti Mitter, *Common Fate, Common Bond: Women in the Global Economy* (London: Pluto P, 1986); Gail Pheterson, ed., *A Vindication of the Rights of Whores* (Seattle: Seal, 1989); Frederique Delacoste and Priscilla Alexander, eds., *Sex Work: Writings by Women in the Sex Industry* (Pittsburgh: Cleis, 1987); Laurie Bell, ed., *Good Girls, Bad Girls: Feminism and Sex Trade Workers Face to Face* (Seattle: Seal, 1987; Toronto: Women's, 1987).

16. Rubin, "Thinking Sex"; cf. Teresa de Lauretis, "Sexual Indifference and Lesbian Representation," *Theatre Journal* 40 (1988): 155–77.

17. Rubin, "Thinking Sex"; Lata Mani, "Multiple Mediations: Feminist Scholarship in the Age of Multi-National Reception," *Feminist Review* 35 (Summer 1990): 24–41.

18. Bernice Johnson Reagon, "Coalition Politics: Turning the Century," in Smith, *Home Girls*, 356–68; Biddy Martin and Chandra Mohanty, "Feminist Politics: What's Home Got To Do with It?" in *Feminist Studies/Critical Studies*, ed. Teresa de Lauretis (Bloomington: Indiana U P, 1986) 191–212; Caren Kaplan, "Deterritorializations: The Rewriting of Home and Exile in Western Feminist Discourse," *Cultural Critique* 9 (1987): 187–98.

19. Todd Jailer, "The Widening Orbit of the University Press," *Small Press* 7 (1989): 10–23; Tonya Bolden Davis, "Publish or Perish," *Small Press* 7 (1989): 31–33.

20. For example, in *Pleasure and Danger*, Hortense Spillers eloquently hungers for a particular naming of sex by Black women, in a particular nonfiction discursive theory. Spillers, "Interstices."

21. See Caren Kaplan's feminist appropriation of Said's "traveling theory" in "Questions of Travel: The Limits of Exile and the Poetics of Displacement" (paper delivered at Modern Language Association, New Orleans, December 30, 1988) and her analysis of mixed genres of deessentialized writing as poetics of displacement in "The Politics of Signification in the Poetics of Displacement: Historical and Literary Dislocation in *Dictee*" (MLA paper, New Orleans, December 28, 1988). See also Sharon Willis, "Feminism's Interrupted Genealogies," *Diacritics* (1988): 29–41. One might also note who is being published in which journals. Now that feminists are published in, for example, *Critical Inquiry, Representations, Diacritics* (examples of cultural analysis), in the major journals of specific disciplines, and with some exciting new academic feminist journals rep-

resenting new political interests and theoretical investments, what has changed in the status of those gatekeeping, brave, academic standbys *Signs* and *Feminist Studies*? Which academic feminists are in each of these locations? Not to mention who is not reading (has never read?) *Sinister Wisdom, Conditions, Calyx, Sage, Trivia, Zeta, Outlook*, for immediate examples? Which of these movement journals has narrowed the range of genres they publish, and for what political reasons?

22. Donna Haraway, "The Promises of Monsters: A Reproductive Politics of the Inappropriate/d Other" (talk at Rochester University, April 20, 1989); Faith Beckett, "Notes on Reading Ogunyemi and Anzaldúa," *HisCon/HerScam: The HistCon Fanzine*, forthcoming.

23. Biddy Martin, "Lesbian Identity and Autobiographical Difference[s]," in *Life/Lines: Theorizing Women's Autobiography*, ed. Bella Brodski and Celeste Schenck (Ithaca: Cornell U P, 1988) 77-103.

24. On radical feminism, Alison Jaggar, *Feminist Politics and Human Nature* (Totowa: Rowman and Allanheld, 1983); Alice Echols, "The New Feminism of Yin and Yang," in *Powers of Desire: The Politics of Sexuality*, ed. Ann Snitow, Christine Stansell, and Sharon Thompson (New York: Monthly Review P/New Feminist Library, 1983) 439-59. On U.S. feminism and Black and lesbian writing, Toril Moi, *Sexual/Textual Politics: Feminist Literary Theory* (New York: Methuen, 1985). For an example of a rehistoricized intervention inscribing a specific definition of feminist theory, Teresa de Lauretis, "Displacing Hegemonic Discourses: Reflections on Feminist Theory in the 1980s," *Inscriptions* 3/4 (1988): 127-44. For an alternative history of radical feminist theory, Alice Echols, "Cultural Feminism: Feminist Capitalism and the Anti-Pornography Movement," *Social Text* 7 (1983): 34-53. Cf. Pamela Allen, *Free Space: A Perspective on the Small Group in Women's Liberation* (Washington: Times Change P, 1970) and Celestine Ware, *Woman Power: The Movement for Women's Liberation* (New York: Tower, 1970); for my alternative analysis, see chapters 1 and 4. For an analysis distinguishing the work of women of color from feminist essentialisms and suggesting a poststructuralist location, see Linda Alcoff, "Cultural Feminism vs. Poststructuralism: The Identity Crisis in Feminist Theory," in *Feminist Theory in Practice and Process*, ed. Micheline R. Malson, Jean F. O'Barr, Sarah Westpahl-Wihe, and Mary Wye (Chicago: U of Chicago P, 1988) 295-326; cf. Sandoval "Oppositional Consciousness." Socialist feminism, its "others" (radical feminism, cultural feminism, Black feminism), and its variants (British and U.S. versions, object-relations or standpoint theorists, and psychoanalytic versions) are implicated in these repositionings and redrawn commonalities.

25. Zap actions, as Celestine Ware points out, are indebted to "elements of Yippie language and psychology," a kind of anarchist protest, sometimes spontaneous, sometimes planned. Here I'm suggesting a genealogy of one strategy in art activism. See Ware, *Woman Power*, 33; compare Douglas Crimp, "AIDS: Cultural Analysis/Cultural Activism," *October* 43 (Winter 1987): 3-16 (look especially at the illustrations documenting various ACT UP actions).

26. Chapter 3 describes some of these, as do: Richard A. Peterson, "Six Constraints on the Production of Literary Works," *Poetics* 14 (1985): 45-68; Robert Escarpit, *Sociology of Literature*, trans. Ernest Pick (London: Frank Cass, 1971; 1st French ed., 1958; 1st English ed., 1965); Mark Schulman, "Gender and Typographic Culture: Beginning to Unravel the 500-Year Mystery," in *Technology and Women's Voices: Keeping in Touch*, ed. Cheris Kramarae (New York: Routledge, 1988) 98-115. See also, Bruce Robbins, "The Politics of Theory," *Social Text* 21 (1987/8).

27. Cf. Donna Haraway, "Situated Knowledges: The Science Question in Feminism and the Privilege of Partial Perspective," *Feminist Studies* 14 (1988): 575-99.

28. A use that might borrow from and revamp the Marxist notion of the proletarian "standpoint." Barbara Christian, "The Race for Theory," *Cultural Critique* 6 (1987): 51-63. Chapters 1 and 2 discuss these issues more fully. Cf. bell hooks, *Talking Back: Thinking Feminist, Thinking Black* (Boston: South End, 1989).

29. Christian's also belongs to a body of work that indicates that no "gay/straight split" can ever again be simply divided over sexual preference, as if outside race or as if white; parallel alli-

ances, coalitions, and shifting momentary commonalities mark political struggles in feminism today (and presumably always did). See also, Lorraine Bethel and Barbara Smith, eds., "Introduction," *conditions five: the black women's issue* (1979): 11–15; Smith, *Home Girls.*

30. For some acute institutional analysis, see June Howard, "Feminist Differings: Recent Surveys of Feminist Literary Theory and Criticism," *Feminist Studies* 14 (1988): 167–90. Christian's work is also, perhaps a little less obviously, an intervention into the narrowing definition of cultural feminism produced in the "sexuality debates." Christian shifts from her analysis of "theory" the product and "theorizing" the activity to a specifically literary-critical critique of the devalued status of the authors of fiction and poetry and the aggrandizement of the authors of criticism and theory. I would differ with her recuperation of the valorized author (either of fiction or criticism) myself, but my own work on the status of "poetry" (parallel to Christian's investment in fiction) as a particular political object suggests that debates about "poetry" and the value of "authors rather than than critics" are often contents that signal struggles about cultural feminism in the eighties. The construction of value of literary forms has been politicized in feminist literary criticism. Not only do feminist literary critics challenge the traditional values of women's writing, but they themselves participate in valuing some forms of writing over others. Genres of writing are highly important in these debates, as objects of knowledge, as producers of knowledge, as the very kinds of knowledge themselves. King, "Canons without Innocence."

31. "Hegemonic feminist theory" is a term pervasive within the debates that critique an unself-conscious feminist theory functioning as a colonial discourse. (See for example, Gayatri Chakravorty Spivak, *In Other Worlds: Essays in Cultural Politics* [New York: Routledge, 1988].) Chandra Mohanty has pointed out to me that hegemonic feminist theory defines all feminist positions in relation to itself such that its centrality then necessitates that all feminisms must in turn define themselves in relation to it. In this chapter, I quote "hegemonic feminist theory" from Sandoval's "Oppositional Consciousness." See section titled "Hegemonic Feminism."

32. Sandra Harding, *The Science Question in Feminism* (Ithaca: Cornell UP, 1986); Donna Haraway, "A Manifesto for Cyborgs: Science, Technology, and Socialist Feminism in the 1980s," *Socialist Review* 80 (1985): 65–107 rpt. in *Simians, Cyborgs, and Women: The Reinvention of Nature* (New York: Routledge, 1991); de Lauretis, "Sexual Indifference" and "Eccentric Subjects."

33. See Diana Russell and Nicole Van de Ven, *The Proceedings of the International Tribunal on Crimes against Women* (East Palo Alto, Calif.: Frog in the Well, 1984); Kathleen Barry, *Female Sexual Slavery* (New York, New York U P, 1985). Robin Morgan, *Sisterhood Is Global: The International Women's Movement Anthology* (New York: Anchor, 1984) and its critique in Chandra Talpade Mohanty, "Feminist Encounters: Locating the Politics of Experience," *Copyright* 1 (1987): 30–44. Joni Seager and Ann Olson, *Women in the World Atlas* (New York: Simon and Schuster/Touchstone/Pluto Press Project, 1986); New Internationalist, *Women: A World Report* (New York: Oxford, 1985). Pheterson, *Rights of Whores;* Bell, *Good Girls, Bad Girls.* Aihwa Ong, "Colonialism and Modernity: Feminist Re-Presentations of Women in Non-Western Societies," *Inscriptions* 3/4 (1988): 79–93; Rey Chow, "Uses of Feminism in a Non-Western Context" (paper delivered at Feminisms and Cultural Imperialism: Politics of Difference conference, Cornell University, April 22, 1989); Kaplan, "Deterritorializations."

34. Rubin, "The Leather Menace"; Echols, "Cultural Feminism"; cf. Kathleen M. Weston and Lisa B. Rofel, "Sexuality, Class, and Conflict in a Lesbian Workplace," *Signs* 9 (1984): 623–46.

35. Rubin, "The Leather Menace"; Combahee River Collective, "A Black Feminist Statement."

36. ACT UP, see for example, *October* 43 (1987), "Issue on AIDS: Cultural Analysis/Cultural Activism." Cf. Simon Watney, *Policing Desire: Pornography, AIDS, and the Media* (Minneapolis: U of Minnesota P, 1987). Also the NAMES Project, for example, Cindy Ruskin, Matt Herron, and Deborah Zemke, *The Quilt: Stories From the NAMES Project* (New York: Pocket, 1988).

37. Cindy Patton, *Sex and Germs: The Politics of AIDS* (Boston: South End, 1985); cf. Hunter

Madsen and Marshall Kirk, *After the Ball: How America Will Conquer Its Fear and Hatred of Gays in the Nineties* (New York: Doubleday, 1989).

38. See landmark series in *San Francisco Examiner* June 4-June 25, 1989, "Gay in America: Sixteen-Part Report."

39. Women's AIDS Network, *Lesbians and AIDS: What's the Connection?* (San Francisco: SF AIDS Foundation and the SF Department of Public Health, July 1986; rev. October 1987); Cindy Patton and Janis Kelly, *Making It: A Woman's Guide to Sex in the Age of AIDS*, Spanish translation by Papusa Molina (Ithaca: Firebrand Sparks Pamphlet #2, 1987); Santa Cruz AIDS Project, "Feeling the Heat: An Evening of Erotic Entertainment, for Women Only" (program from benefit performance, Kuumbwa Jazz Center, Santa Cruz, Calif., February 27, 1988).

40. Sonia Johnson, *Going Out of Our Minds* (Trumansburg: Crossing P 1987); Jackie Winnow, "Lesbians Working on AIDS: Assessing the Impact on Health Care for Women," *Outlook* 5 (1989): 10-18. "PWA Coalition Portfolio," *October* 43 (1987): 147-68; Suki Ports, "Needed (for Women and Children)," *October* 43 (1987): 169-76; Carol Leigh, "Further Violations of Our Rights," *October* 43 (1987): 177-82.

41. Amber Hollibaugh and Cherríe Moraga, "What We're Rollin' Around in Bed with—Sexual Silences in Feminism: A Conversation toward Ending Them," *Heresies* 12 (1981); Frigga Haug and others, *Female Sexualization: A Collective Work of Memory*, trans. Erica Carter (London: Verso, 1987). Trinh T. Minh-ha, "Not You/Like You: Post-Colonial Women and the Interlocking Questions of Identity and Difference," *Inscriptions* 3/4 (1988): 71-77; *Woman, Native, Other: Writing Postcoloniality and Feminism* (Bloomington: Indiana UP, 1989); dir. *Reassemblage*, Idera, 1982; dir. *Naked Spaces—Living Is Round*, Idera, 1985; dir. *Surname Viet Given Name Nam*, Idera, 1989.

42. Barry D. Adam, "Homosexuality without a Gay World: Pasivos y Activos en Nicaragua," *Outlook* 4 (1989): 74-82; Schreiber and Tatiana Schreiber and Lynn Stephen, "AIDS Education—Nicaraguan Style," *Outlook* 4 (1989): 78-80; Ramon A. Gutierrez, "Must We Deracinate Indians to Find Gay Roots?" *Outlook* 4 (1989): 61-67. For a model that might be adapted for imagining gay organization in transnational terms, see *Public Culture: Bulletin of the Project for Transnational Cultural Studies* 1 (1988) and 1 (1989).

43. Cf. Lourdes Arguelles and B. Ruby Rich, "Homosexuality, Homophobia, and Revolution: Notes toward an Understanding of the Cuban Lesbian and Gay Male Experience, Part 1," *Signs* 9 (1984): 683-99; John D'Emilio, "Capitalism and Gay Identity," in *Powers of Desire*, 100-113; and D'Emilio, *Sexual Politics*. For a set of imperatives through which to read emerging lesbianisms in specific global locations, see Lata Mani, "Multiple Mediations"; for a possible model for how to read: Anu, "Sexuality, Lesbianism, and South Asian Feminism," "Who Is a Lesbian?" "Who Are We?" and "Life in the Interstices," in *Between the Lines: An Anthology by Pacific/Asian Lesbians of Santa Cruz, California*, ed. C. Chung, A. Kim, A. K. Lemeshewsky (Santa Cruz: Dancing Bird P, 1987) 10-13; 26-27; 35-36; 42; and *Connexions* 3 (1982), "Global Lesbianism I"; 10 (1983), "Global Lesbianism II"; 29 (1989), "Lesbian Activism issue." Also modeling issues of multiple receptions/agencies, Aihwa Ong, *Spirits of Resistance and Capitalist Discipline, Factory Women in Malaysia* (New York: SUNY P, 1987).

44. See current catalogs from Kitchen Table: Women of Color Press (New York City) and Firebrand Press (Ithaca, New York) for examples, and notice roles in distribution as well as in publication.

45. Sandoval, "Oppositional Consciousness"; see also Sharon Willis, "Feminism's Interrupted Genealogies."

6. GLOBAL GAY FORMATIONS AND LOCAL HOMOSEXUALITIES

This chapter is dedicated with love and appreciation to my friend Jaye Miller, who died of AIDS August 11, 1991. Jaye's love of Japan and Hawaii I mean to represent in my attention to Masami Teraoka's work here; and indeed I thought of Jaye often in relation to it: when I first found the catalog, as I examined the paintings, and while writing about them. Looking at the writing now I can hardly bear that I cannot show it to him. As one of many friends mourning Jaye's death, I wonder with them how to bear and to cherish Jaye's world without Jaye.

I would like to thank Paula Treichler for generously sharing her ongoing work on AIDS discourse. I would also like to thank Caren Kaplan, whose intellectual support over a decade has for me threaded feminist theory and women's studies with excitement, style, the unexpected, and always exemplified shifting political forms and priorities! Many of my thoughts in this chapter have been influenced by her explications.

Somewhat different versions of this paper appeared in *camera obscura* 28 (1992): 79–99, and *Provoking Agents: Theorizing Gender and Agency*, ed. Judith Kegan Gardiner (U of Illinois P, 1995).

1. *Genders* 10 (Spring 1991): 22; ftn. 50. [Emphasis mine.]

2. (New York: Routledge, 1990) 131. [Emphasis mine.]

3. *Coming to Terms* (New York: Routledge, 1989) xx. [Emphasis mine.]

4. Foucault's most influential text in this area is *The History of Sexuality*. Volume I: *An Introduction*, trans. Robert Hurley (New York: Pantheon, 1978). Eve Kosofsky Sedgwick wonderfully describes some of the ironies of defamiliarization when gay theorists deploy Foucauldian periodization: how periods move, how homosexuality today becomes transparent; in *Epistemology of the Closet* (Berkeley: U of California P, 1990) 44–48.

5. I mean here to disentangle a premature reduction of cultural feminism from the much-needed critique of the anti-pornography movement. See chapter 3.

6. See ftns. 37–44 in chapter 5.

7. Fredric Jameson, "Postmodernism, or the Cultural Logic of Late Capitalism," *New Left Review* 146 (July-August 1984). See Sandoval's ftn. 50 for her reading of the essay.

8. AIDS series *Black Ships and Geisha* [1987, Masami Teraoka. Watercolor study on paper, 30 by 57". Space Gallery, Los Angeles] in Howard A. Link, *Waves and Plagues: The Art of Masami Teraoka* (Honolulu: The Contemporary Museum; San Francisco: Chronicle Books, 1988), 69; cat. no. 27.

9. This description is drawn from Link's commentary (above).

10. *I Am Out Therefore I Am* [1989, Adam Rolston. Crack-and-peel sticker, offset lithography, 3 7/8 by 3 7/8" (also used as T-shirt)]. This graphic and others are historicized in Douglas Crimp and Adam Rolston, *AIDS/DEMO/GRAPHICS* (Seattle: Bay P, 1990) 103.

11. Cindy Patton has some choice remarks to make about this reemphasis in Sue O'Sullivan's interview with her, "Mapping: Lesbianism, AIDS, and Sexuality," *Feminist Review* 34 (Spring 1990): 120–33.

12. Program from benefit performance, Kuumbwa Jazz Center, Santa Cruz, Calif., February 27, 1988.

13. Sedgwick, *Epistemology* 41, 43.

14. I'm indebted to Diana Fuss's *Essentially Speaking* (New York: Routledge, 1989) for helping me think through the idea that "essentialism" is not itself the essence of identity formation.

15. See, for example, the premier issue: Winter 1991; 2404 California Street #24, San Francisco CA 94115.

16. 1 (Winter 1989): 101–124.

17. Arjun Appadurai and Carol Breckenridge, "Editor's Comments," *Public Culture* 1 (Fall 1988): 2–3.

18. I'm deliberately confounding entailed dichotomies, such as Hartsock's interlocking concrete/abstract entailing materialist/idealist and entailed by female/male (although the formulation "abstract masculinity" I find very useful). See Nancy Hartsock, *Money, Sex, and Power* (New York: Longman, 1983); esp. 231–51.

19. My understandings of these issues are most indebted to the manifestos and ruminations of the editors of and contributors to that journal *Public Culture*, engaging in transnational cultural

studies, whose historical reframings contain that dynamism shifting *who* gets to count as a center, *where*, why, and how, that I see in examining international art activism.

20. *Genders* 5 (Summer 1989): 50–69.

21. I borrow the term "gender transitivity" from Sedgwick's *Epistemology of the Closet*, 1–2.

22. Reider and Ruppelt (San Francisco: Cleis, 1988) and Reider (San Francisco: Cleis, 1990); Penelope and Valentine (Freedom, Calif.: Crossing, 1990).

23. In my work on feminism and writing technologies discussed in chapter 3, I attempt to anchor some discussion of politicized systems of language, technology, publication, and multinational capital.

24. For the exchange between Gordon and Scott, see mutual reviews of each other's books and responses in *Signs* (Summer 1990): 848–60.

25. Bruno Latour and Steve Woolgar, *Laboratory Life* (Beverly Hills: Sage, 1979). For example, also consider the similar intellectual feminist genealogies producing "woman/women."

26. See the discussion in chapter 2 and "Women Respond to Racism: A Report on the National Women's Studies Association Conference, Storrs, Connecticut" (Oakland: Center for Third World Organizing [n.d. but 1982]). A revised version is reprinted in Gloria Anzaldúa, *Making Face, Making Soul: Haciendo Caras, Creative and Critical Perspectives by Women of Color* (San Francisco: Aunt Lute, 1990) 55–71.

27. Shelley Anderson, *Out in the World: International Lesbian Organizing* (Ithaca: Firebrand, 1991); International Lesbian and Gay Association, *Second ILGA Pink Book* (Utrecht: Interfacultaire Werkgroep Homostudies, 1988).

28. "U.S. feminists of color, insofar as they involved themselves with the 1970s white women's liberation movement, were also enacting one or more of the ideological positionings just outlined, but rarely for long, and rarely adopting the kind of fervid belief systems and identity politics that tend to accompany their construction under hegemonic understanding. This unusual affiliation with the movement was variously interpreted as disloyalty, betrayal, absence, or lack: 'When they *were* there, they were rarely there for long' went the usual complaint, or 'they seemed to shift from one type of women's group to another.' They were the mobile (yet ever present in their 'absence') members of this particular liberation movement. It is precisely the significance of this mobility which most inventories of oppositional ideology cannot register." Sandoval, "Oppositional Consciousness," 14. This listing here is simply my own paraphrasing of the kinds of repetitive critiques of postmodern politics I hear over and over. Some of these are also drawn explicitly and implicitly from the Gordon-Scott debate.

Index

Abbott, Sidney, 130–32, 177n.5, 178n.13
academy: circumstances of production of feminist theory, 56–91; feminist literary criticism and, 42–53; gay/straight split in feminism, 143–47
ACT UP, 153, 155
Afrocentrism, 33
agency, feminist debates on, 152–64
AIDS activism, 148–49, 151–64
AIDS: The Women (Reider and Ruppelt), 161
Allen, Pamela, 2, 127–28
Alonso, Ana Maria, 157–59
anti-pornography activism, 147–48, 176n.1
Anzaldúa, Gloria, 41, 68
Appadural, Arjun, 158
Around 1981 [Academic Feminist Literary Theory] (Gallop), 42–53
Art Against Apartheid, 122
Asian Americans, women writers, 111–13
Atkinson, Ti-Grace, 125, 133, 177n.4

Bananas, Beaches, and Bases (Enloe), 39
Baxandall, Ros, 23–24
Beale, Frances M., 15, 16
Beauvoir, Simone de, 9
Bennett, Paula, 173n.21
Bernikow, Louise, 101
Bianchi, Martha Dickinson, 103
Bird, Caroline, 130
birth control, 16
Black feminism: Collins on feminist standpoint and, 83–86; and Echols's construction of radical feminism, 7–54; Ware on racism and, 133
Black Feminist Thought: Knowledge, Consciousness, and the Politics of Empowerment (Collins), 29–35
The Black Woman (Cade), 13–14, 14–15, 21–22
Black women: oral tradition and writing of, 109–110; standpoint and feminist thought, 83–86; writing of in anthologies of 1969–1973 women's liberation movement, 13–19. *See also* Black feminism

Breaking Bread: Insurgent Black Intellectual Life (hooks and West), 32
Breckenridge, Carol, 158
Brown, Norman O., 142
Brown, Rita Mae, 177n.11

Cade, Toni, 13–14, 14–15, 21–22
canon, literary, 105–106, 110, 113
categories, linguistic, 60–62, 64–66, 75
Center for Third World Organizing, 81
Chicanas: writers and oral tradition, 110–11
Chisholm, Shirley, xvi
Chodorow, Nancy, 170n.30
choice, lesbianism as, 133–35
Chow, Rey, 36–39
Christian, Barbara, 145–46, 181–82n.29, 182n.30
Clausen, Jan, 102, 121–22
Collins, Patricia Hill, 6, 29–35, 56, 63, 82–86
colonialism, 38. *See also* decolonization
Coming to Power (Samois), 136
Common Differences (Joseph and Lewis), 84
Conflicts in Feminism (Hirsch and Keller), 81–82, 88
Conjuring: Black Women, Fiction, and Literary Tradition (Pryse and Spiller), 82, 171n.35
Connexions (magazine), 161
consciousness-raising (CR), 127–28, 136
Cosmopolis (Reider), 161
The Critical Difference (Johnson), 53
cultural feminism: AIDS activism and, 153; apparatus for production of, 92–123, 147–49; and Echols's history of feminist theory, 10; radical feminism and, 136; sexuality debates and, 182n.30

Daring to Be Bad (Echols), 7–54
decolonization, 26, 38
de Lauretis, Teresa, 1, 2, 3, 4–5, 7, 146–47
The Dialectic of Sex: The Case for Feminist Revolution (Firestone), 13, 177n.5
Dickinson, Emily, 101–104, 172n.18, 173n.21
difference: Hartsock on feminist standpoint and,

KATIE KING is Associate Professor of Women's Studies at the University of Maryland, College Park.